Arkansas

Recipes Past and Present

The Old State House, Little Rock, Arkansas

The Old State House, located in downtown Little Rock, served as Arkansas' original state capitol from 1836 to 1911. Now a major tourist attraction, the Old State House has become a museum of Arkansas history and tradition.

This cookbook was prepared especially for the American Cancer Society, Arkansas Division, Inc.

Proceeds from the sale of *Arkansas Heritage: Recipes Past and Present* are used to support the American Cancer Society, Arkansas Division programs of research, education and service. The tax deductible part of the cookbook price is $9.50. Cookbook order blanks follow the index.

The American Cancer Society, Arkansas Division, Inc. has no reason to doubt that these recipes will work successfully. However, the recipes have not necessarily been thoroughly or systematically tested. The recipes in this book have been collected from various sources and neither the American Cancer Society, Arkansas Division, Inc. nor any contributor, publisher, or distributor of the book is responsible for errors or omissions.

Published by: Favorite Recipes® Press
P. O. Box 305142
Nashville, Tennessee 37230

Copyright© 1992
American Cancer Society
Arkansas Division, Inc.
901 N. University
Little Rock, Arkansas 72207

Library of Congress Number: 92-32004
ISBN: 0-87197-356-1

Printed in the United States of America
First Printing: 1992   10,000 copies

Acknowledgements

The American Cancer Society, Arkansas Division, Inc. gratefully acknowledges the hard work and dedication of each cookbook committee member and thanks every person who submitted a recipe. Because of you, this cookbook was made possible.

A heartfelt thanks to PRESENTATIONS PLUS, 3811 Turtle Creek Blvd., Suite 600, Dallas, TX 75219, 214-528-0010, Debbie Woodman, Carol Rognrud, Velva Nelson, Mike Munoz and Andy Davis for donating their time and talent to produce the artwork found in this cookbook. Also a special thank you to Robert Chitwood of MCMANN TATE, 9550 Skillman, Suite 206-LB 132, Dallas, TX 75243, 214-349-3918 who assisted in the artwork and presented the Arkansas Division with a beautiful painting of "The Old State House" to be used at the kickoff for the cookbook. They have truly made the history of Arkansas come to life.

Finally, we thank you the donor for helping us win the fight against cancer through your gift.

We are confident you'll enjoy *Arkansas Heritage: Recipes Past and Present* in the years ahead.

Cookbook Committee Members

Willie Oates, Chairman, Little Rock

Dorothy Deen, Brinkley

Bonnie Harris, Pocahontas

Paula Jackson, Fort Smith

Anne Jennings, Hot Springs Village

Zada Koen, DeWitt

Dorothy Pantier, Danville

Linda Partridge, El Dorado

Stella Rognrud, Pine Bluff

Karen Stevens, Harrison

Patti Kee, Staff

Foreword

The American Cancer Society is a nationwide community-based voluntary health organization dedicated to eliminating cancer as a major health problem by preventing cancer, by saving lives from cancer, and by diminishing suffering from cancer through research, education and service.

RESEARCH

The American Cancer Society is the largest source of private cancer research funds nationally with its overall investment having climbed from $1 million in 1946 to $90 million in 1991.

EDUCATION

Educating the public about ways of preventing or reducing one's cancer risk is an important focus of the American Cancer Society. Target areas include relationship between diet, nutrition and cancer as well as anti-smoking.

Detecting cancer early is also important in saving lives from cancer. American Cancer Society programs on colon/rectum, breast, skin and other cancer sites are available to inform and teach Arkansans about early cancer detection tests.

PATIENT SERVICE AND REHABILITATION

Service and rehabilitation programs offer information, guidance and support both for cancer patients and their families. Trained American Cancer Society volunteers play an important role in providing these programs to local communities. Such programs include:

I Can Cope: A six to eight week series addressing the day to day issues facing cancer patients, their families and close friends.

Reach to Recovery: A visitation program providing support and guidance to breast cancer patients.

Cancer Camp: A week-long summer camp for children with cancer.

Additional services available include gift items such as wigs and turbans, hospital equipment and transportation.

These are only a few of the programs your contribution helps to fund. For more information on these programs, call 1-800-ACS-2345.

One Day Memorial Response

What better way to remember a friend or loved one by making a gift in their memory to the American Cancer Society. It is simple and easy. Just call 1-800-ACS-2345 and charge your gift on VISA/Mastercard/American Express. A memorial card will be sent to the family of the deceased the day you place your call.

Eat Smart

This cookbook does not necessarily contain recipes which fit into the American Cancer Society's dietary guidelines. Nutritional analysis information is included to help you make choices regarding the food you prepare and eat.

The American Cancer Society Dietary Guidelines for Reducing One's Cancer Risk are as follows:

* Avoid obesity.

* Cut down on total fat intake.

* Eat more high fiber foods.

* Include more foods rich in vitamins A and C in your daily diet.

* Include cruciferous (cabbage-family) vegetables in your diet.

* Cut down on salt-cured, smoked and nitrite-cured foods.

* Keep consumption of alcohol moderate, if you drink.

THERE'S NOTHING MIGHTIER THAN THE SWORD
AMERICAN CANCER SOCIETY®

FOR MORE INFORMATION CALL THE AMERICAN CANCER SOCIETY TOLL FREE: 1-800-ACS-2345

Contributors

** Due to limited space we were unable to use every recipe
which was submitted, but again we want to thank every one who
contributed recipes and made this cookbook possible.*

Mattie Adkison, Dardanelle
Elizabeth Almond, Brinkley
Sandy Anderson, Lonoke
Nelda Antonetti, Marion
Coma Austin, Atkins
Mary Anna Bailey, Atkins
Priscilla Baker, Marshall
Virginia Baker, Warm Springs
Bettye Sue Baratti, Marion
Bootsie Barré, Pocahontas
Cindy Baswell, Hot Springs
Wanda Bateman, Pine Bluff
Martha Beebe, El Dorado
Vada Beebe, El Dorado
Dessie Mae Bell, Augusta
Polly Bell, Batesville
Margaret Benafield, Lonoke
Kay Lynn Bennett, Pocahontas
Loraine Bennett, Little Rock
Mildred Bennett, Pine Bluff
Wanda Bennett, Atkins
Ci Berry, Fort Smith
Vivian Beukers, Edmonds, WA
Willie Mae Bigger, Marion
Denise Black, DeWitt
Virginia Bland, Walnut Ridge
Nita Bluford, Havana
Evelyn Bowden, Ola
Carolyn Bowen, Booneville
Katherine Brady, Pine Bluff
Sue Brand, Walnut Ridge
Marilyn Braswell, DeWitt
Donna Bratton, Havana
Laura Brown, Pine Bluff
Nita Buford, Danville
Lucille Burkett, McCrory
Sonia Byrd, Pine Bluff
Donna Camp, Pocahontas
Mildred Capps, DeWitt
Jacalyn Carfagno, Atkins
Rita Carfagno, Atkins
Susan Carfagno, Atkins
Rhonda Carroll, Brinkley
Lanita Carver, Stuttgart
Nita Mae Cater, Crocketts Bluff
Mary Jo Chambers, Maumelle
Pat Chambers, Danville
Margaret Cheek, Atkins
Sherry Cheek, DeWitt
Diane Chester, Pocahontas
Dorothy Clayton, Hazen

Mrs. B. E. Cobb, Fort Smith
Evelyn Cobb, Nashville
Patricia Cole, Arkadelphia
Shelby Conrad, White Hall
Melissa Cook, Pine Bluff
Peggy Cooke, Fishers, IN
Alice Corbin, Havana
Betty Cotner, DeWitt
Florence Courtney, Marion
Barbara Cunningham, Walnut Ridge
Mary Lou Cunningham, DeWitt
Dorothy Deane Currie, DeWitt
Bill Davidson, Hot Springs Village
Beatrice Davis, Augusta
Elowese Davis, Marion
Rosemary Davis, Danville
Carrie Davison, Marvell
Margaret Dearing, DeWitt
Dorothy Deen, Brinkley
Lisa Defoor, Bluffton
Sherry Defoor, Danville
Mildred G. Delamar, Prescott
Beverly Denman, DeWitt
Joann Devries, Lonoke
Aggie Doss, Fort Smith
Etta Doss, Hazen
Ethelyn Dow, Danville
Fern B. Downs, Little Rock
Ara Scott Drum, Fort Smith
Mary Ella Du Bois, Pocahontas
Debbie Dupuy, Gillett
Aletha Durrett, Little Rock
Carolyn Edwards, West Helena
Phyllis Elam, Lonoke
Norryce Eldridge, Stuttgart
Patty Eldridge, Stuttgart
Barbara Ellenburg, DeWitt
Marilyn Elliott, Searcy
Louise Elmore, Belleville
Glenda Faith, Searcy
Bessie Fengler, Atkins
Jannis Ferguson, DeWitt
Berta Fikes, Pine Bluff
Pam Fisher, Fort Smith
Marion Flake, Little Rock
Mrs. Robert Foster, Fort Smith
Sandra Franklin, Springdale
Debbie Franks, Russellville
Bonnie Franz, Arkadelphia
Myrle Frazier, Danville
Kathy Freeman, Dover

Janie Freeze, Fort Smith
Darleen Frizzell, DeWitt
Helen Fulton, Clarksville
Jane Galyean, Helena
Carlie Gamble, Marvell
Janice Garrett, San Diego, CA
Jeannette Garrett, Marion
Katherine Garrett, Clarksville
Monica Gates, Danville
Faye Geisler, Brinkley
Christine George, Belleville
Marguerite Gibson, Russellville
Linda Glidewell, Lavaca
Daniel Golden, San Diego, CA
Barbara (Bobbi) Goldman, Pine Bluff
Patty Gonzales, West Memphis
Marjorie Gray, Marshall
Becky Green, Stuttgart
Mary Green, Stuttgart
Diane Griffin, Conway
Evelyn Griffin, Helena
Suzy Griffin, Russellville
Laverne B. Gwyn, Brinkley
Jeff Hall, Belleville
Polly Hall, Belleville
Janet Hall-Davis, Naples, FL
Elizabeth Haltom, Prescott
Lyn Haralson, Dardanelle
Betty Harris, Brinkley
Bonnie Harris, Pocahontas
Daniel Harris, Pocahontas
Helen Harrison, Prescott
Marjie Hart, Pine Bluff
Joyce Hartnett, Harrison
Mildred Heise, Russellville
Wincie Hendricks, Fort Smith
Sara Henry, Atkins
Elizabeth Hickman, Atkins
Jean Highsmith, Batesville
Jack Hill, Russellville
Dorinda Hix, Belleville
E. M. Hogan, Kodiak, AK
Emma Hoke, Brinkley
Stan Holleman, Fort Smith
Jauana Holt, Danville
Thelma Hood, Russellville
Elizabeth Horn, Belleville
Barbara Hornbeck, DeWitt
Cheryl Hornbeck, DeWitt
Pattie Hornbeck, DeWitt
Nancy Hornberger, Fort Smith
Mary House, Batesville
Mary Webb Hubbard, Prescott
Delia Mae Hudspeth, DeWitt
Markie Hudspeth, Rover
Ruby Humphrey, Russellville
Darlene Hunt, Brinkley
Jackie Hynum, DeWitt
Paul Jackson, North Carolina
Paula Jackson, Fort Smith
Clara Jacobs, DeWitt
Molly James, Pocahontas
Vera James, Pocahontas
Anne Jennings, Hot Springs Village
Agnes Jimerson, Augusta
America Jones, Almyra
Betty Jones, Russellville
Lenela Jones, Ola

Marjorie Kagels, Peoria, IL
Leona Keener, Atkins
Nancy Kelly, Helena
Patsy Keys, Dardanelle
Vicki Knight, Little Rock
Louise Koen, DeWitt
Zada Koen, DeWitt
Stephanie Kratts, Pine Bluff
Becca Lane, DeWitt
Louise LaRue, Hot Springs Village
Patricia Latham, Danville
Bobbye Laws, Russellville
John Le Maire, Helena
Faye Lemley, Atkins
Polly Livingston, Batesville
Tricia Long, Little Rock
Estelle Loomis, Poplar Grove
JimmieLou Fisher Lumpkin, Little Rock
Carolyn Lutes, Blytheville
Juanita Luttrell, El Dorado
Marilyn Lyons, Danville
Patty MacDonald, Hot Springs Village
Lois Madonia, Helena
Linda Maienschein, Bella Vista
Nila Mansker, Pocahontas
Margland II Bed & Breakfast Inn, Pine Bluff
Syble Marple, Atkins
Donna Marshall, Dardanelle
Pam Marshall, DeWitt
Gracie Jo Martin, Danville
Hazel Martin, Pocahontas
Dorothy Mattison, Conway
Eleanor McCann, Fort Smith
Ron McConnell, Magazine
Kay McCord, Pocahontas
Amy McGee, DeWitt
Kathy McKinney, El Dorado
Francine McKnight, Walnut Ridge
Eunice Merritt, DeWitt
Barbara Meyer, Lavaca
Bobbie and James Miner, Prescott
Mary Couch Moll, Fort Smith
Ann Moore, Osceola
Frances Moore, Walnut Ridge
Joanne Moore, Camden
Joyce Moore, Bella Vista
Virginia Moore, Dardanelle
Margaret Ann Morgan, Little Rock
Ruby Morgan, West Memphis
Retha Morrison, Danville
Inas Moseley, Jasper
Ruth Moseley, Little Rock
Ginger Jones Motes, Pine Bluff
Bettye Moulton, Fort Smith
Betty Muck, Danville
Mrs. Gerald Mullen, Bella Vista
Eloise Muncy, Searcy
Nora Murray, Pine Bluff
Pat Nelson, Danville
Verna Mae Newman, Cherokee Village
Leona Newton, Hot Springs Village
Fran Nichols, North Little Rock
Pat Norman, Brinkley
Willie Oates, Little Rock
Linda O'Daniel, Jonesboro
Jane Overcash, Brinkley
Helen Oxner, Brinkley
Dorothy Pantier, Danville

Sallye Parker, Fort Smith
Robbie Partain, Dardanelle
Linda Partridge, El Dorado
Blanche Patterson, Little Rock
Zada Payne, Marion
Diane Perryman, Dardanelle
Erma Petty, North Little Rock
Isabelle Phillips, Fort Smith
Frances Plafcan, Stuttgart
Geneva Pledger, Danville
Libby Pledger, Danville
Winifred Pledger, Danville
Mary Lou Plumb, Mena
Louise Ponder, Walnut Ridge
Jean Prange, Crocketts Bluff
Laura Jo Prange, Wabbaseka
Rev. N. Lorene Pritchett, West Memphis
Ruby Nell Pugh, Rover
Dixie Pulliam, Walnut Ridge
Mrs. G. S. Puryear, Little Rock
Vickie Rabeneck, DeWitt
Dora Rainey, Casa
Sallie Jane Rainey, Little Rock
Mary Rainwater, Walnut Ridge
Beatrice Ray, Brinkley
Alice Reinsch, Dardanelle
Shelly Richardson, Dumas, TX
Thelma Ridgway, Pine Bluff
Imogene Riggs, Walnut Ridge
Shirley Robins, Walnut Ridge
Rhonda Robinson, Bluffton
Susie Robison, Danville
Catherine Rogers, Danville
Marlee Rognrud, Naples, FL
Stella Rognrud, Pine Bluff
Clara Lee Rose, Brinkley
Jean Sabatier, Brinkley
Kathleen Safreed, Fort Smith
Merle Sartini, Marion
Jane Saviers, Fort Smith
Pam Schimmel, DeWitt
Violet Scott, Doniphan, MO
Lottie Shackelford, Little Rock
Paula Shafer, Havana
Doris, Sharp, Pocahontas
Helen Shinn, Russellville
Margaret Shockley, Fort Smith
Chris Shoemake, Marion
Lola Short, Danville
Mary Silkenson, Russellville
June Simmons, Hot Springs
Becky Singleton, Marion
Bonnye Sisk, Parkin
Freda Skarda, Pine Bluff
Barbara Skouras, Brinkley
Ruth Ann Sloan, Danville
Elva Smith, Danville
Kim Smith, Walnut Ridge
Marlene Smith, Brinkley
Murrial Smith, Danville
Stephanie Smith, DeWitt
Jewel Snapp, Walnut Ridge
Linda Southard, Dardanelle
Rose Spencer, Crocketts Bluff
Mildred Spillers, Russellville
Sue Statler, Pocahontas
Bobbie Stigall, Hot Springs Village

Nancy Stiles, Fort Smith
Elizabeth Stinnett, Dardanelle
Lucille Stolt, Pocahontas
Janice Stratton, Tumbling Shoals
Doris Tanner, Pocahontas
Martha Tatum, Danville
Willie Taylor, McCrory
Charlie Teeter, Prescott
Martha Tehan, Edmond, OK
Joyce Thielemier, Pocahontas
Bettye Thompson, Little Rock
Jeanne Thompson, Forrest City
Sandra Thompson, El Dorado
Sarah Traugh, Marion
Monica Trayler, Brinkley
Renee Tucker, Searcy
Helen Tull, Hazen
Ginnie Tyson, Atkins
Mrs. Van Tyson, Atkins
Dorothy Umfress, Helena
Charlotte Vaughn, Piggott
Kathy Vining, Little Rock
Peggy Vining, Little Rock
Myrtle Volz, Dover
Jane Vos, Almyra
Alice Waddell, Pocahontas
Karen Wagner, El Dorado
Jane Walcott, Fort Smith
Claudette Walker, Pocahontas
Donna Walker, Crossett
Mary Howard Walker, Walnut Ridge
Ora Walker, Pine Bluff
Verlee Walter, Hot Springs Village
Bettye Ward, Marion
Dorothy B. Ward, Prescott
Sue Ward, Danville
Mrs. Wendell Ward, Fayetteville
Mary Watermann, Hot Springs
Toni Weatherford, Russellville
Carol Weathers, DeWitt
Rosemary Weaver, Pocahontas
Tonya Webber, Pine Bluff
Sally Wellman, Pocahontas
Thelma Wells, DeWitt
Hilly Wendland, Hot Springs Village
Myrtle Wesson, Carlisle
Debbie West, St. Charles
Sylvia West, Dardanelle
Irene White, Clarksville
Nancy White, Blytheville
Adell Whitfield, El Dorado
Thomas Wiggins, Hot Springs
Ruby Wilcoxson, Walnut Ridge
Martha Willett, Danville
Carolyn Williams, DeWitt
Marion Williams, Morrilton
Utanah Williams, Pocahontas
Wanda Williams, Nashville
Bonnie Williamson, Pine Bluff
Joyce Wilson, Danville
LaJean Wilson, Hot Springs
Nita Wilson, Lonoke
Gail Wiser, Havana
Marge Woods, Moose Pass, AK
R. M. Woods, Conway
Charlotte Woody, Tullahoma, TN
Diann Yarber, Gatewood, MO

Contents

Nutritional Guidelines

The editors have attempted to present these family recipes in a form that allows approximate nutritional values to be computed. Persons with dietary or health problems or whose diets require close monitoring should not rely solely on the nutritional information provided. They should consult their physicians or a registered dietitian for specific information.

ABBREVIATIONS FOR NUTRITIONAL ANALYSIS

Cal — Calories	Dietary Fiber — Fiber	Sod — Sodium
Prot — Protein	T Fat — Total Fat	g — gram
Carbo — Carbohydrates	Chol — Cholesterol	mg — milligrams

Nutritional information for these recipes is computed from information derived from many sources, including materials supplied by the United States Department of Agriculture, computer databanks and journals in which the information is assumed to be in the public domain. However, many specialty items, new products and processed foods may not be available from these sources or may vary from the average values used in these analyses. More information on new and/or specific products may be obtained by reading the nutrient labels. Unless otherwise specified, the nutritional analysis of these recipes is based on all measurements being level.

* **Artificial sweeteners** vary in use and strength so should be used "to taste," using the recipe ingredients as a guideline. Sweeteners using aspartame (NutraSweet and Equal) should not be used as a sweetener in recipes involving prolonged heating which reduces the sweet taste. For further information, refer to package information.
* **Alcoholic ingredients** have been analyzed for the basic ingredients, although cooking causes the evaporation of alcohol thus decreasing caloric content.
* **Buttermilk, sour cream** and **yogurt** are types available commercially.
* **Cake mixes** which are prepared using package directions include 3 eggs and 1/2 cup vegetable oil.
* **Chicken**, cooked for boning and chopping, has been roasted; this method yields the lowest caloric values.
* **Cottage cheese** is cream-style with 4.2% creaming mixture. Dry-curd cottage cheese has no creaming mixture.
* **Eggs** are all large. To avoid raw eggs that may carry salmonella as in eggnog or 6-week muffin batter, use an equivalent amount of commercial egg substitute.
* **Flour** is unsifted all-purpose flour.
* **Garnishes**, serving suggestions and other optional additions and variations are not included in the analysis.
* **Margarine** and **butter** are regular, not whipped or presoftened.
* **Milk** is whole milk, 3.5% butterfat. Lowfat milk is 1% butterfat. Evaporated milk is whole milk with 60% of the water removed.
* **Oil** is any type of vegetable cooking oil. Shortening is hydrogenated vegetable shortening.
* **Salt** and other ingredients to taste as noted in the ingredients have not been included in the nutritional analysis.
* If a choice of ingredients has been given, the nutritional analysis information reflects the first option. If a choice of amounts has been given, the nutritional analysis reflects the greater amount.

Starters

The Major Black Home

The Major Black Home

The Major Black home at 311 West Ash Street, has been a Brinkley landmark since 1895. It was placed on the National Register of Historic Places in 1977. This home, with its Queen Anne Victorian-style architecture, is the only structure of its kind in the area. The house stands as a monument to Major William Black who was largely responsible for the development of Brinkley and the surrounding area.

Appetizers

Beefy Cheese Ball

8 ounces light cream cheese, softened
1   12-ounce package dried beef, chopped

3 or 4 green onions, finely chopped
Garlic or garlic salt to taste
1/2 cup chopped pecans

Combine cream cheese, dried beef and onions in bowl; mix well. Add garlic or garlic salt; mix well. Shape into ball; roll in chopped pecans. Chill, wrapped in plastic wrap, in refrigerator until serving time. Serve with wheat thins or crackers. May substitute ham for dried beef. Yield: 50 (1-tablespoon) servings.

Approx Per Serving: Cal 30; Prot 3 g; Carbo 1 g; Fiber <1 g;
    T Fat 2 g; 56% Calories from Fat; Chol 14 mg; Sod 262 mg.

Fruited Cheese Ball

16 ounces cream cheese, softened
1   8-ounce can crushed pineapple, drained
1/4 cup chopped red and green bell pepper

1 tablespoon chopped onion
1 cup cooked rice, chilled
1 tablespoon seasoning salt
1 cup chopped walnuts

Combine cream cheese and pineapple in bowl; mix well. Add bell pepper, onion, rice and seasoning salt; mix well. Shape into ball; roll in chopped walnuts. Chill, wrapped, in refrigerator until serving time. May chill for 24 to 48 hours to enhance flavor. Yield: 80 (1-tablespoon) servings.

Approx Per Serving: Cal 34; Prot 1 g; Carbo 1 g; Fiber <1 g;
    T Fat 3 g; 75% Calories from Fat; Chol 6 mg; Sod 66 mg.

Garlic-Cheese Roll

16 ounces American cheese, softened
16 ounces cream cheese, softened
2 cloves of garlic, minced

1 cup chopped pecans
1 tablespoon chili powder

Combine American cheese and cream cheese in bowl; mix well. Add garlic and pecans; mix well. Shape into ball; roll in chili powder. Chill, wrapped in plastic wrap, in refrigerator until serving time. May substitute garlic powder for garlic. Yield: 140 (1-tablespoon) servings.

Approx Per Serving: Cal 29; Prot 1 g; Carbo <1 g; Fiber <1 g;
 T Fat 3 g; 82% Calories from Fat; Chol 7 mg; Sod 57 mg.

Parmesan Cheese Spread

12 ounces cream cheese, softened
1/3 cup grated Parmesan cheese
1/4 cup mayonnaise

1/2 teaspoon oregano
1/8 teaspoon garlic powder

Combine cream cheese, Parmesan cheese, mayonnaise, oregano and garlic powder in bowl; mix well. Chill in refrigerator. Form into pine cone shape on cheese board; garnish with nuts. May be shaped into ball and rolled in chopped parsley. Serve with fruit and/or crackers. Yield: 28 (1-tablespoon) servings.

Approx Per Serving: Cal 61; Prot 1 g; Carbo <1 g; Fiber 0 g;
 T Fat 6 g; 89% Calories from Fat; Chol 15 mg; Sod 65 mg.

Sausage-Cheese Mold

2 pounds hot sausage
16 ounces Velveeta cheese, chopped
16 ounces extra sharp Cheddar
 cheese, chopped

16 ounces Cheddar cheese, chopped
1 jalapeño pepper, seeded, chopped
1 cup finely chopped onion

Brown sausage in skillet, stirring until crumbly; drain on paper towels. Melt Velveeta and Cheddar cheeses together in top of double boiler, stirring frequently. Remove from heat. Stir in sausage, pepper and onion. Line oiled bundt pan with plastic wrap. Press mixture into pan. Chill in refrigerator until firm. Unmold onto serving plate. Serve with crackers. May substitute chili pepper for jalapeño pepper. Yield: 60 servings.

Approx Per Serving: Cal 116; Prot 7 g; Carbo 1 g; Fiber <1 g;
 T Fat 10 g; 74% Calories from Fat; Chol 29 mg; Sod 294 mg.

Shrimp-Cheese Balls

6 ounces cream cheese, softened
1½ teaspoons prepared mustard
1 teaspoon grated onion
1 teaspoon lemon juice

Salt and cayenne pepper to taste
1 4-ounce can shrimp, drained
⅔ cup chopped salted peanuts

Combine cream cheese, mustard, onion, lemon juice, salt and cayenne pepper in bowl; mix well. Break shrimp into small pieces. Add to mixture; mix well. Chill in refrigerator. Shape into ½-inch balls; roll in chopped peanuts. May substitute ¾ cup chopped cooked shrimp for canned shrimp. Yield: 42 (½-inch ball) servings.

Approx Per Serving: Cal 29; Prot 1 g; Carbo 1 g; Fiber <1 g;
T Fat 2 g; 73% Calories from Fat; Chol 9 mg; Sod 27 mg.

Shrimp-Cheese Mold

1 10-ounce can tomato soup
8 ounces cream cheese, softened
2 envelopes unflavored gelatin
½ cup cold water
1 medium onion, grated

1 cup mayonnaise
1 1-pound package frozen cooked
  shrimp, thawed
¾ cup finely chopped celery

Combine soup and cream cheese in saucepan. Cook over low heat until cheese is melted, stirring constantly. Remove from heat. Beat until smooth. Soften gelatin in cold water. Stir into hot mixture until gelatin is dissolved. Add onion, mayonnaise, shrimp and celery; mix well. Pour into greased mold. Chill in refrigerator overnight. Unmold onto serving plate. May substitute two 6-ounce cans shrimp, drained, for frozen shrimp. Yield: 100 (1-tablespoon) servings.

Approx Per Serving: Cal 31; Prot 1 g; Carbo 1 g; Fiber <1 g;
T Fat 3 g; 75% Calories from Fat; Chol 13 mg; Sod 50 mg.

Dilled Salmon-Cheese Ball

1 16-ounce can red salmon
8 ounces cream cheese, softened
1 tablespoon lemon juice
2 teaspoons grated onion

2 teaspoons minced celery
2 teaspoons dillweed
½ cup chopped parsley

Remove skin and bones from salmon; discard. Combine salmon, cream cheese, lemon juice, onion, celery and dillweed in bowl; mix well. Shape into ball. Roll in chopped parsley to coat. Chill, wrapped, in refrigerator until serving time. Serve with crackers. Yield: 40 (1-tablespoon) servings.

Approx Per Serving: Cal 36; Prot 3 g; Carbo <1 g; Fiber <1 g;
T Fat 3 g; 67% Calories from Fat; Chol 12 mg; Sod 80 mg.

Smoked Salmon-Cheese Roll

1 16-ounce can red salmon
8 ounces cream cheese, softened
1 tablespoon lemon juice
1/4 teaspoon liquid smoke
1 teaspoon horseradish

1/4 teaspoon dillweed
1/4 teaspoon salt
11/2 teaspoons grated onion
1/2 cup chopped pecans
1/2 cup chopped parsley

Drain salmon; remove and discard skin and bones. Combine salmon, cream cheese, lemon juice, liquid smoke, horseradish, dillweed, salt and onion in bowl; mix well. Shape mixture into roll. Combine pecans and parsley on waxed paper; mix well. Roll cheese roll in mixture to coat. Chill, wrapped, in refrigerator until serving time. Serve with crackers or pumpernickel rounds. Yield: 40 (1-tablespoon) servings.

Approx Per Serving: Cal 46; Prot 3 g; Carbo 1 g; Fiber <1 g;
    T Fat 4 g; 71% Calories from Fat; Chol 12 mg; Sod 93 mg.

Southwest Cheesecake

16 ounces cream cheese, softened
2 cups shredded sharp Cheddar
    cheese
2 cups sour cream
11/2 envelopes taco seasoning mix

3 eggs
1 4-ounce can green chilies
2/3 cup salsa
1 10-ounce package tortilla chips

Combine cream cheese and Cheddar cheese in mixer bowl; beat until fluffy. Add 1 cup sour cream and taco seasoning mix; mix well. Beat in eggs 1 at a time. Fold in green chilies. Spoon into greased 9-inch springform pan. Bake at 350 degrees for 35 to 40 minutes or until center is firm. Cool for 10 minutes. Spoon remaining 1 cup sour cream over top of cheesecake. Bake for 5 minutes longer. Cool completely on wire rack. Chill, covered, in refrigerator overnight. Remove side of springform pan; place cheesecake on serving plate. Top with salsa. Serve with tortilla chips. Yield: 125 (1-tablespoon) servings.

Approx Per Serving: Cal 43; Prot 1 g; Carbo 2 g; Fiber <1 g;
    T Fat 3 g; 69% Calories from Fat; Chol 13 mg; Sod 93 mg.

Artichoke-Mozzarella Dip

1 cup mayonnaise
1 cup shredded mozzarella cheese
1 cup grated Parmesan cheese

1 16-ounce can artichoke hearts,
    finely chopped

Combine mayonnaise, cheeses and artichoke hearts in bowl; mix well. Pour into greased 8x8-inch baking dish. Bake at 350 degrees for 15 to 20 minutes or until bubbly. Serve warm with crackers or chips. Yield: 70 (1-tablespoon) servings.

Approx Per Serving: Cal 35; Prot 1 g; Carbo 1 g; Fiber 0 g;
    T Fat 3 g; 83% Calories from Fat; Chol 4 mg; Sod 62 mg.

Creamy Artichoke-Parmesan Dip

8 ounces cream cheese, softened
1 cup mayonnaise
1 cup grated Parmesan cheese

1 16-ounce can artichoke hearts,
   drained, chopped

Combine cream cheese, mayonnaise and Parmesan cheese in bowl; mix well. Add drained chopped artichoke hearts; mix well. Spoon into greased 8x8-inch baking dish. Bake at 350 degrees for 20 minutes or until bubbly and light brown. Serve with chunks of French bread or breadsticks. Yield: 70 (1-tablespoon) servings.

Approx Per Serving: Cal 41; Prot 1 g; Carbo 1 g; Fiber 0 g;
    T Fat 4 g; 86% Calories from Fat; Chol 6 mg; Sod 65 mg.

Broccoli Dip

3 stalks celery, chopped
1 4-ounce can mushroom pieces
1/2 large onion, finely chopped
1 tablespoon butter
1 10-ounce package frozen chopped
   broccoli

1 8-ounce roll garlic cheese,
   coarsely chopped
1 10-ounce can cream of mushroom
   soup

Sauté celery, mushroom pieces and onion in butter in skillet until celery is tender; drain. Cook broccoli using package directions; drain. Place garlic cheese in microwave-safe bowl. Microwave on Low until cheese is melted. Combine sautéed vegetables, broccoli, cheese and mushroom soup in bowl; mix well. Pour into serving dish. Serve with crackers or chips. Yield: 80 (1-tablespoon) servings.

Approx Per Serving: Cal 12; Prot 1 g; Carbo 1 g; Fiber <1 g;
    T Fat 1 g; 59% Calories from Fat; Chol 2 mg; Sod 53 mg.

Ay Chihuahua Dip

1 pound hot sausage
1 16-ounce can refried beans
1 4-ounce can chopped green chilies

8 ounces Monterey Jack cheese,
   shredded

Brown sausage in skillet, stirring until crumbly; drain. Spread beans in greased 9x13-inch baking dish. Layer sausage, chilies and cheese over beans. Chill until 15 minutes before serving time. Bake at 350 degrees for 15 minutes. Serve hot with tortilla chips. Yield: 80 (1-tablespoon) servings.

Approx Per Serving: Cal 27; Prot 2 g; Carbo 1 g; Fiber <1 g;
    T Fat 2 g; 59% Calories from Fat; Chol 5 mg; Sod 84 mg.

Hot Crab Dip

*I use this dip whenever I have a group. Given to me by a good friend;
it is always good. —Marilyn S. Lyons*

8 ounces cream cheese, softened
1 tablespoon milk
1 6-ounce can crab meat
2 tablespoons finely chopped onion

1/2 teaspoon cream-style horseradish
1/4 teaspoon salt
Pepper to taste
1/3 cup sliced almonds, toasted

Combine cream cheese, milk, crab meat, onion, horseradish, salt and pepper in bowl; mix well. Spoon into small greased casserole; sprinkle with almonds. Bake at 375 degrees for 20 to 25 minutes or until hot and bubbly. Serve hot with wheat crackers or cocktail rye bread. Yield: 36 (1-tablespoon) servings.

Approx Per Serving: Cal 32; Prot 2 g; Carbo <1 g; Fiber <1 g;
    T Fat 3 g; 75% Calories from Fat; Chol 11 mg; Sod 50 mg.

Dill Dip

1 cup mayonnaise-type salad dressing
1 cup sour cream
3 tablespoons grated onion
5 teaspoons dillweed

3 tablespoons parsley flakes
1 teaspoon Worcestershire sauce
Garlic salt to taste

Combine all ingredients in bowl; mix well. Chill, covered, in refrigerator for several hours to overnight before serving. Yield: 30 (1-tablespoon) servings.

Approx Per Serving: Cal 47; Prot <1 g; Carbo 2 g; Fiber <1 g;
    T Fat 4 g; 78% Calories from Fat; Chol 5 mg; Sod 61 mg.

Layered Dip

2 16-ounce cans bean dip
16 ounces guacamole dip
1 cup mayonnaise
1 cup sour cream
1 1/3 envelopes taco seasoning mix
2 4-ounce cans chopped black
    olives, drained

1/2 cup chopped onion
2 tomatoes, seeded, chopped
1 green bell pepper, chopped
1 cup shredded Cheddar cheese
1 cup shredded Monterey Jack cheese

Layer bean dip evenly in large deep bowl. Spread guacamole dip and mixture of mayonnaise, sour cream and taco seasoning mix over bean dip. Sprinkle with remaining ingredients. Chill, covered, in refrigerator until serving time. Serve with corn chips or tortilla chips. Yield: 200 (1-tablespoon) servings.

Approx Per Serving: Cal 27; Prot 1 g; Carbo 1 g; Fiber <1 g;
    T Fat 2 g; 73% Calories from Fat; Chol 2 mg; Sod 88 mg.

Mexican Dip

2 4-ounce cans chopped black
    olives, drained
2 4-ounce cans chopped green
    chilies, drained
2 large tomatoes, chopped
1 tablespoon oil

1 tablespoon wine vinegar
Garlic powder to taste
Seasoned salt to taste
Cumin to taste
Jalapeño pepper to taste

Combine black olives, green chilies, tomatoes, oil, vinegar, garlic powder, seasoned salt, cumin and jalapeño pepper in bowl; mix well. Chill, covered, in refrigerator for 24 hours. Serve with tortilla chips. Yield: 60 (1-tablespoon) servings.

Approx Per Serving: Cal 10; Prot <1 g; Carbo 1 g; Fiber <1 g;
    T Fat 1 g; 79% Calories from Fat; Chol 0 mg; Sod 56 mg.

Sherry-Shrimp Dip

8 ounces cream cheese, softened
¹/₄ cup mayonnaise
1 teaspoon wine and pepper
    Worcestershire sauce
¹/₄ teaspoon minced fresh garlic
1 tablespoon sherry

6 tablespoons chopped green olives
2 tablespoons finely chopped green
    onions
1 tablespoon horseradish sauce
¹/₄ teaspoon Tabasco sauce
1 6-ounce can small shrimp, drained

Combine cream cheese, mayonnaise, Worcestershire sauce, garlic, sherry, olives, green onions, horseradish sauce and Tabasco sauce in bowl; mix well. Stir in shrimp. Pour into refrigerator container. Chill, covered, for 2 hours. Serve with toast points or chips. Yield: 40 (1-tablespoon) servings.

Approx Per Serving: Cal 37; Prot 1 g; Carbo <1 g; Fiber <1 g;
    T Fat 3 g; 81% Calories from Fat; Chol 14 mg; Sod 72 mg.

Shrimp-Onion Dip

1 6-ounce can tiny cocktail shrimp   8 ounces French onion dip

Rinse and drain shrimp. Combine shrimp and French onion dip in bowl; mix well. Chill, covered, in refrigerator for 1 hour or longer. Serve with chips. Yield: 20 (1-tablespoon) servings.

Approx Per Serving: Cal 39; Prot 2 g; Carbo 2 g; Fiber 0 g;
    T Fat 2 g; 48% Calories from Fat; Chol 15 mg; Sod 128 mg.

Spinach-Cheese Dip

1 8-ounce package frozen chopped
  spinach, thawed, drained
¹/₄ cup chopped artichoke hearts
1 cup whipping cream
1 tablespoon grated Parmesan cheese

¹/₂ cup shredded mozzarella cheese
1 cup sour cream
1 cup salsa
1 10-ounce package corn chips

Process spinach and artichoke hearts in blender container until puréed. Add cream gradually, processing until well mixed. Pour into saucepan. Add Parmesan cheese. Cook over low heat until bubbly, stirring constantly. Spoon into individual serving bowls; sprinkle with mozzarella cheese. Serve with sour cream and salsa on the side and corn chips to dip. Yield: 10 servings.

Approx Per Serving: Cal 322; Prot 5 g; Carbo 21 g; Fiber 3 g;
    T Fat 24 g; 67% Calories from Fat; Chol 48 mg; Sod 451 mg.

Bacon Roll-Ups

1 14-ounce can sweetened
  condensed milk
¹/₄ cup prepared mustard
1 tablespoon Worcestershire sauce

20 slices bread, crusts removed
1 pound bacon, cut into halves
2 cups shredded mild Cheddar cheese

Combine first 3 ingredients in bowl; mix well. Cut each bread slice into 3 strips. Lay 1 bread strip on each half bacon slice; spread mustard mixture on bread. Sprinkle with cheese. Roll to enclose filling; secure with wooden pick. Place on baking sheet. Bake at 350 degrees for 30 minutes or until golden brown. Place on serving dish. May be frozen before or after baking. Yield: 60 servings.

Approx Per Serving: Cal 68; Prot 3 g; Carbo 7 g; Fiber <1 g;
    T Fat 3 g; 43% Calories from Fat; Chol 8 mg; Sod 117 mg.

Ham Rolls

16 ounces cream cheese, softened
2 bunches green onions with tops,
  chopped
1¹/₂ teaspoons chili powder

1 tablespoon Greek seasoning
1 tablespoon lemon pepper
2 pounds cooked ham, thinly sliced

Combine cream cheese, green onions, chili powder, seasoning and lemon pepper in bowl; mix well. Spread about 2 tablespoons mixture over each slice ham; roll to enclose filling. Place seam side down on tray. Chill, covered, in refrigerator. Cut each into 5 bite-sized pieces just before serving. Secure with wooden picks.
Yield: 200 servings.

Approx Per Serving: Cal 15; Prot 1 g; Carbo <1 g; Fiber <1 g;
    T Fat 1 g; 62% Calories from Fat; Chol 5 mg; Sod 79 mg.
    Nutritional information does not include Greek seasoning.

Sweet and Sour Meatballs

1¹/₂ pounds ground chuck
2 pounds ground pork
1 cup seasoned bread crumbs
¹/₂ cup chopped almonds, toasted
2 cloves of garlic, minced
2 eggs, beaten
3 tablespoons soy sauce
Nutmeg to taste
2 teaspoons salt
Tabasco sauce to taste
¹/₂ cup cornstarch

2 cups pineapple juice
2 cups water
2 cups white vinegar
3 cups sugar
¹/₂ cup cornstarch
1 cup soy sauce
1 8-ounce can pineapple chunks,
   drained
1 large green bell pepper, cut into
   strips

Combine ground chuck, ground pork, bread crumbs, almonds, garlic, eggs, soy sauce, nutmeg, salt and Tabasco sauce in bowl; mix well. Shape into 1-inch meatballs. Roll in cornstarch to coat. Brown meatballs several at a time in skillet; drain. Cool. Freeze in single layer. Store in freezer container. Combine pineapple juice, water, vinegar, sugar, cornstarch and soy sauce in saucepan; mix well. Cook for 10 minutes, stirring frequently. Place meatballs in baking dish; pour sauce over meatballs. Let stand, covered, in refrigerator for 24 hours. Bake at 350 degrees for 50 minutes. Add pineapple and green pepper. Bake for 15 minutes longer.
Yield: 20 servings.

Approx Per Serving: Cal 365; Prot 20 g; Carbo 48 g; Fiber 1 g;
    T Fat 11 g; 27% Calories from Fat; Chol 77 mg; Sod 1282 mg.

Margland II's Mushroom Puffs

We serve this at wedding receptions. —Wanda Bateman, Innkeeper

2 8-count cans crescent rolls
8 ounces cream cheese, softened
2 4-ounce cans mushrooms, drained,
   chopped

2 green onions, chopped
1 teaspoon seasoned salt
1 egg, beaten
2 teaspoons poppy seed

Unroll crescent roll dough. Separate into rectangles. Lay on lightly floured surface, sealing perforations. Combine cream cheese, mushrooms, green onions and seasoned salt in bowl; mix well. Spread mixture on dough; roll jelly roll fashion to enclose filling. Cut into 1-inch slices. Brush with egg; sprinkle with poppy seed. Place on baking sheet. Bake at 375 degrees for 10 minutes. Serve hot. May freeze rolls before cutting into slices. Rolls are easy to slice while frozen. Yield: 48 servings.

Approx Per Serving: Cal 53; Prot 1 g; Carbo 4 g; Fiber <1 g;
    T Fat 4 g; 61% Calories from Fat; Chol 10 mg; Sod 139 mg.

Marriages are made in heaven, but so are thunder and lightning.

Appetizer Cream Puffs

¹/₂ cup butter	¹/₄ teaspoon salt
1 cup hot water	4 eggs
1 cup flour	

Combine butter and hot water in saucepan. Bring to a boil, stirring occasionally. Stir in flour and salt all at once. Cook until mixture leaves side of pan, stirring constantly. Remove from heat. Cool slightly. Beat in eggs 1 at a time. Drop by tablespoonfuls 2 inches apart onto greased baking sheet. Bake at 400 degrees for 25 minutes or until puffed and golden brown. Cool on wire rack. Cut off tops; remove soft dough inside. May fill with chicken or tuna salad; replace tops. Serve immediately. May also fill with chocolate, lemon or vanilla pudding. Yield: 24 servings.

Approx Per Serving: Cal 66; Prot 2 g; Carbo 4 g; Fiber <1 g;
    T Fat 5 g; 66% Calories from Fat; Chol 46 mg; Sod 66 mg.

Appetizer Tortilla Pinwheels

1 cup sour cream	1 cup shredded Cheddar cheese
8 ounces cream cheese, softened	¹/₂ cup chopped green onions
1 4-ounce can chopped green chilies, drained	Garlic powder to taste
	Seasoned salt to taste
1 4-ounce can chopped black olives, drained	5 10-inch flour tortillas

Combine sour cream, cream cheese, green chilies, black olives, Cheddar cheese, green onions, garlic powder and seasoned salt in bowl; mix well. Divide into 5 portions. Spread 1 portion on each tortilla; roll to enclose filling. Enclose each tortilla in plastic wrap, twisting ends to seal tightly. Chill in refrigerator for several hours. Cut into ¹/₂ to ³/₄-inch slices; place on serving dish. Yield: 48 servings.

Approx Per Serving: Cal 55; Prot 1 g; Carbo 3 g; Fiber <1 g;
    T Fat 4 g; 68% Calories from Fat; Chol 10 mg; Sod 83 mg.

Sausage Balls

1 pound sausage	¹/₄ teaspoon garlic powder
1 pound Cheddar cheese, melted	1 tablespoon Worcestershire sauce
3 cups baking mix	

Combine sausage, melted cheese, baking mix, garlic powder and Worcestershire sauce in bowl; mix well. Shape into 1-inch balls; place on greased baking sheet. Bake at 300 degrees for 15 minutes or until brown. Yield: 120 servings.

Approx Per Serving: Cal 36; Prot 2 g; Carbo 2 g; Fiber 0 g;
    T Fat 2 g; 58% Calories from Fat; Chol 5 mg; Sod 87 mg.

Soups

Bush Bean Soup

*This recipe belonged to a dear friend, Faye Hollingsworth of
El Dorado, Arkansas, who died of cancer. —Sandra Thompson*

1 pound extra-lean ground beef
1   20-ounce can Bush's pinto beans
1   20-ounce can Bush's navy beans
**1   20-ounce can Bush's hot chili
   beans**

**1   20-ounce can Bush's Great
   Northern beans**
**2   10-ounce cans Ro-Tel tomatoes,
   chopped**

Brown ground beef in skillet, stirring until crumbly; drain. Combine ground beef, pinto beans, navy beans, hot chili beans, Great Northern beans and tomatoes in slow cooker; mix well. Cook, covered, on Low for 6 to 8 hours or on High for 3 to 4 hours, stirring occasionally. Yield: 12 servings.

Approx Per Serving: Cal 267; Prot 19 g; Carbo 36 g; Fiber <1 g;
   T Fat 6 g; 20% Calories from Fat; Chol 25 mg; Sod 1025 mg.

Cherish yesterday.
Dream tomorrow.
Live today.

Ozark Bean Soup

1 1-pound package mixed dried beans
1 48-ounce can vegetable cocktail
   juice
1 onion, chopped
1 cup chopped carrot
1 cup chopped celery
1 cup chopped green bell pepper

4 cups water
1/4 teaspoon garlic powder
1 tablespoon each basil, thyme and
   oregano
2 tablespoons Worcestershire sauce
8 ounces Italian turkey sausage or
   ground turkey

Combine dry beans, vegetable juice, onion, carrot, celery, green pepper, water, garlic powder, basil, thyme, oregano, Worcestershire sauce and turkey sausage in slow cooker. Cook, covered, on High until mixture comes to a boil. Cook on Low for 6 to 8 hours, stirring occasionally. Yield: 10 servings.

Approx Per Serving: Cal 218; Prot 14 g; Carbo 37 g; Fiber 9 g;
    T Fat 2 g; 9% Calories from Fat; Chol 9 mg; Sod 619 mg.

Baby Lima Bean Soup

1 1-pound package dried baby lima
   beans
Meat tenderizer to taste
2 rings Polish sausage, chopped

1 or 2 potatoes, chopped
4 carrots, chopped
1 medium onion, chopped
12 ounces baked ham, chopped

Combine lima beans, tenderizer and water to cover in saucepan. Let stand for 30 minutes; drain. Cover with fresh water. Cook over medium heat for 35 minutes or until beans are tender. Brown sausage in skillet, stirring until crumbly; drain. Add sausage, potatoes, carrots, onion and ham to beans; mix well. Cook for 30 minutes or until vegetables are tender. Yield: 12 servings.

Approx Per Serving: Cal 324; Prot 21 g; Carbo 33 g; Fiber 13 g;
    T Fat 12 g; 34% Calories from Fat; Chol 41 mg; Sod 697 mg.

Broccoli-Cheese Soup

2 cups water
2 pounds fresh broccoli, chopped
2 chicken bouillon cubes
1 small onion, chopped

2 tablespoons butter
3/4 cup flour
2 cups milk
16 ounces American cheese, cubed

Combine water, broccoli and bouillon cubes in saucepan. Cook over medium heat until broccoli is tender. Sauté onion in butter in skillet until tender. Stir in flour until well mixed. Add milk; mix well. Add cheese. Cook over medium heat until thick and creamy, stirring frequently. Stir into undrained broccoli mixture; mix well. Yield: 6 servings.

Approx Per Serving: Cal 474; Prot 26 g; Carbo 27 g; Fiber 6 g;
    T Fat 31 g; 57% Calories from Fat; Chol 94 mg; Sod 1573 mg.

Cabbage Soup

8 ounces ground turkey
1 onion, chopped
1 tablespoon oil
1/2 head cabbage, shredded
3 large carrots, sliced
2 16-ounce cans stewed tomatoes

3 cups low-fat chicken broth
1/4 teaspoon black pepper
1/8 teaspoon cayenne pepper
1 tablespoon minced garlic
1 16-ounce can red kidney beans,
   drained, rinsed

Sauté turkey and onion in oil in 4-quart saucepan until onion is tender, stirring frequently. Add cabbage, carrots, tomatoes, chicken broth, black pepper, cayenne pepper, garlic and kidney beans. Bring to a boil. Simmer for 1 hour or until vegetables are tender, stirring occasionally. May substitute 1/4 teaspoon garlic powder for garlic. Yield: 8 servings.

Approx Per Serving: Cal 177; Prot 11 g; Carbo 24 g; Fiber 6 g;
      T Fat 5 g; 25% Calories from Fat; Chol 20 mg; Sod 659 mg.

Chicken Stew with Peppers

3 pounds chicken pieces, skinned
4 teaspoons oil
2 cups chopped onions
2 cups chopped celery
2 cups chopped red and green bell
   peppers
4 cups canned whole tomatoes
1/2 cup green beans

1/2 cup sliced carrots
1 green chili pepper, minced
2 bay leaves
1 tablespoon chopped fresh parsley
1 teaspoon salt
1/2 teaspoon each thyme, basil, chili
   powder and pepper

Rinse chicken and pat dry. Brown in hot oil in 5-quart saucepan. Remove chicken to bowl. Add onions, celery and bell peppers to saucepan. Sauté until onions are golden brown. Add tomatoes, green beans, carrots, chili pepper, bay leaves, parsley, salt, thyme, basil, chili powder and pepper; mix well. Bring to a boil. Add chicken. Simmer, covered, for 1 hour or until chicken and vegetables are tender, stirring occasionally. Discard bay leaves. Yield: 4 servings.

Approx Per Serving: Cal 472; Prot 54 g; Carbo 24 g; Fiber 6 g;
      T Fat 18 g; 35% Calories from Fat; Chol 152 mg; Sod 1130 mg.

You may be the only gospel your neighbor ever reads.

Good Chicken Stew

1 pound boneless chicken, chopped
1 10-ounce can Ro-tel tomatoes
1 16-ounce can stewed tomatoes
1 16-ounce can tomato sauce
1 small onion, chopped
1 clove of garlic, minced
2 stalks celery, coarsely chopped

6 carrots, coarsely chopped
3 large potatoes, coarsely chopped
3 to 4 tablespoons pearl barley
1 tablespoon sugar
3/4 teaspoon salt
Pepper to taste
3 8-ounce cans mushrooms

Rinse chicken and pat dry. Combine with Ro-tel tomatoes, stewed tomatoes, tomato sauce, onion, garlic, celery, carrots, potatoes, barley, sugar, salt and pepper in roasting pan; mix well. Add enough water to make of desired consistency. Bake, covered, at 250 degrees for 6 hours. Add undrained mushrooms 10 minutes before removing from oven. May also simmer over low heat for 2 hours, stirring occasionally. Yield: 16 servings.

Approx Per Serving: Cal 108; Prot 7 g; Carbo 19 g; Fiber 3 g;
   T Fat 1 g; 11% Calories from Fat; Chol 13 mg; Sod 642 mg.

Garlic Soup with Summer Greens

This recipe is dedicated to my mom, Stella Rognrud. —Marlee Rognrud

1 bulb of garlic, separated into cloves
2 onions, chopped
3 bay leaves
1 teaspoon thyme
2 whole allspice, crushed

1 tablespoon olive oil
3 cups chicken stock
1 cup milk
1 cup shredded fresh spinach

Sauté garlic and onions with bay leaves, thyme and allspice in hot olive oil in large stockpot. Add chicken stock. Bring to a boil. Reduce heat. Simmer for 15 minutes or until garlic is tender, stirring occasionally. Discard bay leaves. Remove garlic and onions with slotted spoon to blender container. Add a small amount of hot chicken stock. Process until vegetables are puréed. Return puréed mixture to stockpot. Add milk gradually. Cook over low heat until mixture is hot. Add spinach. Cook until heated through. Yield: 4 servings.

Approx Per Serving: Cal 136; Prot 7 g; Carbo 12 g; Fiber 2 g;
   T Fat 7 g; 44% Calories from Fat; Chol 9 mg; Sod 621 mg.

Fish Chowder

4 ounces salt pork, finely chopped
1 large onion, sliced
3 medium potatoes, chopped
1 cup (about) water

16 ounces haddock, cubed
1½ quarts milk
2 tablespoons butter

Cook salt pork over low heat in saucepan until fat is rendered and pork is brown. Remove pork to paper towels to drain. Sauté onion in drippings in saucepan until tender. Add potatoes and water to cover. Cook over medium heat until potatoes are tender. Add fish. Cook for 5 minutes or until fish flakes easily, adding water to cover as necessary. Add milk. Heat to the boiling point. Remove from heat. Add butter. Spoon into bowls. Garnish with pork. May substitute water for half the milk. Yield: 6 servings.

Approx Per Serving: Cal 353; Prot 28 g; Carbo 27 g; Fiber 1 g;
T Fat 16 g; 39% Calories from Fat; Chol 93 mg; Sod 281 mg.

Monastery-Style Lentil Soup

2 large onions, chopped
1 carrot, chopped
¼ cup olive oil
½ teaspoon each thyme and
   marjoram
3 cups seasoned stock

1 cup dried lentils
Salt to taste
¼ cup chopped fresh parsley
1   16-ounce can tomatoes
¼ cup dry sherry
⅔ cup shredded Swiss cheese

Sauté onions and carrot in hot olive oil in large soup pot for 3 to 5 minutes or until tender. Add thyme and marjoram. Sauté for 1 minute. Add stock, lentils, salt, parsley and tomatoes. Cook, covered, over medium heat for 45 minutes or until lentils are tender, stirring occasionally. Add sherry. Sprinkle 2 tablespoons cheese in each soup bowl. Fill with soup. Yield: 6 servings.

Approx Per Serving: Cal 305; Prot 17 g; Carbo 28 g; Fiber 6 g;
T Fat 14 g; 41% Calories from Fat; Chol 12 mg; Sod 554 mg.

You're judged by the company you keep.

Cream of Mushroom Soup

3 tablespoons unsalted butter
3 tablespoons flour
4 cups chicken stock
8 ounces fresh mushrooms, sliced
1 tablespoon butter

1 cup Madeira
1 cup whipping cream
1 tablespoon chopped fresh tarragon
Salt and pepper to taste

Melt butter in soup pot over low heat. Add flour gradually, mixing well. Add chicken stock gradually, mixing well. Cook over low heat for 20 to 25 minutes or until thickened, stirring frequently. Sauté mushrooms in butter in skillet over high heat until golden brown. Remove from heat. Stir in wine. Add mushroom mixture, cream, tarragon, salt and pepper to chicken stock mixture. Cook over low heat for 10 minutes, stirring occasionally. Yield: 4 servings.

Approx Per Serving: Cal 423; Prot 8 g; Carbo 10 g; Fiber 1 g;
    T Fat 35 g; 75% Calories from Fat; Chol 114 mg; Sod 829 mg.

Cheese and Potato Soup

2 stalks celery, chopped
1 onion, chopped
2 tablespoons margarine
6 to 10 red potatoes, peeled
2 carrots, sliced
3 cups water
5 chicken bouillon cubes

$3/4$ teaspoon seasoned salt
$1/2$ teaspoon rosemary
1 teaspoon thyme
Pepper and garlic powder to taste
2 cups milk
2 cups shredded Cheddar cheese

Sauté celery and onion in margarine in skillet until tender. Cut potatoes into cubes. Combine potatoes, carrots, water, bouillon cubes, seasoned salt, rosemary, thyme, pepper, garlic powder and sautéed vegetables in large soup pot. Cook, covered, for 20 minutes or until vegetables are tender. Remove from heat. Mash potatoes with potato masher. Add milk and cheese; mix well. Cook until cheese is melted. Yield: 6 servings.

Approx Per Serving: Cal 458; Prot 17 g; Carbo 55 g; Fiber 5 g;
    T Fat 20 g; 38% Calories from Fat; Chol 52 mg; Sod 1467 mg.

There are two sides to every story.

Sausage Stew

Always double the recipe because everyone eats double servings.
Men love this! —Pattie Hornbeck

1 pound sausage
1 medium green bell pepper, chopped
1 medium onion, chopped
1 28-ounce can whole tomatoes,
    chopped
2 8-ounce cans tomato sauce

2 tomato sauce cans water
1 tablespoon instant chicken bouillon
³/₄ teaspoon garlic salt
³/₄ cup uncooked small shell
    macaroni
1 cup shredded mozzarella cheese

Brown sausage with green pepper and onion in skillet, stirring until sausage is crumbly; drain. Combine tomatoes, tomato sauce, water, chicken instant bouillon and garlic salt in large soup pot. Cook, covered, for 15 minutes, stirring occasionally. Add macaroni. Simmer, covered, for 15 minutes or until macaroni is tender, stirring occasionally. Add sausage. Heat to serving temperature. Spoon into bowls; top with shredded cheese. Yield: 6 servings.

Approx Per Serving: Cal 277; Prot 15 g; Carbo 21 g; Fiber 3 g;
    T Fat 16 g; 50% Calories from Fat; Chol 44 mg; Sod 2035 mg.

Scotch Broth

Salt to taste
8 cups water
³/₄ cup barley
2 carrots, thinly sliced

1 whole small onion
1 meaty lamb bone
Freshly chopped parsley to taste
Pepper to taste

Bring salted water to a boil in large saucepan. Add barley, carrots, onion and lamb bone. Cook over medium heat until barley is tender. Remove onion. Add parsley, salt and pepper. Cook until of creamy consistency. Remove lamb bone. Remove meat from bone; add to broth. May use bone from roasted leg of lamb. Yield: 6 servings.

Approx Per Serving: Cal 132; Prot 6 g; Carbo 24 g; Fiber 5 g;
    T Fat 2 g; 12% Calories from Fat; Chol 10 mg; Sod 19 mg.

One of the best things a man can have up
his sleeve is a funny-bone.

Shrimp Chowder

Discovered this recipe several years ago for my family who is very fond of seafood.
It is excellent without shrimp as a potato soup base. —Bonnie Franz

4 large onions, thinly sliced
1/4 cup margarine
1 cup boiling water
6 medium potatoes, peeled, cubed
1 tablespoon salt

1/2 teaspoon pepper
1 1/2 quarts milk
2 cups shredded Cheddar cheese
2 pounds peeled uncooked shrimp
3 tablespoons chopped parsley

Sauté onions in margarine in soup pot until tender. Add boiling water, potatoes, salt and pepper. Cook, covered, over medium heat for 20 minutes or until potatoes are tender. Heat milk and cheese together in saucepan until cheese is melted. Do not boil. Add shrimp to potato mixture. Cook for 3 minutes or until shrimp turn pink. Add hot milk mixture. Heat over low heat until of serving temperature. Spoon into bowls. Sprinkle with parsley. Yield: 8 servings.

Approx Per Serving: Cal 481; Prot 35 g; Carbo 35 g; Fiber 3 g;
T Fat 23 g; 42% Calories from Fat; Chol 231 mg; Sod 1371 mg.

Tortilla Soup

4 cups each chicken and beef stock
1 large onion, cut into quarters
2 carrots, julienned
1 zucchini, chopped
1 14-ounce can whole tomatoes, chopped

1 medium potato, peeled, chopped
1 tablespoon salt
1 teaspoon freshly ground pepper
8 tortillas
8 ounces each Monterey Jack cheese and Cheddar cheese, shredded

Bring chicken and beef stock to a boil in soup pot. Cut onion quarters into slices. Add onion and next 6 ingredients to stock. Simmer for 3 hours, adding more stock if necessary and stirring occasionally. Crumble tortillas into soup bowls; add cheeses. Ladle soup into bowls. May add jalapeño peppers to soup. Yield: 8 servings.

Approx Per Serving: Cal 354; Prot 21 g; Carbo 24 g; Fiber 4 g;
T Fat 20 g; 50% Calories from Fat; Chol 57 mg; Sod 1996 mg.

Icy Watermelon Soup

2 cups chopped watermelon
2 cups orange juice

1 tablespoon thawed frozen orange juice concentrate

Purée all ingredients in blender. Chill for 1 hour or longer. Process again briefly just before serving. Pour into chilled bowls. Garnish with orange rind or mint sprigs. Yield: 4 servings.

Approx Per Serving: Cal 88; Prot 1 g; Carbo 20 g; Fiber 1 g;
T Fat 1 g; 6% Calories from Fat; Chol 0 mg; Sod 3 mg.

Salads

Trulock-Cook Home

Trulock-Cook Home

The Trulock-Cook home in Pine Bluff, built in 1903, now serves as a bed and breakfast known as Margland II. The "shingle style" architecture is one of two remaining in the city. The original owner, Harry E. Trulock, bought the lot from his mother and built the house shortly thereafter. Joe Q. Cook, a wholesale grocery business owner, bought the house in 1918 and lived there until he died. The house has been beautifully restored and is on the National Register of Historic Places.

Apple Salad

1 20-ounce can sliced pineapple
1 egg, slightly beaten
Juice of 1 lemon
1/2 teaspoon prepared mustard
1/2 cup sugar
1 1/2 tablespoons (heaping) flour

3 or 4 large apples, chopped
1 10-ounce package miniature
   marshmallows
1 7-ounce can shredded coconut
8 ounces Cheddar cheese, shredded

Drain pineapple, reserving juice. Combine reserved juice, egg, lemon juice, mustard, sugar and flour in saucepan. Cook over medium heat until thickened, stirring constantly. Cool. Chop pineapple. Combine pineapple, apples and marshmallows in bowl; mix well. Add sauce; mix well. Press into 8x14-inch glass dish. Sprinkle with coconut and cheese. Chill, covered, until serving time. Yield: 15 servings.

Approx Per Serving: Cal 270; Prot 5 g; Carbo 42 g; Fiber 2 g;
    T Fat 10 g; 33% Calories from Fat; Chol 30 mg; Sod 153 mg.

Apricot-Cheese Delight

1 9-ounce can apricots, chilled
1 16-ounce can crushed pineapple,
   chilled
2 3-ounce packages orange gelatin
2 cups boiling water
3/4 cup miniature marshmallows

1/2 cup sugar
3 tablespoons flour
1 egg, slightly beaten
2 tablespoons margarine
1 cup whipping cream, whipped
1 cup shredded mild Cheddar cheese

Drain apricots and pineapple, reserving juices. Dissolve gelatin in boiling water in bowl. Add 1 cup combined reserved juices; mix well. Chill in refrigerator until partially set. Chop apricots. Combine apricots, pineapple and marshmallows in bowl; mix well. Add to gelatin; mix well. Pour into 7x11-inch dish. Chill until firm. Combine sugar, flour, egg and 1 cup combined reserved juices in saucepan. Cook over low heat until thickened, stirring constantly. Stir in margarine. Remove from heat. Cool slightly. Fold in whipped cream. Spread over gelatin; sprinkle with cheese. Chill until serving time. Yield: 15 servings.

Approx Per Serving: Cal 224; Prot 4 g; Carbo 31 g; Fiber 1 g;
    T Fat 10 g; 40% Calories from Fat; Chol 44 mg; Sod 115 mg.

The time you enjoy wasting is not wasting time.

Blueberry Salad

2 3-ounce packages black cherry
   gelatin
2 cups boiling water
1 16-ounce can blueberries
1 8-ounce can crushed pineapple

2 cups sour cream
8 ounces cream cheese, softened
1/2 cup sugar
1/2 cup chopped pecans

Dissolve gelatin in boiling water in bowl. Drain blueberries and pineapple, reserving 1 cup juice. Add blueberries, pineapple and 1 cup reserved juice to gelatin; mix well. Pour into 9x13-inch serving dish. Chill in refrigerator until partially set. Add 1 cup sour cream, swirling through mixture. Chill until set. Combine remaining 1 cup sour cream, cream cheese and sugar in bowl; mix well. Spread over congealed gelatin; sprinkle with pecans. Chill until serving time. Yield: 12 servings.

Approx Per Serving: Cal 314; Prot 5 g; Carbo 36 g; Fiber 1 g;
   T Fat 18 g; 50% Calories from Fat; Chol 38 mg; Sod 123 mg.

Cranberry Salad

2 3-ounce packages cherry gelatin
3 cups boiling water
1 16-ounce can crushed pineapple

1 16-ounce can whole cranberry
   sauce
1 cup chopped pecans

Dissolve gelatin in boiling water in bowl. Chill until partially congealed. Add pineapple, cranberry sauce and pecans; mix well. Pour into 9x9-inch glass dish or mold. Chill until set. May substitute pineapple tidbits for crushed pineapple. Yield: 8 servings.

Approx Per Serving: Cal 308; Prot 3 g; Carbo 55 g; Fiber 3 g;
   T Fat 10 g; 28% Calories from Fat; Chol 0 mg; Sod 85 mg.

Easy-But-Delicious Fruit Salad

4 bananas, sliced
4 apples, peeled, chopped
2 kiwifruit, peeled, chopped
2 cups sliced strawberries

2 cups seedless grapes
1 large package sugar-free Hawaiian
   pineapple gelatin

Combine bananas, apples, kiwifruit, strawberries and grapes in bowl; mix well. Sprinkle in dry gelatin; mix well. Chill in refrigerator for 2 hours. Garnish with whipped topping. Yield: 6 servings.

Approx Per Serving: Cal 194; Prot 3 g; Carbo 48 g; Fiber 6 g;
   T Fat 1 g; 5% Calories from Fat; Chol 0 mg; Sod 78 mg.

Frozen Fruit Salad

2 8-ounce cans crushed pineapple, drained
2 21-ounce cans cherry pie filling
1 14-ounce can sweetened condensed milk
16 ounces whipped topping

Combine pineapple, pie filling and condensed milk in bowl; mix well. Fold in whipped topping. Spoon into 12 individual molds. Freeze until firm. Unmold onto lettuce-lined salad plates. May substitute strawberry or blueberry pie filling for cherry. Yield: 12 servings.

Approx Per Serving: Cal 340; Prot 4 g; Carbo 57 g; Fiber 2 g;
    T Fat 13 g; 32% Calories from Fat; Chol 11 mg; Sod 82 mg.

Fruity Frog's Eye Salad

1 cup sugar
$1/2$ teaspoon salt
2 eggs, beaten
2 tablespoons flour
$1^3/4$ cups pineapple juice
1 tablespoon lemon juice
2 quarts water
2 teaspoons salt
1 tablespoon oil
1 8-ounce package acini-di-pepe
4 11-ounce cans mandarin oranges, drained
2 20-ounce cans pineapple chunks, drained
2 20-ounce cans crushed pineapple, drained
2 cups miniature marshmallows
1 cup flaked coconut
12 ounces whipped topping

Combine sugar, $1/2$ teaspoon salt, eggs, flour and pineapple juice in saucepan. Cook over medium heat until thickened, stirring constantly. Add lemon juice; mix well. Cool to room temperature. Combine water, 2 teaspoons salt and oil in saucepan. Bring to a boil. Add pasta. Cook until tender, stirring occasionally; drain. Rinse pasta; drain. Cool to room temperature. Combine cooked mixture and pasta in bowl; mix well. Chill, covered, in refrigerator overnight. Add mandarin oranges, pineapple, marshmallows and coconut to chilled mixture; mix well. Fold in whipped topping. Chill until serving time. May keep for several days in refrigerator. Yield: 40 servings.

Approx Per Serving: Cal 148; Prot 2 g; Carbo 29 g; Fiber 1 g;
    T Fat 4 g; 21% Calories from Fat; Chol 11 mg; Sod 145 mg.

Your mother is your best friend.

Real Good Fruit Salad

1 7-ounce jar maraschino cherries
1 16-ounce can pineapple chunks
1 16-ounce can sliced peaches
1 6-ounce package vanilla instant
   pudding mix

3 apples, chopped
Sections of 3 oranges
2 cups seedless grapes
2 or 3 kiwifruit, sliced
5 bananas, sliced

Drain maraschino cherries, pineapple and peaches, reserving juices. Combine reserved juices and pudding mix in bowl; mix well. Combine maraschino cherries, pineapple, peaches, apples, oranges, grapes, kiwifruit and bananas in bowl; mix well. Pour pudding over fruit; mix well. Pour into large serving dish. Chill until serving time. Yield: 20 servings.

Approx Per Serving: Cal 145; Prot 1 g; Carbo 38 g; Fiber 2 g;
   T Fat <1 g; 2% Calories from Fat; Chol 0 mg; Sod 60 mg.

Grapefruit Salad

2 3-ounce packages orange gelatin
1 3-ounce package lemon gelatin
3 cups boiling water

3 grapefruit
1 20-ounce can crushed pineapple

Dissolve orange and lemon gelatin in boiling water in bowl. Chill in refrigerator until partially congealed. Cut grapefruit into halves. Remove grapefruit segments to bowl. Remove membranes from grapefruit shells; discard. Add pineapple to grapefruit segments; mix well. Stir fruit into partially congealed gelatin. Fill grapefruit shells with mixture; place on tray. Chill until set. Garnish with whipped cream cheese. Yield: 6 servings.

Approx Per Serving: Cal 270; Prot 5 g; Carbo 66 g; Fiber 2 g;
   T Fat <1 g; 1% Calories from Fat; Chol 0 mg; Sod 136 mg.

Lime Gelatin Salad

2 20-ounce cans crushed pineapple
1 6-ounce package lime gelatin
12 ounces cream cheese, softened
2 cups whipped topping

2 cups chopped celery
2 cups chopped pecans
2/3 cup chopped pimento

Bring pineapple to a boil in saucepan, stirring frequently. Stir in gelatin until dissolved. Pour into bowl. Chill in refrigerator until partially congealed. Combine cream cheese and whipped topping in bowl; mix well. Stir into partially congealed gelatin mixture. Add celery, pecans and pimento; mix well. Pour into 9x13-inch glass dish. Chill until set. Yield: 12 servings.

Approx Per Serving: Cal 401; Prot 6 g; Carbo 40 g; Fiber 3 g;
   T Fat 27 g; 57% Calories from Fat; Chol 31 mg; Sod 139 mg.

Nanny's Lime Gelatin Salad

*This has been a favorite for years. My Grandmother "Nanny"
makes it for special occasions. —Suzy Griffin*

1   3-ounce package lime gelatin
1¹/₂ cups boiling water
3 ounces cream cheese, softened

1   16-ounce can pears, drained
1 cup miniature marshmallows
¹/₂ cup chopped pecans

Dissolve gelatin in boiling water in bowl. Add cream cheese, stirring until almost melted. Cut pears into small pieces. Add to mixture. Pour into 9x9-inch glass dish. Sprinkle with marshmallows and pecans. Chill until set. Yield: 12 servings.

Approx Per Serving: Cal 170; Prot 3 g; Carbo 17 g; Fiber 1 g;
    T Fat 10 g; 53% Calories from Fat; Chol 24 mg; Sod 92 mg.

Mandarin Orange Salad

¹/₄ cup oil
¹/₄ cup red wine vinegar
3 tablespoons sugar
¹/₂ teaspoon each salt and pepper
Tabasco sauce to taste
1 teaspoon minced parsley

¹/₂ head lettuce, shredded
2 green onions, sliced
1 cup chopped celery
1   11-ounce can mandarin oranges,
    drained
¹/₄ cup slivered almonds, toasted

Combine oil, vinegar, sugar, salt, pepper, Tabasco sauce and minced parsley in jar. Shake, covered, until sugar and salt are dissolved. Chill in refrigerator until serving time. Combine lettuce, green onions, celery, mandarin oranges and almonds in bowl; mix well. Shake dressing well. Pour over salad, tossing to mix. Yield: 6 servings.

Approx Per Serving: Cal 177; Prot 2 g; Carbo 18 g; Fiber 1 g;
    T Fat 12 g; 58% Calories from Fat; Chol 0 mg; Sod 201 mg.

Orange Salad

1   6-ounce package orange gelatin
2 cups boiling water
2 tea bags
2 teaspoons prepared mustard
1   8-ounce can crushed pineapple

2   11-ounce cans mandarin oranges,
    drained
1   8-ounce can sliced water
    chestnuts, drained

Dissolve gelatin in boiling water. Add tea bags. Steep for 5 minutes; remove tea bags. Add mustard; mix well. Add undrained pineapple, mandarin oranges and water chestnuts; mix well. Pour into 9x13-inch glass dish. Chill, covered, overnight. Yield: 12 servings.

Approx Per Serving: Cal 109; Prot 2 g; Carbo 27 g; Fiber 1 g;
    T Fat <1 g; 1% Calories from Fat; Chol 0 mg; Sod 61 mg.

Orange-Almond Salad

½ cup sliced almonds
2 tablespoons sugar
½ teaspoon salt
½ teaspoon pepper
¼ cup oil
2 tablespoons vinegar

2 tablespoons sugar
½ head lettuce, shredded
1 tablespoon chopped parsley
2 green onions with tops, sliced
1 11-ounce can mandarin oranges, chilled, drained

Cook almonds and 2 tablespoons sugar in small skillet over medium heat until sugar melts, browns and sticks to almonds, stirring constantly. Spread on foil. Cool and crumble. Combine salt, pepper, oil, vinegar and 2 tablespoons sugar in jar. Shake, covered, until sugar and salt are dissolved. Combine lettuce, parsley, green onions and mandarin oranges in salad bowl. Add dressing, tossing to coat. Top with almonds just before serving. May also add sliced red onion and sliced celery. Yield: 6 servings.

Approx Per Serving: Cal 194; Prot 2 g; Carbo 19 g; Fiber 1 g;
   T Fat 13 g; 58% Calories from Fat; Chol 0 mg; Sod 184 mg.

Peach Salad

1 16-ounce can crushed pineapple
1 cup water
1 cup sugar
1 6-ounce package peach gelatin

8 ounces cream cheese, softened
5 tablespoons milk
9 ounces whipped topping

Combine undrained pineapple, water and sugar in saucepan. Bring to a boil over medium heat, stirring occasionally. Stir in gelatin until dissolved. Pour into bowl. Chill in refrigerator until partially set. Combine cream cheese and milk in bowl; beat well. Add whipped topping; beat well. Whip partially congealed mixture slightly. Fold in whipped topping mixture. Pour into 9x13-inch glass dish. Chill until set. Yield: 12 servings.

Approx Per Serving: Cal 284; Prot 3 g; Carbo 42 g; Fiber <1 g;
   T Fat 12 g; 38% Calories from Fat; Chol 22 mg; Sod 110 mg.

Creative minds are seldom tidy.

Pineapple Salad

1 20-ounce can crushed pineapple
1¹/₂ cups sugar
2 eggs, beaten
2 tablespoons flour
Salt to taste

10 marshmallows
Sections of 2 oranges
1 cup chopped pecans
1 cup whipped topping

Drain juice from pineapple into double boiler. Reserve pineapple. Cook over medium heat until hot. Add mixture of sugar, eggs, flour and salt. Cook until thickened, stirring constantly. Cool. Add marshmallows, oranges, pecans and pineapple; mix well. Fold in whipped topping. Spoon into serving bowl. Chill until serving time. Yield: 12 servings.

Approx Per Serving: Cal 270; Prot 3 g; Carbo 47 g; Fiber 2 g;
    T Fat 9 g; 30% Calories from Fat; Chol 36 mg; Sod 20 mg.

Pistachio Salad

1 4-ounce package pistachio instant
    pudding mix
1 16-ounce can crushed pineapple

8 ounces whipped topping
¹/₂ cup miniature marshmallows
¹/₂ cup chopped pecans

Combine pudding mix and crushed pineapple with juice in bowl; mix well. Fold in whipped topping, marshmallows and pecans. Spoon into serving bowl. Chill until serving time. Yield: 8 servings.

Approx Per Serving: Cal 248; Prot 1 g; Carbo 36 g; Fiber 1 g;
    T Fat 12 g; 43% Calories from Fat; Chol 0 mg; Sod 106 mg.

Pretzel Salad

1¹/₂ cups crushed pretzels
4¹/₂ tablespoons sugar
³/₄ cup melted margarine
8 ounces cream cheese, softened
8 ounces whipped topping
³/₄ cup sugar

1 6-ounce package strawberry
    gelatin
2 cups boiling water
1 16-ounce package frozen sliced
    strawberries

Combine pretzels, 4¹/₂ tablespoons sugar and margarine in bowl; mix well. Press into greased 9x13-inch baking dish. Bake at 350 degrees for 10 minutes. Cool. Combine cream cheese, whipped topping and ³/₄ cup sugar in bowl; mix well. Spread over cooled crust. Chill in refrigerator. Dissolve gelatin in boiling water in bowl. Add frozen strawberries, stirring until thawed. Chill until partially set. Spoon over cream cheese layer. Chill until set. Yield: 12 servings.

Approx Per Serving: Cal 403; Prot 4 g; Carbo 47 g; Fiber 1 g;
    T Fat 23 g; 51% Calories from Fat; Chol 21 mg; Sod 412 mg.

Strawberry Salad

2 3-ounce packages strawberry
　 gelatin
1 cup boiling water
1 10-ounce package frozen
　 strawberries

1 cup cold water
1 8-ounce can crushed pineapple
2 bananas, mashed
1 cup sour cream

Dissolve gelatin in boiling water in bowl. Stir in strawberries until thawed. Add cold water; mix well. Add pineapple and juice and mashed bananas; mix well. Pour half the mixture into 8x12-inch glass dish. Chill in refrigerator until congealed. Spread sour cream over congealed gelatin. Pour remaining gelatin mixture over top. Chill until set. Yield: 10 servings.

Approx Per Serving: Cal 161; Prot 3 g; Carbo 29 g; Fiber 1 g;
　　T Fat 5 g; 26% Calories from Fat; Chol 10 mg; Sod 67 mg.

Striped Salad

8 ounces whipped topping
1 6-ounce package vanilla instant
　 pudding mix
1 cup buttermilk

1 11-ounce can mandarin oranges,
　 drained
1 10-ounce package striped
　 shortbread cookies

Combine whipped topping and pudding mix in bowl; mix well. Add buttermilk; mix well. Stir in mandarin oranges. Break shortbread cookies into small pieces. Fold into mixture. Spoon into serving dish. Chill until serving time. Yield: 10 servings.

Approx Per Serving: Cal 316; Prot 2 g; Carbo 47 g; Fiber <1 g;
　　T Fat 13 g; 38% Calories from Fat; Chol 1 mg; Sod 259 mg.

Yankee Salad

1 11-ounce can mandarin oranges,
　 drained
1 cup juice-pack pineapple chunks,
　 drained

1$\frac{1}{3}$ cups low-fat cottage cheese
1 cup low-fat whipped topping
2 small packages sugar-free orange
　 gelatin

Combine mandarin oranges and pineapple in bowl; mix well. Add cottage cheese and whipped topping; mix well. Sprinkle in dry gelatin, stirring to mix. Pour into 8x8-inch glass dish. Chill until serving time. Yield: 4 servings.

Approx Per Serving: Cal 197; Prot 13 g; Carbo 30 g; Fiber 1 g;
　　T Fat 4 g; 16% Calories from Fat; Chol 6 mg; Sod 423 mg.

Avocado and Chicken Salad

6 cups chopped cooked chicken
1/2 cup minced onion
1 cup finely chopped celery
2 tablespoons capers
1/4 cup fresh lemon juice
1/4 cup minced parsley

3 hard-boiled eggs, chopped
1 to 1 1/2 cups mayonnaise
Salt and pepper to taste
8 avocados
1/2 head lettuce, shredded
Paprika to taste

Combine chicken, onion, celery, capers, lemon juice and parsley in bowl. Add eggs, mayonnaise, salt and pepper; mix well. Peel avocados; cut into halves, removing seeds. Place 2 avocado halves on bed of shredded lettuce on salad plates. Fill avocados with chicken salad; sprinkle with paprika. Garnish with tomato quarters and parsley. Yield: 8 servings.

Approx Per Serving: Cal 859; Prot 38 g; Carbo 19 g; Fiber 20 g;
    T Fat 74 g; 75% Calories from Fat; Chol 198 mg; Sod 385 mg.
    Nutritional information does not include capers.

Chicken-Spinach Salad

8 ounces fresh spinach
2 cups chopped cooked chicken
2 cups broccoli flowerets
1   8-ounce can sliced water
    chestnuts, drained
4 slices crisp-fried bacon, crumbled
3 tablespoons wine vinegar

3 tablespoons soy sauce
3 tablespoons oil
1 teaspoon minced onion
1 teaspoon sugar
1/8 teaspoon pepper
1/2 cup chow mein noodles
1/4 cup grated Parmesan cheese

Combine spinach, chicken, broccoli, water chestnuts and bacon in bowl; mix well. Chill, covered, until serving time. Combine vinegar, soy sauce, oil, onion, sugar and pepper in jar. Shake, covered, until sugar is dissolved. Chill in refrigerator until serving time. Shake dressing. Pour over chicken mixture, tossing to mix. Spoon into salad bowl. Top with chow mein noodles and cheese. Yield: 4 servings.

Approx Per Serving: Cal 375; Prot 29 g; Carbo 18 g; Fiber 5 g;
    T Fat 22 g; 51% Calories from Fat; Chol 72 mg; Sod 1145 mg.

There is no cosmetic for beauty like happiness.

Crunchy Chicken Salad

1½ cups chopped cooked chicken
5 hard-boiled eggs, chopped
1 cup chopped celery
1 cup cubed sweet pickles
1 cup chopped pecans, toasted
1 cup seedless green grape halves
1 8-ounce can water chestnuts, drained, chopped

1 8-ounce can pineapple tidbits, drained, chopped
½ cup chopped pimento-stuffed olives
1 small onion, chopped
1 2-ounce jar chopped pimento, drained
1 tablespoon lemon juice
1 cup mayonnaise

Combine chicken, eggs, celery, sweet pickles, pecans, grapes, water chestnuts, pineapple, olives, onion and pimento in bowl; mix well. Add lemon juice and mayonnaise; mix well. Chill, covered, for 4 hours to enhance flavors. Yield: 8 servings.

Approx Per Serving: Cal 493; Prot 14 g; Carbo 27 g; Fiber 3 g;
T Fat 39 g; 68% Calories from Fat; Chol 173 mg; Sod 566 mg.

Fruity Chicken Salad

2 cups chopped cooked chicken
1 cup grape halves
1 cup coarsely chopped peaches
½ cup chopped celery

½ cup (or more) sour cream
Curry powder to taste
Salt and pepper to taste

Combine chicken, grapes, peaches and celery in bowl; mix well. Add sour cream, curry powder, salt and pepper; mix well. Chill, covered, in refrigerator. Serve on lettuce-lined salad plates. Yield: 6 servings.

Approx Per Serving: Cal 175; Prot 15 g; Carbo 12 g; Fiber 1 g;
T Fat 8 g; 39% Calories from Fat; Chol 50 mg; Sod 60 mg.

Crab Pasta Salad

2 cups cooked noodles
1½ cups imitation crab meat
½ cup chopped green bell pepper
½ cup chopped tomato
¼ cup chopped green onions

1 cup broccoli flowerets, blanched
½ cup mayonnaise
¼ cup Italian salad dressing
¼ cup grated Parmesan cheese

Combine noodles, crab meat, green pepper, tomato, green onions and broccoli in bowl; mix well. Combine mayonnaise, Italian dressing and Parmesan cheese in small bowl; mix well. Pour over noodle mixture, tossing to mix. Chill, covered, until serving time. Yield: 10 servings.

Approx Per Serving: Cal 182; Prot 5 g; Carbo 12 g; Fiber 1 g;
T Fat 14 g; 64% Calories from Fat; Chol 22 mg; Sod 303 mg.

Tortellini and Ham Salad

9 ounces uncooked cheese tortellini
1 cup julienned ham
8 ounces Cheddar cheese, cubed
3/4 cup thawed frozen tiny peas
2 tablespoons minced green onions
2 cups ranch salad dressing

Cook tortellini using package directions; drain. Cool. Combine tortellini, ham, cheese cubes, peas and green onions in bowl; mix well. Add salad dressing; mix well. Chill, covered, until serving time. May use cheese of your choice. Yield: 6 servings.

Approx Per Serving: Cal 625; Prot 25 g; Carbo 27 g; Fiber 1 g;
    T Fat 47 g; 67% Calories from Fat; Chol 104 mg; Sod 1069 mg.

Seafood Pasta Salad

4 1/2 cups water
1 1/2 pounds fresh medium shrimp
10 ounces uncooked linguine
3/4 cup olive oil
1 envelope garlic salad dressing mix
1/2 cup chopped fresh parsley
2/3 cup wine vinegar
1 teaspoon oregano
1 1/2 teaspoons basil
1 1/2 teaspoons garlic salt
1/2 teaspoon coarsely ground pepper
1   6-ounce package frozen snow
    peas, thawed, drained
6 green onions, chopped
4 medium tomatoes, peeled,
    chopped, drained
3/4 cup crab meat

Bring water to a boil in saucepan. Add shrimp. Cook for 3 minutes; drain. Rinse in cold water. Chill, covered, in refrigerator. Peel and devein shrimp. Cook linguine using package directions, omitting salt; drain. Rinse in cold water; drain. Cool. Combine olive oil, salad dressing mix, parsley, vinegar, oregano, basil, garlic salt and pepper in bowl; mix well. Combine snow peas, green onions, tomatoes, crab meat, shrimp and linguine in bowl; mix well. Add dressing, tossing to mix. Chill, covered, in refrigerator for 2 hours to overnight before serving. Yield: 16 servings.

Approx Per Serving: Cal 210; Prot 11 g; Carbo 17 g; Fiber 2 g;
    T Fat 11 g; 47% Calories from Fat; Chol 73 mg; Sod 350 mg.

*Happiness is the sense that
one matters.*

Avocado-Shrimp Salad

2 teaspoons Dijon mustard
1 teaspoon salt
1/2 teaspoon pepper
1 teaspoon garlic salt
1/3 cup red wine vinegar
2/3 cup olive oil

1 tablespoon lemon juice
1 14-ounce can hearts of palm,
   drained
1/2 cup sliced green onions
3 cups cooked small shrimp
3 avocados

Process first 7 ingredients in blender until well mixed. Cut hearts of palm into 1/4-inch slices. Combine hearts of palm, green onions and shrimp in bowl; mix well. Add dressing, tossing to mix. Chill, covered, in refrigerator for several hours to overnight. Peel avocados; cut into halves, removing seeds. Place avocado halves on lettuce-lined salad plates. Spoon shrimp salad into avocado halves. Garnish with watercress sprigs. Yield: 6 servings.

Approx Per Serving: Cal 481; Prot 21 g; Carbo 10 g; Fiber 10 g;
    T Fat 41 g; 75% Calories from Fat; Chol 166 mg; Sod 1279 mg.

Greek Salad with Shrimp

1 cup uncooked rice
1 4-ounce can shrimp, drained
Flowerets of 1 head cauliflower
1 green bell pepper, chopped
20 stuffed green olives, sliced

Juice of 1 lemon
1/2 teaspoon salt
1/4 teaspoon pepper
Hot pepper sauce to taste
1 cup mayonnaise

Cook rice using package directions. Cool. Combine rice, shrimp, cauliflower, green pepper and olives in bowl; mix well. Combine next 5 ingredients in bowl; mix well. Add to vegetables, tossing to mix. Chill, covered, until serving time. Yield: 8 servings.

Approx Per Serving: Cal 325; Prot 6 g; Carbo 23 g; Fiber 2 g;
    T Fat 24 g; 65% Calories from Fat; Chol 41 mg; Sod 556 mg.

Shrimp Salad Mold

2 envelopes unflavored gelatin
1/2 cup cold water
1 10-ounce can tomato soup
8 ounces cream cheese, softened
1 cup mayonnaise

1/2 cup chopped green onions
1/4 cup chopped celery
Salt, pepper and Tabasco sauce to taste
1 6-ounce can shrimp, drained,
   chopped

Soften gelatin in cold water in bowl. Bring soup to a boil in saucepan over medium heat. Add gelatin, stirring until dissolved. Add cream cheese, stirring until melted. Remove from heat. Cool. Add next 6 ingredients; mix well. Stir in shrimp. Pour into oiled mold. Chill until set. Unmold onto lettuce-lined serving plate. Yield: 8 servings.

Approx Per Serving: Cal 354; Prot 10 g; Carbo 7 g; Fiber 1 g;
    T Fat 33 g; 82% Calories from Fat; Chol 84 mg; Sod 527 mg.

Macaroni Salad

2 cups cooked small macaroni
8 green onions, finely chopped
8 slices American cheese, chopped
2 dill pickles, chopped
6 hard-boiled eggs, chopped
1 green bell pepper, chopped

1 tomato, chopped
2 tablespoons (heaping) mayonnaise
1 teaspoon prepared mustard
8 ounces bacon, crisp-fried, crumbled
Salt, pepper and paprika to taste

Combine macaroni, green onions, cheese, pickles, eggs, green pepper and tomato in bowl; mix well. Add mayonnaise, mustard, bacon, salt, pepper and paprika; mix well. Chill, covered, for 2 hours before serving. Yield: 10 servings.

Approx Per Serving: Cal 222; Prot 12 g; Carbo 7 g; Fiber 1 g;
   T Fat 16 g; 65% Calories from Fat; Chol 157 mg; Sod 644 mg.

Sweet Macaroni Salad

16 ounces macaroni, cooked
1 large onion, chopped
1 large green bell pepper, chopped
3 carrots, grated
1/2 cup vinegar
1 cup sugar

2 cups mayonnaise-type salad
   dressing
1   14-ounce can sweetened
   condensed milk
2 teaspoons pepper

Combine macaroni, onion, green pepper and carrots in bowl; mix well. Combine vinegar, sugar and salad dressing in bowl; mix well. Add condensed milk and pepper; mix well. Add to macaroni mixture; mix well. Chill, covered, until serving time. Yield: 8 servings.

Approx Per Serving: Cal 570; Prot 7 g; Carbo 85 g; Fiber 2 g;
   T Fat 24 g; 37% Calories from Fat; Chol 32 mg; Sod 492 mg.

Italian Garden Pasta Salad

1 1/2 cups uncooked elbow macaroni
1 medium tomato, chopped
1 or 2 medium zucchini, sliced
1 cup pitted black olives
1/4 cup sliced green onions
3 tablespoons tarragon vinegar

2 tablespoons oil
1 teaspoon dillweed
1/4 teaspoon dry mustard
1/8 teaspoon pepper
1 small clove of garlic, minced
1/4 teaspoon salt

Cook macaroni using package directions; drain. Rinse under cold water; drain. Cool. Combine macaroni, tomato, zucchini, olives and green onions in bowl; mix well. Combine remaining ingredients in bowl; mix well. Pour dressing over macaroni mixture, tossing to mix. Chill, covered, until serving time. Yield: 12 servings.

Approx Per Serving: Cal 65; Prot 1 g; Carbo 7 g; Fiber 1 g;
   T Fat 4 g; 52% Calories from Fat; Chol 0 mg; Sod 100 mg.

Rainbow Pasta Salad

12 ounces uncooked rainbow rotini
2 cups chopped celery
1 medium cucumber, chopped
1/2 cup chopped radishes
1 cup chopped green bell pepper

4 green onions, chopped
1 8-ounce bottle of ranch salad
   dressing
1/2 cup mayonnaise
Salt to taste

Cook pasta using package directions; drain. Rinse; drain. Cool. Combine pasta, celery, cucumber, radishes, green pepper and green onions in bowl; mix well. Add salad dressing, mayonnaise and salt; mix well. Chill, covered, until serving time. Yield: 12 servings.

Approx Per Serving: Cal 250; Prot 5 g; Carbo 25 g; Fiber 2 g;
    T Fat 15 g; 53% Calories from Fat; Chol 13 mg; Sod 155 mg.

Spaghetti Salad

2 16-ounce packages uncooked
   spaghetti
1 large green bell pepper, chopped
1 large red bell pepper, chopped

1 large onion, chopped
1 10-ounce bottle of Italian salad
   dressing
1 jar Salad Supreme seasoning

Cook spaghetti using package directions; drain. Rinse spaghetti 8 times; drain. Cool. Combine spaghetti, green pepper, red pepper and onion in bowl; mix well. Combine Italian dressing and salad supreme seasoning in bowl; mix well. Add to spaghetti mixture, tossing to mix. Chill, covered, overnight before serving. Yield: 12 servings.

Approx Per Serving: Cal 411; Prot 13 g; Carbo 62 g; Fiber 4 g;
    T Fat 16 g; 33% Calories from Fat; Chol 0 mg; Sod 401 mg.

Rice and Artichoke Salad

1 6-ounce package chicken-flavored
   Rice-A-Roni
1 6-ounce jar marinated artichoke
   hearts

3/4 teaspoon curry powder
1/3 cup mayonnaise
4 green onions, chopped
12 pimento-stuffed olives, sliced

Cook rice using package directions, omitting butter. Cool. Drain artichoke hearts, reserving marinade. Combine reserved marinade, curry powder and mayonnaise in bowl; mix well. Combine rice, artichoke hearts, green onions and olives in bowl. Add dressing; mix well. Chill, covered, for several hours. Yield: 8 servings.

Approx Per Serving: Cal 168; Prot 3 g; Carbo 18 g; Fiber 2 g;
    T Fat 10 g; 51% Calories from Fat; Chol 5 mg; Sod 602 mg.

Marinated Rice Salad

1/2 cup water
1 1/2 cups sugar
1 cup vinegar
1/2 cup oil
2 teaspoons salt
4 cups cooked rice
1   8-ounce can sliced water
   chestnuts, drained
1   16-ounce can whole kernel corn,
   drained

1   2-ounce jar chopped pimento,
   drained
1   16-ounce can carrots, drained,
   chopped
1   16-ounce can green peas, drained
1 cup chopped celery
1/2 cup chopped green bell pepper
1/2 cup chopped red onion

Combine water, sugar, vinegar, oil and salt in saucepan. Bring to a boil, stirring until sugar and salt are dissolved. Remove from heat. Cool. Combine rice, water chestnuts, corn, pimento, carrots, peas, celery, green pepper and onion in bowl; mix well. Pour dressing over mixture; mix well. Marinate, covered, in refrigerator overnight or for up to 2 weeks. Yield: 25 servings.

Approx Per Serving: Cal 160; Prot 2 g; Carbo 29 g; Fiber 2 g;
   T Fat 5 g; 25% Calories from Fat; Chol 0 mg; Sod 302 mg.

Rice Salad

3 cups chicken broth
1 1/4 cups uncooked rice
1 cup oil
2 tablespoons vinegar
1 teaspoon salt
1/8 teaspoon black pepper
1/8 teaspoon red pepper
1 cup chopped black olives
2 hard-boiled eggs, chopped

1 1/2 cups chopped celery
1/4 cup chopped dill pickle
1 small onion, chopped
1   2-ounce jar chopped pimento,
   drained
1 green bell pepper, chopped
1/2 cup mayonnaise
2 tablespoons prepared mustard

Bring chicken broth to a boil in saucepan. Add rice. Reduce heat. Simmer, covered, for 25 minutes or until rice is tender and broth is absorbed. Combine oil, vinegar, salt, black pepper and red pepper in large bowl; mix well. Stir in rice. Cool. Add black olives, eggs, celery, dill pickle, onion, pimento and green pepper; mix well. Add mayonnaise and mustard; mix well. Chill, covered, overnight before serving. Yield: 10 servings.

Approx Per Serving: Cal 424; Prot 5 g; Carbo 23 g; Fiber 2 g;
   T Fat 36 g; 75% Calories from Fat; Chol 49 mg; Sod 771 mg.

Antipasto

2/3 cup vinegar
2/3 cup olive oil
1 teaspoon salt
1 teaspoon sugar
1 teaspoon oregano
1 16-ounce can artichoke hearts,
   drained
1 4-ounce can black olives, drained
1 4-ounce can green olives, drained

1 16-ounce can chopped carrots,
   drained
1 cup chopped celery
1 2-ounce jar chopped pimento,
   drained
1 4-ounce can mushrooms, drained
1 onion, sliced into rings
1 16-ounce can cut green beans,
   drained

Combine vinegar, olive oil, salt, sugar and oregano in saucepan. Bring to a boil, stirring occasionally. Remove from heat. Combine artichoke hearts, black olives, green olives, carrots, celery, pimento, mushrooms, onion and green beans in bowl; mix well. Add dressing; mix well. Chill, tightly covered, in refrigerator. May be stored for several weeks in refrigerator. Yield: 16 servings.

Approx Per Serving: Cal 129; Prot 1 g; Carbo 7 g; Fiber 2 g;
   T Fat 12 g; 77% Calories from Fat; Chol 0 mg; Sod 637 mg.

Asparagus Mold

1¹/2 envelopes unflavored gelatin
¹/4 cup cold water
1 11-ounce can cut asparagus
¹/2 cup mayonnaise
Juice of ¹/2 lemon

1 teaspoon salt
MSG to taste
¹/8 teaspoon Worcestershire sauce
¹/2 cup whipping cream, whipped

Soften gelatin in cold water. Drain liquid from asparagus into saucepan. Bring asparagus liquid to a boil. Add gelatin, stirring until dissolved. Remove from heat. Cool slightly. Combine mayonnaise, lemon juice, salt, MSG, Worcestershire sauce and gelatin mixture in bowl; mix well. Fold in whipped cream and asparagus. Pour into 6 individual salad molds. Chill until set. Unmold onto lettuce-lined salad plates. Yield: 6 servings.

Approx Per Serving: Cal 217; Prot 3 g; Carbo 3 g; Fiber 1 g;
   T Fat 22 g; 89% Calories from Fat; Chol 38 mg; Sod 650 mg.

Age only matters in cheese.

Asparagus Vinaigrette

2 bunches fresh asparagus
1/2 cup olive oil
1/4 cup red wine vinegar
2 tablespoons Dijon mustard
2 tablespoons chopped fresh parsley
1 tablespoon chopped chives

2 tablespoons chopped green onions
  with tops
1 teaspoon tarragon
2 hard-boiled eggs, finely chopped
1 head Bibb lettuce, torn

Wash and trim asparagus. Cut into 3-inch lengths. Cook asparagus in steamer for 3 to 4 minutes or until tender-crisp. Cool. Place asparagus in shallow refrigerator container. Combine olive oil, vinegar, mustard, parsley, chives, green onions, tarragon and eggs in bowl; mix well. Pour over asparagus. Chill, tightly covered, for 4 to 8 hours. Place lettuce in salad bowl. Pour asparagus and dressing over lettuce, tossing to mix. Yield: 6 servings.

Approx Per Serving: Cal 210; Prot 4 g; Carbo 4 g; Fiber 1 g;
    T Fat 21 g; 85% Calories from Fat; Chol 71 mg; Sod 158 mg.

Jessie's Vegetable Aspic

This recipe came out of a 1920 handwritten cookbook belonging
to my mother. It can also be put into small molds. —Marguerite Gibson

2 envelopes unflavored gelatin
1/2 cup cold water
1/2 cup vinegar
Juice of 1 lemon
1/4 teaspoon salt
1/4 teaspoon pepper
1/2 cup sugar

2 cups water
2 cups chopped celery
1 16-ounce can tiny peas, drained
1 2-ounce jar chopped pimento,
  drained
1 onion, chopped
2 cups chopped pecans

Soften gelatin in 1/2 cup cold water. Combine vinegar, lemon juice, salt, pepper, sugar and 2 cups water in saucepan. Bring to a boil, stirring occasionally. Stir in gelatin until dissolved. Cool. Add celery, peas, pimento, onion and pecans; mix well. Pour into 10x10-inch glass dish. Chill, covered, until set. Yield: 10 servings.

Approx Per Serving: Cal 247; Prot 5 g; Carbo 24 g; Fiber 5 g;
    T Fat 16 g; 56% Calories from Fat; Chol 0 mg; Sod 176 mg.

When you are through changing, you're through.

Black-Eyed Pea Salad

2 15-ounce cans black-eyed peas,
    drained
1/2 cup chopped red onion
1/2 cup chopped green bell pepper
1/2 clove of garlic
1/4 cup vinegar

1/4 cup sugar
1/4 cup oil
1/2 teaspoon salt
Pepper to taste
Tabasco sauce to taste

Combine peas, onion, green pepper and garlic in bowl; toss lightly to mix. Combine vinegar, sugar, oil, salt, pepper and Tabasco sauce in bowl; mix well. Pour over vegetables, tossing to mix. Chill, covered, for 12 hours. Remove garlic before serving. Yield: 6 servings.

Approx Per Serving: Cal 229; Prot 7 g; Carbo 30 g; Fiber 10 g;
    T Fat 10 g; 38% Calories from Fat; Chol 0 mg; Sod 603 mg.

Broccoli and Pecan Salad

3/4 cup mayonnaise
1/4 cup sugar
3 tablespoons vinegar
4 cups broccoli flowerets

1/4 cup chopped onion
1/4 cup raisins
1/2 cup pecans
2 slices crisp-fried bacon, crumbled

Combine mayonnaise, sugar and vinegar in bowl; mix well. Combine broccoli, onion, raisins, pecans and bacon in bowl; mix well. Add dressing, tossing to mix. Yield: 10 servings.

Approx Per Serving: Cal 208; Prot 2 g; Carbo 12 g; Fiber 2 g;
    T Fat 18 g; 74% Calories from Fat; Chol 11 mg; Sod 124 mg.

Broccoli and Raisin Salad

1 bunch broccoli, chopped
1/2 cup raisins
10 to 12 slices crisp-fried bacon,
    crumbled

1/4 cup chopped red onion
1 cup mayonnaise
1/4 cup sugar
2 tablespoons vinegar

Combine broccoli, raisins, bacon and onion in bowl; mix well. Combine mayonnaise, sugar and vinegar in bowl; mix well. Add dressing to broccoli mixture, tossing to mix. Chill, covered, for 1 to 2 hours before serving. Yield: 8 servings.

Approx Per Serving: Cal 321; Prot 5 g; Carbo 18 g; Fiber 2 g;
    T Fat 27 g; 72% Calories from Fat; Chol 24 mg; Sod 321 mg.

Canary Salad

1 cup grated carrots
1/2 cup finely chopped celery
1/2 cup chopped apple

1/2 cup finely chopped orange
sections
1/2 cup (or more) mayonnaise

Combine carrots, celery, apple and orange in bowl. Add mayonnaise; mix well. Serve on lettuce-lined salad plates. Yield: 4 servings.

Approx Per Serving: Cal 242; Prot 1 g; Carbo 12 g; Fiber 3 g;
    T Fat 22 g; 79% Calories from Fat; Chol 16 mg; Sod 179 mg.

Carrot Salad

3 to 4 cups shredded carrots
1/2 cup raisins
1 8-ounce can crushed pineapple,
    drained

1/2 (or more)   6-ounce can frozen
    orange juice concentrate

Combine carrots, raisins and pineapple in bowl; mix well. Add orange juice concentrate, mixing until all ingredients are moist. Chill, covered, until serving time. Yield: 8 servings.

Approx Per Serving: Cal 87; Prot 1 g; Carbo 22 g; Fiber 3 g;
    T Fat <1 g; 2% Calories from Fat; Chol 0 mg; Sod 21 mg.

My Favorite Carrot Salad

5 large carrots, grated
1 apple, peeled, grated
1 cup crushed pineapple
1/2 cup grated coconut
1/4 cup chopped pecans

24 maraschino cherry halves
12 dates, chopped
1 teaspoon sugar
1 tablespoon mayonnaise-type salad
    dressing

Combine carrots, apple, pineapple, coconut, pecans, maraschino cherries and dates in bowl; mix well. Add sugar and salad dressing; toss to mix. Chill, covered, until serving time. Yield: 8 servings.

Approx Per Serving: Cal 152; Prot 1 g; Carbo 29 g; Fiber 4 g;
    T Fat 5 g; 27% Calories from Fat; Chol <1 mg; Sod 31 mg.

Lighthouses don't toot horns, they just shine.

Cauliflower and Olive Salad

This recipe was given to me by my sister, Mary Ann Lacy,
who died of cancer 6 years ago. —Jewel Snapp

4 cups thinly sliced cauliflower
1 cup sliced black olives
1/2 cup chopped pimento
2/3 cup chopped green bell pepper
1/2 cup chopped onion
3 tablespoons wine vinegar

1 tablespoon sugar
3 tablespoons lemon juice
2 teaspoons salt
1/4 teaspoon pepper
1/2 cup vegetable oil

Combine cauliflower, olives, pimento, green pepper and onion in bowl; mix well. Combine vinegar, sugar, lemon juice, salt, pepper and oil in bowl; mix well. Add to salad; toss to mix. Chill, covered, for several hours to overnight. May store in refrigerator for 1 week. May substitute 2 teaspoons Greek seasoning for salt and pepper. Yield: 12 servings.

Approx Per Serving: Cal 123; Prot 1 g; Carbo 5 g; Fiber 2 g;
    T Fat 12 g; 82% Calories from Fat; Chol 0 mg; Sod 468 mg.

Cauliflower Salad

1/2 head lettuce, shredded
Flowerets of 1 head cauliflower
2 cups mayonnaise
1 onion, chopped

1 pound bacon, crisp-fried, crumbled
1/3 cup grated Parmesan cheese
1/2 cup sugar

Layer lettuce, cauliflower, mayonnaise, onion, bacon, Parmesan cheese and sugar in glass bowl. Chill, covered, overnight. Toss just before serving. Yield: 12 servings.

Approx Per Serving: Cal 384; Prot 6 g; Carbo 12 g; Fiber 1 g;
    T Fat 36 g; 82% Calories from Fat; Chol 33 mg; Sod 437 mg.

Corn Bread Salad

1   9x9-inch pan corn bread, crumbled
1 large green bell pepper, chopped
1 large onion, chopped
3 tomatoes, chopped

6 slices crisp-fried bacon, crumbled
Garlic powder, oregano, salt and
  pepper to taste
2 tablespoons (rounded) mayonnaise

Combine corn bread, green pepper, onion, tomatoes, bacon, garlic powder, oregano, salt and pepper in bowl; mix well. Add mayonnaise; mix well. Yield: 12 servings.

Approx Per Serving: Cal 352; Prot 8 g; Carbo 50 g; Fiber 1 g;
    T Fat 14 g; 34% Calories from Fat; Chol 38 mg; Sod 518 mg.

Cucumbers in Sour Cream

1 large cucumber, peeled, thinly
  sliced
1/2 teaspoon salt
1 cup sour cream
2 tablespoons lemon juice

1 1/2 tablespoons finely chopped
  onion
1/2 teaspoon sugar
Salt and pepper to taste
2 tablespoons chopped dill pickle

Combine cucumber and salt in bowl; toss to mix. Chill in refrigerator. Combine sour cream, lemon juice, onion, sugar, salt, pepper and dill pickle in bowl; mix well. Drain cucumber. Add to dressing; mix well. Chill, covered, until serving time. Serve on lettuce-lined salad plates. Garnish with chopped parsley. May also be served as a dip. Yield: 2 servings.

Approx Per Serving: Cal 277; Prot 5 g; Carbo 13 g; Fiber 2 g;
    T Fat 24 g; 76% Calories from Fat; Chol 51 mg; Sod 759 mg.

Sunflower Salad

2 cups broccoli flowerets
2 cups cauliflowerets
1/2 cup chopped purple onion
1/2 cup sunflower seed
8 slices crisp-fried bacon, crumbled

1/2 cup raisins
1/2 cup mayonnaise
2 tablespoons vinegar
1/4 cup sugar

Combine broccoli, cauliflower, onion, sunflower seed, bacon and raisins in bowl; mix well. Combine mayonnaise, vinegar and sugar in bowl; mix well. Add dressing to vegetables 10 minutes before serving. Yield: 4 servings.

Approx Per Serving: Cal 514; Prot 12 g; Carbo 40 g; Fiber 6 g;
    T Fat 37 g; 62% Calories from Fat; Chol 27 mg; Sod 381 mg.

Classic Potato Salad

1 cup mayonnaise
3 tablespoons red wine vinegar
1 1/2 teaspoons salt
2 tablespoons sugar
1/4 teaspoon pepper
1 teaspoon prepared mustard

1/4 cup pickle relish
4 cups chopped cooked potatoes
1/2 cup chopped onion
1 cup chopped celery
2 hard-boiled eggs, chopped

Combine mayonnaise, vinegar, salt, sugar, pepper, mustard and pickle relish in bowl; mix well. Combine potatoes, onion, celery and egg in bowl; mix well. Add dressing; toss to mix. Chill, covered, until serving time. Yield: 4 servings.

Approx Per Serving: Cal 608; Prot 7 g; Carbo 44 g; Fiber 3 g;
    T Fat 47 g; 68% Calories from Fat; Chol 139 mg; Sod 1302 mg.

Cottage Cheese Potato Salad

6 to 8 medium potatoes, boiled,
  cooled
1½ cups chopped celery
1 medium onion, finely chopped
1 tablespoon oil
1 tablespoon chopped pimento

1 tablespoon white vinegar
1½ teaspoons salt
⅛ teaspoon pepper
1 cup mayonnaise
16 ounces cottage cheese

Peel potatoes; cut into slices. Combine potatoes, celery and onion in bowl; mix well. Combine oil, pimento, vinegar, salt and pepper in bowl; mix well. Add to potato mixture; mix well. Chill, covered, until serving time. Combine mayonnaise and cottage cheese in bowl; mix well. Add to salad just before serving; toss to mix. Yield: 8 servings.

Approx Per Serving: Cal 397; Prot 10 g; Carbo 32 g; Fiber 3 g;
   T Fat 26 g; 58% Calories from Fat; Chol 25 mg; Sod 813 mg.

German Potato Salad

7 medium potatoes, boiled, chopped
4 hard-boiled eggs, chopped
1 cup chopped sweet pickles
1 large yellow onion, chopped
5 stalks celery, chopped

¾ cup mayonnaise-type salad
  dressing
½ cup prepared mustard
¼ cup sweet pickle juice
Salt to taste

Combine potatoes, eggs, pickles, onion and celery in bowl; mix well. Add remaining ingredients; mix well. Chill, covered, for 24 hours before serving. May substitute 1 bunch green onions, chopped, for yellow onion. Yield: 6 servings.

Approx Per Serving: Cal 358; Prot 9 g; Carbo 50 g; Fiber 4 g;
   T Fat 15 g; 36% Calories from Fat; Chol 149 mg; Sod 686 mg.
   Nutritional information does not include pickle juice.

Hot German Potato Salad

4 slices bacon
½ cup chopped onion
1   10-ounce can cream of celery soup
3 tablespoons vinegar
¼ cup water

½ cup sugar
⅛ teaspoon pepper
½ teaspoon salt
4 cups sliced cooked potatoes

Fry bacon in skillet until crisp; drain, reserving bacon drippings. Sauté onion in reserved bacon drippings in skillet until tender. Add soup, vinegar, water, sugar, pepper and salt. Bring to a boil, stirring constantly. Crumble bacon. Add bacon and potatoes to mixture. Cook for 5 minutes, stirring occasionally. Serve hot. Yield: 10 servings.

Approx Per Serving: Cal 159; Prot 2 g; Carbo 24 g; Fiber 1 g;
   T Fat 7 g; 37% Calories from Fat; Chol 29 mg; Sod 405 mg.

Potato Salad

10 to 12 potatoes, peeled
6 hard-boiled eggs
1 medium onion, chopped
1 16-ounce jar sweet pickles,
   chopped

1 16-ounce jar sandwich spread
3 tablespoons prepared mustard
1/2 cup sugar
1/4 cup pickle juice

Cut potatoes into quarters. Combine potatoes and water to cover in saucepan. Cook over medium heat for 15 minutes or until tender; drain. Beat at medium speed until creamy. Add eggs, onion, sweet pickles, sandwich spread, mustard, sugar and pickle juice; mix well. Yield: 8 servings.

Approx Per Serving: Cal 500; Prot 13 g; Carbo 83 g; Fiber 4 g;
      T Fat 15 g; 26% Calories from Fat; Chol 182 mg; Sod 1112 mg.
      Nutritional information does not include pickle juice.

Nine-Day Coleslaw

1 medium head cabbage, shredded
1 medium carrot, shredded
1 onion, finely chopped
1 green bell pepper, chopped
1 cup sugar

1/2 cup oil
1/2 cup vinegar
1 teaspoon salt
1 teaspoon celery seed

Combine cabbage, carrot, onion and green pepper in bowl; mix well. Combine sugar, oil, vinegar, salt and celery seed in saucepan. Bring to a boil, stirring occasionally. Pour over cabbage mixture; mix well. Chill, covered, overnight before serving. Yield: 10 servings.

Approx Per Serving: Cal 192; Prot 1 g; Carbo 25 g; Fiber 1 g;
      T Fat 11 g; 50% Calories from Fat; Chol 0 mg; Sod 222 mg.

Cabbage and Pepper Slaw

4 cups shredded cabbage
1/2 cup chopped green bell pepper
2 tablespoons sugar
1 teaspoon salt
Pepper to taste

1 teaspoon celery seed
2 tablespoons cider vinegar
1 teaspoon prepared mustard
1/2 cup mayonnaise

Combine cabbage, green pepper, sugar, salt, pepper and celery seed in bowl; mix well. Combine vinegar, mustard and mayonnaise in bowl; mix well. Add to slaw; mix well. Chill, covered, until serving time. Yield: 6 servings.

Approx Per Serving: Cal 163; Prot 1 g; Carbo 8 g; Fiber 1 g;
      T Fat 15 g; 79% Calories from Fat; Chol 11 mg; Sod 479 mg.

Crunchy Slaw

4 cups shredded cabbage
4 to 6 green onions, chopped
2 ounces slivered almonds, toasted
2 tablespoons sesame seed, toasted
2 3-ounce packages oriental
   noodles, crumbled

1/2 cup oil
3 tablespoons vinegar
1/2 teaspoon pepper
Garlic powder to taste
2 tablespoons minced onion
2 tablespoons sugar

Combine cabbage and green onions in bowl; mix well. Chill, covered, until serving time. Combine almonds, sesame seed and oriental noodles in bowl; mix well. Combine oil, vinegar, seasoning packages from oriental noodles, pepper, garlic powder, onion and sugar in bowl; mix well. Toss crunchy ingredients with cabbage mixture just before serving. Add dressing; mix well. Yield: 6 servings.

Approx Per Serving: Cal 439; Prot 9 g; Carbo 28 g; Fiber 3 g;
    T Fat 35 g; 68% Calories from Fat; Chol 0 mg; Sod 526 mg.

Spinach and Mushroom Salad

2 tablespoons Dijon mustard
1/4 cup oil
2 tablespoons lemon juice
1 tablespoon grated Parmesan cheese
1 teaspoon sugar
1 teaspoon Worcestershire sauce

1/2 teaspoon salt
1/8 teaspoon pepper
1 pound fresh spinach, torn
1 cup sliced fresh mushrooms
6 slices crisp-fried bacon, crumbled
2 hard-boiled eggs, chopped

Combine mustard, oil, lemon juice, cheese, sugar, Worcestershire sauce, salt and pepper in bowl; mix well. Chill, covered, in refrigerator. Combine spinach, mushrooms, bacon and eggs in bowl; mix well. Add mustard dressing; toss to mix. Yield: 6 servings.

Approx Per Serving: Cal 179; Prot 7 g; Carbo 5 g; Fiber 3 g;
    T Fat 15 g; 74% Calories from Fat; Chol 77 mg; Sod 517 mg.

Surprise Salad

1 6-ounce package lemon gelatin
1 1/2 cups boiling water
1 cup chopped cucumber
1 cup chopped celery

1 cup chopped onion
2 cups small curd cottage cheese
1 1/2 cups mayonnaise

Dissolve gelatin in boiling water in bowl. Chill in refrigerator until partially congealed. Stir in cucumber, celery, onion, cottage cheese and mayonnaise. Pour into serving dish. Chill until set. Yield: 12 servings.

Approx Per Serving: Cal 295; Prot 6 g; Carbo 16 g; Fiber 1 g;
    T Fat 23 g; 70% Calories from Fat; Chol 21 mg; Sod 353 mg.

Marinated Zucchini and Artichoke Salad

2 or 3 small zucchini, sliced
2 or 3 tomatoes, cut into wedges
1   16-ounce can artichoke hearts,
   drained
1/4 cup sliced green onions
2 tablespoons chopped fresh parsley
1/4 cup red wine vinegar

1/2 teaspoon salt
1/4 teaspoon garlic salt
1/4 teaspoon seasoned pepper
1/4 cup olive oil
1/2 cup vegetable oil
1 teaspoon lemon juice

Combine zucchini, tomatoes, artichoke hearts and green onions in bowl; mix well. Combine parsley, vinegar, salt, garlic salt, pepper, olive oil, vegetable oil and lemon juice in jar. Shake, covered, until well mixed. Add to salad, tossing to mix. Chill, covered, for several hours. Serve on lettuce-lined salad plates. Yield: 6 servings.

Approx Per Serving: Cal 289; Prot 3 g; Carbo 9 g; Fiber 2 g;
    T Fat 28 g; 84% Calories from Fat; Chol 0 mg; Sod 459 mg.

Marinated Vegetable Toss

Flowerets of 1 bunch broccoli
Flowerets of 1 head cauliflower
2 carrots, sliced
Salt to taste
4 to 6 large fresh mushrooms, sliced

1   4-ounce jar stuffed olives, drained
1   3-ounce can black olives, drained
1   8-ounce bottle of Italian salad
   dressing

Combine broccoli, cauliflower and carrots in a small amount of boiling salted water in saucepan. Cook for 3 minutes; drain. Immerse in cold water; drain. Cool slightly. Combine with mushrooms, olives and salad dressing in bowl; mix well. Chill, covered, for 3 hours or longer. Yield: 12 servings.

Approx Per Serving: Cal 134; Prot 2 g; Carbo 7 g; Fiber 3 g;
    T Fat 15 g; 78% Calories from Fat; Chol 0 mg; Sod 390 mg.

You never learn anything while you are talking.

Eight-Layer Salad

¹/₂ to ³/₄ package fresh spinach,
  chopped
12 to 15 slices crisp-fried bacon,
  crumbled
1 small head lettuce, chopped
6 hard-boiled eggs, sliced
1 bunch green onions with tops,
  chopped

1 16-ounce can green peas, drained
¹/₂ cup mayonnaise
¹/₂ cup mayonnaise-type salad
  dressing
8 ounces Swiss cheese, shredded

Layer spinach, bacon, lettuce, eggs, green onions and green peas in 9x13-inch glass dish. Mix mayonnaise and salad dressing together in bowl. Spread over top, sealing to edge. Sprinkle with cheese. Chill, covered with plastic wrap, for 24 hours. Yield: 12 servings.

Approx Per Serving: Cal 294; Prot 14 g; Carbo 10 g; Fiber 3 g;
    T Fat 23 g; 69% Calories from Fat; Chol 138 mg; Sod 428 mg.

Texas Salad Dressing

2 hard-boiled eggs
2 tablespoons capers
2 cups mayonnaise-type salad
  dressing

2 cloves of garlic
1 teaspoon MSG
Freshly ground pepper to taste

Combine eggs, capers, salad dressing, garlic, MSG and pepper in blender or food processor container. Process until of desired consistency. Store in covered container in refrigerator. Yield: 10 servings.

Approx Per Serving: Cal 200; Prot 2 g; Carbo 12 g; Fiber <1 g;
    T Fat 17 g; 74% Calories from Fat; Chol 55 mg; Sod 776 mg.
    Nutritional information does not include capers.

⁓

*A person who is wrapped up in himself
makes a very small bundle.*

Entrées

The Arlington Resort Hotel & Spa

The Arlington
Resort Hotel & Spa

The Arlington Resort Hotel & Spa is a historical landmark located in the heart of downtown Hot Springs National Park. When the original Arlington first opened on April 15, 1875, it was the largest hotel in the state and boasted 120 guest rooms. The original structure was razed to make way for a new 300-room luxury hotel which opened in March of 1893. The second Arlington Hotel was destroyed by fire on April 5, 1923. The present and third structure (pictured) opened its doors on New Year's Eve 1924. With 486 guest rooms and 22 meeting rooms, it remains the largest hotel in the state.

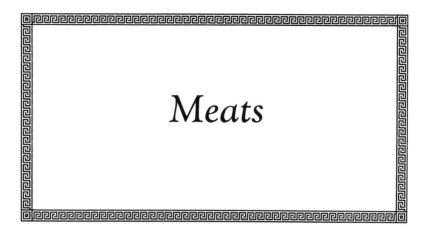

Meats

Beef Parmigiana

2 pounds cube steak
1 egg, beaten
1/4 teaspoon salt
1/8 teaspoon pepper
3/4 cup dry bread crumbs
3 tablespoons grated Parmesan
  cheese

1/8 teaspoon oregano
1/4 cup oil
1 8-ounce can tomato sauce
8 ounces mozzarella cheese, thinly
  sliced
2 tablespoons grated Parmesan
  cheese

Tenderize steaks with meat mallet. Season egg with salt and pepper. Mix bread crumbs, 3 tablespoons Parmesan cheese and oregano. Dip steaks into egg mixture; coat with bread crumb mixture. Sauté in hot oil in skillet until browned. Place in shallow baking dish. Pour tomato sauce over steaks. Top with cheese slices. Sprinkle with remaining 2 tablespoons Parmesan cheese. Bake at 375 degrees for 20 minutes. Yield: 6 servings.

Approx Per Serving: Cal 478; Prot 41 g; Carbo 13 g; Fiber 1 g;
    T Fat 28 g; 54% Calories from Fat; Chol 154 mg; Sod 687 mg.

Don't tell tall tales.

Beef Paprika

1¹/₂ pounds round steak
2 tablespoons oil
1   14-ounce can whole tomatoes
1   4-ounce can mushrooms
1 envelope stroganoff sauce mix

1 tablespoon paprika
1 cup uncooked rice
1 tablespoon chopped parsley
1 cup sour cream

Cut beef into ³/₄-inch cubes. Brown in oil in skillet. Drain tomatoes, reserving liquid. Chop tomatoes. Add reserved tomato liquid, undrained mushrooms, sauce mix and paprika to beef. Simmer, covered, for 45 to 60 minutes or until steak is tender. Prepare rice using package directions. Stir in chopped tomatoes and parsley. Stir sour cream into beef mixture just before serving. Serve over rice. Yield: 6 servings.

Approx Per Serving: Cal 425; Prot 26 g; Carbo 34 g; Fiber 2 g;
    T Fat 20 g; 43% Calories from Fat; Chol 83 mg; Sod 532 mg.

Sweet Glazed Brisket

1   3 to 3¹/₂-pound beef brisket
2 cups sliced celery
1 large onion, chopped
2 bay leaves
1   9-ounce jar sweet and sour sauce

³/₄ cup red wine vinegar and oil salad
    dressing
2 teaspoons ground ginger
¹/₄ teaspoon ground allspice

Place brisket fat side up in shallow baking dish. Top with celery, onion and bay leaves. Mix sweet and sour sauce, salad dressing, ginger and allspice in bowl. Pour over brisket. Bake, covered, at 300 degrees for 3¹/₂ to 4 hours or until tender. Remove bay leaves. May serve over rice. Yield: 8 servings.

Approx Per Serving: Cal 407; Prot 38 g; Carbo 10 g; Fiber 1 g;
    T Fat 23 g; 53% Calories from Fat; Chol 112 mg; Sod 167 mg.

Biddy's Chuck Roast

*Good served with buns for patio picnic. I like it with
Ratatouille (page 117) and green salad. —Paula Jackson*

1   10 to 12-pound chuck roast
Salt and pepper to taste

Worcestershire sauce to taste
2 onions, sliced

Season roast with salt and pepper. Brown in large Dutch oven. Sprinkle with Worcestershire sauce. Top with onion slices. Add ¹/₂ inch water. Bake, covered, at 300 degrees for 30 minutes per pound. Yield: 18 servings.

Approx Per Serving: Cal 403; Prot 57 g; Carbo 1 g; Fiber <1 g;
    T Fat 17 g; 40% Calories from Fat; Chol 170 mg; Sod 93 mg.

London Broil

1/2 cup steak sauce
2 tablespoons lemon juice
1 large onion, thinly sliced

2 medium cloves of garlic, minced
1 1/2 pounds flank steak
Salt and pepper to taste

Mix steak sauce, lemon juice, onion and garlic in shallow glass dish. Add steak, turning to coat. Marinate, covered, in refrigerator for 1 hour. Drain, reserving marinade. Season steak with salt and pepper. Grill over medium-hot coals for 10 to 15 minutes or until done to taste, turning and basting frequently with reserved marinade. May marinate steak in refrigerator overnight if desired. Yield: 6 servings.

Approx Per Serving: Cal 181; Prot 22 g; Carbo 6 g; Fiber 1 g;
  T Fat 7 g; 34% Calories from Fat; Chol 64 mg; Sod 35 mg.

Marinated Eye-of-Round

1/4 cup oil
1/2 cup wine vinegar
1/2 cup lemon juice
1/2 cup soy sauce

1/2 cup Worcestershire sauce
2 tablespoons lemon pepper
1   3-pound eye-of-round roast

Mix oil, vinegar, lemon juice, soy sauce, Worcestershire sauce and lemon pepper in bowl. Place roast in shallow glass dish. Pour marinade over top. Marinate, covered, in refrigerator for 1 to 3 days, turning at least once a day. Place roast in baking pan. Bake at 250 degrees for 2 to 3 hours or until done to taste. Yield: 6 servings.

Approx Per Serving: Cal 419; Prot 44 g; Carbo 10 g; Fiber <1 g;
  T Fat 22 g; 48% Calories from Fat; Chol 128 mg; Sod 2448 mg.

Peppered Roast Beef

1/4 cup coarsely ground pepper
1 teaspoon ground cardamom
1   4 to 5-pound beef roast
2/3 cup soy sauce

1/2 cup vinegar
1 teaspoon paprika
1 clove of garlic, crushed
1 tablespoon catsup

Mix pepper and cardamom on waxed paper. Coat beef evenly with mixture, pressing to push spices into surface. Place roast in large glass dish. Mix soy sauce, vinegar, paprika, garlic and catsup in bowl. Pour over beef. Marinate, covered, in refrigerator overnight, turning occasionally. Drain marinade. Wrap roast tightly in foil. Place in baking pan. Bake at 300 degrees for 3 hours or until tender. Serve hot or cold. Yield: 12 servings.

Approx Per Serving: Cal 259; Prot 36 g; Carbo 2 g; Fiber <1 g;
  T Fat 11 g; 39% Calories from Fat; Chol 106 mg; Sod 988 mg.
  Nutritional information includes entire amount of marinade.

Sirloin with Mushrooms

2 pounds sirloin steak
1 cup flour
1 tablespoon salt
1/4 teaspoon pepper
2 tablespoons oil

1 14-ounce can beef broth
1/2 cup white cooking wine
1/2 cup water
1 4-ounce can mushrooms

Cut steak into 3-inch strips. Mix flour, salt and pepper. Coat meat with mixture. Sauté in hot oil in skillet until lightly browned. Stir in broth, wine, water and mushrooms. Simmer for 30 minutes. Yield: 8 servings.

Approx Per Serving: Cal 239; Prot 22 g; Carbo 13 g; Fiber 1 g;
    T Fat 10 g; 39% Calories from Fat; Chol 51 mg; Sod 1067 mg.

Bacon and Steak Rolls

3 pounds sirloin steak
Salt to taste
1/2 cup flour

1 pound bacon
1 10-ounce can cream of mushroom
    soup

Cut steak into 1x4-inch strips. Season with salt. Coat with flour. Wrap strips in bacon; secure with wooden pick. Brown in skillet, turning often. Place browned meat in baking pan. Top with soup. Bake at 350 degrees for 1 hour. Yield: 6 servings.

Approx Per Serving: Cal 487; Prot 47 g; Carbo 12 g; Fiber <1 g;
    T Fat 27 g; 51% Calories from Fat; Chol 122 mg; Sod 834 mg.

Family Steak

1 3-pound chuck roast
2 teaspoons unseasoned meat
    tenderizer
1 teaspoon MSG
1/3 cup wine vinegar
1/4 cup catsup

2 tablespoons soy sauce
1 tablespoon Worcestershire sauce
1 teaspoon prepared mustard
1 teaspoon salt
1/4 teaspoon pepper
1/4 teaspoon garlic pepper

Sprinkle roast with meat tenderizer; pierce with fork. Place in shallow baking dish. Mix MSG, vinegar, catsup, soy sauce, Worcestershire sauce, prepared mustard, salt, pepper and garlic pepper in bowl. Pour over roast. Marinate, covered, in refrigerator for 3 to 4 hours, turning and basting frequently. Grill 6 inches from hot coals for 35 to 45 minutes or until done to taste. Yield: 6 servings.

Approx Per Serving: Cal 318; Prot 43 g; Carbo 5 g; Fiber <1 g;
    T Fat 13 g; 38% Calories from Fat; Chol 128 mg; Sod 2223 mg.

Creole Swiss Steak

1¹/₂ pounds round steak
¹/₃ cup flour
1 teaspoon salt
¹/₈ teaspoon pepper

¹/₄ cup oil
1 green bell pepper, sliced
1 onion, sliced
1¹/₂ cups chopped tomatoes

Coat steak with mixture of flour, salt and pepper. Tenderize with meat mallet. Brown steak in hot oil in large saucepan. Arrange green pepper, onion and tomatoes over steak. Simmer, covered, for 1 hour or until tender; add additional liquid if needed. Yield: 4 servings.

Approx Per Serving: Cal 413; Prot 34 g; Carbo 15 g; Fiber 2 g;
    T Fat 24 g; 52% Calories from Fat; Chol 96 mg; Sod 592 mg.

Barbecued Hamburger

1 pound ground beef
1 small onion, chopped
1 stalk celery, chopped
2 tablespoons flour

¹/₂ cup catsup
1¹/₂ tablespoons brown sugar
1 tablespoon vinegar
Salt and pepper to taste

Brown ground beef with onion, celery and flour in skillet, stirring until ground beef is crumbly; drain. Stir in catsup, brown sugar, vinegar, salt and pepper. Simmer for 20 to 30 minutes. Yield: 6 servings.

Approx Per Serving: Cal 208; Prot 15 g; Carbo 13 g; Fiber 1 g;
    T Fat 11 g; 47% Calories from Fat; Chol 49 mg; Sod 288 mg.

Barge Beef and Rice

1 pound ground beef
1 medium green bell pepper, chopped
1 medium onion, chopped
1 teaspoon salt
¹/₂ teaspoon pepper
1 tablespoon Worcestershire sauce
1 tablespoon chili powder
2 teaspoons Louisiana hot sauce

1 4-ounce can chopped green chilies
1 10-ounce can Ro-Tel tomatoes
2 cups cooked rice
1 cup beer
1 cup grated Parmesan cheese
2 jalapeño peppers, chopped
1 cup sour cream

Brown ground beef with green pepper and onion in skillet, stirring until ground beef is crumbly; drain. Add salt, pepper, Worcestershire sauce, chili powder, hot sauce, green chilies, tomatoes, rice, beer, Parmesan cheese and jalapeño peppers; mix well. Simmer for 5 to 10 minutes. Stir in sour cream just before serving; do not boil. May serve as a hot dip with chips. Yield: 6 servings.

Approx Per Serving: Cal 420; Prot 24 g; Carbo 27 g; Fiber 2 g;
    T Fat 23 g; 51% Calories from Fat; Chol 77 mg; Sod 1041 mg.

Ground Beef and Bean Casserole

1¹/₂ pounds ground beef
¹/₂ teaspoon dry mustard
3 tablespoons brown sugar
1 16-ounce can green lima beans
1 16-ounce can pork and beans

1 16-ounce can kidney beans
1 small onion, finely chopped
¹/₂ cup catsup
2 teaspoons vinegar
¹/₂ teaspoon salt

Brown ground beef in Dutch oven, stirring until crumbly; drain. Add dry mustard, brown sugar, lima beans, pork and beans, kidney beans, onion, catsup, vinegar and salt; mix well. Bake at 350 degrees for 30 minutes. Yield: 8 servings.

Approx Per Serving: Cal 370; Prot 25 g; Carbo 39 g; Fiber 12 g;
    T Fat 13 g; 32% Calories from Fat; Chol 59 mg; Sod 940 mg.

Beefy Ro-Tel and Bean Dish

1 pound dried pinto beans
2 slices bacon
¹/₄ teaspoon ground ginger
¹/₂ teaspoon salt

2 pounds ground beef
1 onion, chopped
1 10-ounce can Ro-Tel tomatoes
1 envelope chili seasoning mix

Cook beans using package directions and adding bacon, ginger and salt. Brown ground beef with onion in skillet, stirring until ground beef is crumbly. Add to beans. Stir in tomatoes and chili seasoning mix. Cook until flavors blend and beans are tender. Serve with rice and corn bread. Yield: 16 servings.

Approx Per Serving: Cal 222; Prot 18 g; Carbo 19 g; Fiber 6 g;
    T Fat 9 g; 35% Calories from Fat; Chol 38 mg; Sod 200 mg.

Stuffed Cabbage

1 pound ground beef
1 pound ground pork
2 eggs, beaten
1 cup uncooked rice
¹/₂ cup bread crumbs
2 small onions, chopped

1 teaspoon salt
¹/₂ teaspoon pepper
1 head cabbage
1 10-ounce can tomato soup
2 6-ounce cans mixed vegetable
    juice cocktail

Combine ground beef, ground pork, eggs, rice, bread crumbs, onions, salt and pepper in bowl; mix well. Remove core from cabbage. Place cabbage in glass bowl. Microwave, covered with waxed paper, on High for 8 minutes. Fill cabbage leaves with meat mixture. Roll up; secure with wooden picks. Place in large saucepan. Pour soup and juice over top. Bring to a boil. Reduce heat to low. Simmer for 3 hours. May omit ground pork and use 2 pounds ground beef. Yield: 6 servings.

Approx Per Serving: Cal 522; Prot 40 g; Carbo 45 g; Fiber 3 g;
    T Fat 20 g; 35% Calories from Fat; Chol 177 mg; Sod 1073 mg.

Mom's Chili

*Mom adapted this version from a newspaper
clipping years ago. —Betty J. Jones*

3 pounds beef chuck, cut into 1/4-inch
   cubes
Juice of 1 lemon
1/4 cup oil
2 large onions, chopped
3 cloves of garlic, finely chopped
6 to 8 tablespoons chili powder

2 teaspoons ground cumin
2 14-ounce cans beef broth
2 15-ounce cans tomato sauce
1 teaspoon (heaping) crushed red
   pepper
Oregano to taste

Rub beef with lemon juice. Cook in oil in skillet until lightly browned. Add onions, garlic, chili powder, cumin, beef broth, tomato sauce, red pepper and oregano; mix well. Simmer for 3 to 4 hours. May add beans if desired and may thicken with 2 tablespoons cornmeal. Yield: 12 servings.

Approx Per Serving: Cal 242; Prot 24 g; Carbo 10 g; Fiber 3 g;
    T Fat 12 g; 44% Calories from Fat; Chol 64 mg; Sod 730 mg.

Dinner-in-a-Dish

1 medium onion, chopped
2 medium green bell peppers, sliced
   1/4 inch thick
2 tablespoons oil
1 pound lean ground beef
1 teaspoon salt

1/2 teaspoon pepper
2 eggs
1 16-ounce can whole kernel corn
2 medium tomatoes, peeled, sliced
1 cup bread crumbs
2 tablespoons butter

Sauté onion and green peppers in oil in skillet until tender but not brown. Add ground beef. Cook until brown and crumbly, stirring frequently; drain. Stir in salt and pepper; remove from heat. Stir in eggs. Layer corn, ground beef mixture and tomatoes 1/2 at a time in greased baking dish. Top with bread crumbs; dot with butter. Bake at 400 degrees for 30 minutes. May substitute egg whites for eggs if preferred. Yield: 6 servings.

Approx Per Serving: Cal 388; Prot 21 g; Carbo 29 g; Fiber 3 g;
    T Fat 22 g; 51% Calories from Fat; Chol 132 mg; Sod 773 mg.

A narrow mind has a broad tongue.

Cheesy Enchiladas

1 pound Velveeta cheese
1 10-ounce can tomatoes with green
   chilies
1 pound ground beef

1 envelope taco seasoning mix
1 cup water
8 large flour tortillas

Microwave cheese in glass dish on Medium until melted, stirring occasionally. Stir in undrained tomatoes with chilies. Microwave on High for 2 minutes. Brown ground beef in skillet, stirring until crumbly; drain. Stir in taco seasoning mix and water. Simmer for 5 minutes. Spoon 1/4 cup ground beef mixture onto each tortilla; roll to enclose filling. Place seam side down in 8x11-inch baking dish. Spoon cheese sauce over top. Bake at 350 degrees for 20 minutes or until light brown and bubbly. Serve with sour cream. Yield: 8 servings.

Approx Per Serving: Cal 520; Prot 28 g; Carbo 37 g; Fiber 2 g;
    T Fat 31 g; 54% Calories from Fat; Chol 91 mg; Sod 1637 mg.

Ground Beef Main Dish

1 pound ground chuck
1 14-ounce can mixed Chinese
   vegetables

1 8-ounce can tomato sauce
Salt and pepper to taste
1 5-ounce can chow mein noodles

Brown ground chuck in skillet, stirring until crumbly; drain. Stir in mixed vegetables, tomato sauce, salt and pepper. Cook for 10 to 15 minutes or until of desired consistency. Serve over noodles. Yield: 4 servings.

Approx Per Serving: Cal 492; Prot 29 g; Carbo 33 g; Fiber 2 g;
    T Fat 29 g; 51% Calories from Fat; Chol 78 mg; Sod 1074 mg.

Italian Casserole

12 ounces uncooked ziti
1 pound Italian sausage
1 pound lean ground round
1 24-ounce jar spaghetti sauce

12 ounces ricotta cheese
12 ounces cottage cheese
16 ounces mozzarella cheese,
   shredded

Cook pasta using package directions; drain. Brown sausage and ground round in skillet, stirring until crumbly; drain. Add spaghetti sauce. Combine ricotta cheese and cottage cheese in bowl; mix well. Layer pasta, ricotta cheese mixture, meat sauce and mozzarella cheese in 9x13-inch baking dish. Bake at 350 degrees for 15 minutes or until cheese melts and casserole is heated through. Yield: 10 servings.

Approx Per Serving: Cal 582; Prot 35 g; Carbo 40 g; Fiber 2 g;
    T Fat 31 g; 48% Calories from Fat; Chol 103 mg; Sod 897 mg.

Johnnie Marzetti

1 16-ounce package wide egg
   noodles
1½ pounds ground beef
8 ounces onions, chopped
4 ounces green bell pepper, chopped
½ bunch celery, chopped
1 4-ounce can mixed vegetable juice
   cocktail
1 10-ounce can tomato soup

1 10-ounce can cream of mushroom
   soup
1 8-ounce can tomato sauce
2 cups shredded Cheddar cheese
1 4-ounce can sliced mushrooms,
   drained
1 4-ounce bottle of green olives,
   drained, sliced

Cook noodles using package directions; drain. Brown ground beef in skillet, stirring until crumbly; remove with slotted spoon. Add onions, green pepper and celery to skillet. Sauté for several minutes; drain. Add vegetable juice, soups and tomato sauce; mix well. Fold in noodles, ground beef and half the cheese, mushrooms and olives. Spoon into 9x13-inch baking dish. Top with remaining cheese, mushrooms and olives. Bake at 325 degrees for 30 minutes. Yield: 10 servings.

Approx Per Serving: Cal 490; Prot 27 g; Carbo 44 g; Fiber 2 g;
    T Fat 24 g; 43% Calories from Fat; Chol 148 mg; Sod 1127 mg.

Easy Lasagna

12 ounces uncooked lasagna noodles
1 pound ground beef
2 tablespoons chopped onion
1 32-ounce jar spaghetti sauce with
   mushrooms

2 eggs, beaten
16 ounces cottage cheese
8 ounces mozzarella cheese, shredded
½ cup grated Parmesan cheese

Cook noodles using package directions; drain. Brown ground beef with onion in skillet, stirring until ground beef is crumbly; drain. Stir in spaghetti sauce. Simmer for several minutes. Combine eggs, cottage cheese and mozzarella cheese in bowl; mix well. Alternate layers of noodles, meat sauce and cheese mixture in 9x13-inch baking dish until all ingredients are used. Top with Parmesan cheese. Bake, covered, at 325 degrees for 50 minutes. Bake, uncovered, for 10 minutes longer. Yield: 8 servings.

Approx Per Serving: Cal 580; Prot 35 g; Carbo 52 g; Fiber 1 g;
    T Fat 26 g; 40% Calories from Fat; Chol 125 mg; Sod 1045 mg.

*Treat your mate as you would want your
children's mates to treat them.*

Barbecued Meatballs

1 cup soft bread crumbs
1 cup milk
1¹/2 pounds ground beef
1 egg, beaten
1 teaspoon finely chopped onion
Salt and black pepper to taste
¹/2 cup catsup

1 cup water
2 tablespoons (about) vinegar
2 tablespoons (about) brown sugar
2 tablespoons Worcestershire sauce
3 slices lemon
1 teaspoon chili powder
Red pepper to taste

Soak bread crumbs in milk in bowl. Add ground beef, egg, onion, salt and black pepper; mix well. Shape into meatballs; arrange in baking dish. Combine catsup, water, vinegar, brown sugar, Worcestershire sauce, lemon slices, chili powder and red pepper in saucepan. Bring to a boil. Cook for several minutes. Pour over meatballs. Bake at 350 degrees for 1 hour. Yield: 10 servings.

Approx Per Serving: Cal 202; Prot 15 g; Carbo 11 g; Fiber <1 g;
    T Fat 11 g; 50% Calories from Fat; Chol 69 mg; Sod 252 mg.

Meatballs and Gravy

2 cups hot water
1 envelope onion soup mix
1¹/2 pounds ground chuck
1 egg
2 slices white bread, crumbled
¹/2 cup milk

¹/4 teaspoon pepper
3 tablespoons olive oil
2 tablespoons flour
7 ounces uncooked wide egg noodles
¹/4 cup sour cream

Mix water and half the soup mix in bowl; set aside. Combine remaining soup mix with ground chuck, egg, bread crumbs, milk and pepper in bowl; mix well. Shape into small balls. Brown in olive oil in large skillet over medium heat. Push meatballs to 1 side. Stir flour into drippings in skillet. Add soup mixture; mix well. Simmer for 20 minutes. Cook noodles using package directions; drain. Stir in sour cream. Serve meatballs and gravy over noodles. Yield: 6 servings.

Approx Per Serving: Cal 501; Prot 29 g; Carbo 32 g; Fiber <1 g;
    T Fat 29 g; 51% Calories from Fat; Chol 175 mg; Sod 248 mg.

No-Work Meat Loaf

1¹/2 pounds ground beef
1 cup herb-seasoned stuffing mix
1 8-ounce can seasoned tomato sauce

1 egg
1¹/2 teaspoons salt
¹/4 teaspoon pepper

Combine all ingredients in bowl; mix well. Shape into loaf in loaf pan or shallow baking pan. Bake at 350 degrees for 1 hour. Yield: 6 servings.

Approx Per Serving: Cal 298; Prot 24 g; Carbo 11 g; Fiber 1 g;
    T Fat 18 g; 53% Calories from Fat; Chol 110 mg; Sod 993 mg.

Saucy Meat Loaves

1¹/₂ pounds ground beef
1 cup soft bread crumbs
1 medium onion, finely chopped
1 egg, beaten
1¹/₄ teaspoons salt
¹/₄ teaspoon pepper

1 cup tomato sauce
2 tablespoons brown sugar
2 tablespoons vinegar
2 tablespoons prepared mustard
¹/₂ cup water

Combine ground beef, bread crumbs, onion, egg, salt, pepper and ¹/₂ cup tomato sauce in large bowl; mix well. Shape into 6 individual meat loaves; place in greased 9-inch baking dish. Combine remaining tomato sauce, brown sugar, vinegar, mustard and water in bowl; mix well. Spoon over loaves. Bake at 350 degrees for 35 to 40 minutes or until cooked through. Yield: 6 servings.

Approx Per Serving: Cal 306; Prot 24 g; Carbo 14 g; Fiber 1 g;
    T Fat 18 g; 51% Calories from Fat; Chol 110 mg; Sod 874 mg.

Unusual Meat Loaf

2 slices bread
1 cup milk
3 eggs
1¹/₂ pounds ground beef
¹/₄ cup chopped onion
1 hot pepper, chopped
1 cup drained sauerkraut
1   10-ounce can cream of mushroom
    soup

¹/₂ teaspoon sage
¹/₈ teaspoon salt
¹/₈ teaspoon pepper
¹/₂ cup catsup
¹/₃ cup sugar
¹/₃ cup prepared mustard
¹/₄ teaspoon nutmeg

Soak bread in milk in bowl. Add eggs; beat well. Add ground beef, onion, hot pepper, sauerkraut, soup, sage, salt and pepper; mix well. Shape into loaf in greased baking pan. Mix catsup, sugar, prepared mustard and nutmeg in small bowl. Spread on meat loaf. Bake at 350 degrees for 1 hour. Yield: 6 servings.

Approx Per Serving: Cal 458; Prot 29 g; Carbo 31 g; Fiber 2 g;
    T Fat 25 g; 49% Calories from Fat; Chol 187 mg; Sod 1263 mg.

*It's better to say a flat "no"—than to say
"yes" and back out at the last minute.*

Hamburger Pie

1 8-count can crescent rolls
1 egg, beaten
1 pound ground beef
1 16-ounce can French-style green
   beans
1 6-ounce can sliced mushrooms

1 green bell pepper, chopped
1 onion, chopped
1 14-ounce can stewed tomatoes,
   sliced
Paprika to taste
8 ounces Cheddar cheese, shredded

Fit roll dough into bottom and side of deep-dish pie plate. Brush with beaten egg. Brown ground beef in skillet, stirring until crumbly. Stir in green beans, mushrooms, green pepper, onion, tomatoes and paprika. Cook until heated through; drain. Sprinkle a small amount of cheese in pie shell. Spoon in ground beef mixture. Top with remaining cheese. Bake at 350 degrees for 25 to 30 minutes or until bubbly in center. Yield: 6 servings.

Approx Per Serving: Cal 503; Prot 29 g; Carbo 27 g; Fiber 2 g;
    T Fat 32 g; 56% Calories from Fat; Chol 125 mg; Sod 1208 mg.

Ground Beef Pizza

2 pounds ground beef
1 large green bell pepper, chopped
1 medium onion, chopped
1 8-ounce can tomato sauce
1 envelope taco seasoning mix
2 6-ounce packages pizza dough mix

1 pound American cheese, shredded
1 pound mozzarella cheese, shredded
1 6-ounce can sliced mushrooms,
   drained
1 2-ounce can sliced black olives,
   drained

Brown ground beef with green pepper and onion in skillet, stirring until ground beef is crumbly; drain. Stir in tomato sauce and taco seasoning mix. Simmer for 10 minutes. Prepare pizza dough using package directions. Fit into bottom and side of large pizza pan. Spread half the meat sauce over dough. Layer American cheese, remaining meat sauce, mozzarella cheese, mushrooms and black olives over top. Bake at 350 degrees for 30 to 40 minutes or until crust is golden brown.
Yield: 8 servings.

Approx Per Serving: Cal 801; Prot 46 g; Carbo 36 g; Fiber 2 g;
    T Fat 52 g; 59% Calories from Fat; Chol 172 mg; Sod 1906 mg.

*When you are a mother sometimes you
need to tie a knot in your tongue.*

Scotch Pie

This recipe came from Scotland in 1922 in my grandma's head.
She always made small individual pies. —Joyce Moore

1 recipe 2-crust pie pastry
1¹/₂ pounds lean ground beef
1 slice bread, crumbled

1 tablespoon Worcestershire sauce
¹/₂ teaspoon salt
¹/₈ teaspoon pepper

Fit half the pastry into pie plate. Mix ground beef, bread crumbs, Worcestershire sauce, salt and pepper in bowl. Spread into prepared pie shell. Top with remaining pastry, sealing edge and cutting vents. Bake at 375 degrees for 30 minutes or until golden brown. Yield: 6 servings.

Approx Per Serving: Cal 515; Prot 25 g; Carbo 26 g; Fiber 1 g;
T Fat 34 g; 60% Calories from Fat; Chol 74 mg; Sod 658 mg.

Pizza Casserole

2 pounds ground beef
1 onion, chopped
¹/₂ green bell pepper, chopped
2 15-ounce cans Italian-style tomato
  sauce
1 6-ounce can black olives, sliced

1 6-ounce jar sliced mushrooms
2 tablespoons sugar
Salt and pepper to taste
1 12-ounce package egg noodles
8 ounces Cheddar cheese, shredded
8 ounces mozzarella cheese, shredded

Brown ground beef with onion and green pepper in skillet, stirring until ground beef is crumbly; drain. Stir in next 6 ingredients. Simmer for 15 to 20 minutes. Prepare egg noodles using package directions. Mix cheeses together. Layer egg noodles, meat sauce and cheese into baking dish. Bake at 400 degrees for 15 to 20 minutes. May use meat sauce for sandwiches. Yield: 8 servings.

Approx Per Serving: Cal 684; Prot 41 g; Carbo 42 g; Fiber 3 g;
T Fat 40 g; 52% Calories from Fat; Chol 200 mg; Sod 871 mg.

Creamy Tacos

1¹/₂ pounds ground beef
1 onion, chopped
1 green bell pepper, chopped
1 10-ounce can Ro-Tel tomatoes

1 brick chili
16 ounces Velveeta cheese, chopped
1 cup whipping cream

Brown ground beef in skillet, stirring until crumbly; drain. Add onion, green pepper, tomatoes and chili. Cook until heated through. Stir in cheese and whipping cream. Cook until cheese melts, stirring frequently. Serve over tortilla chips. Yield: 8 servings.

Approx Per Serving: Cal 501; Prot 30 g; Carbo 5 g; Fiber 1 g;
T Fat 41 g; 73% Calories from Fat; Chol 150 mg; Sod 1013 mg.
Nutritional information does not include brick chili.

Taco-Beef Corn Bread

3 cups corn bread mix
1   16-ounce can cream-style corn
1 egg
1/4 to 1/2 cup milk

1 pound ground beef
1 envelope taco seasoning mix
1 to 1 1/2 cups shredded Cheddar
   cheese

Combine corn bread mix, corn and egg in bowl; mix well. Stir in enough milk to make corn bread batter of desired consistency. Pour half the batter into oiled 10-inch cast-iron skillet. Brown ground beef in skillet, stirring until crumbly; drain. Stir in taco seasoning mix. Spoon over corn bread batter in cast-iron skillet. Top with remaining batter. Sprinkle with cheese. Bake at 375 degrees for 45 minutes. Serve with cheese dip or pinto beans. May add onions, peppers and cheese to corn bread batter if desired. Yield: 6 servings.

Approx Per Serving: Cal 668; Prot 30 g; Carbo 74 g; Fiber 3 g;
   T Fat 28 g; 37% Calories from Fat; Chol 117 mg; Sod 1783 mg.

Hot Tamale Pie

1 large onion, chopped
1 large green bell pepper, chopped
2 cloves of garlic, chopped
2 pounds ground beef
1   16-ounce can tomatoes
2 tablespoons chili powder

1 tablespoon ground cumin
2 cups cornmeal
1 cup cold water
5 cups boiling water
1 tablespoon salt

Combine onion, green pepper and garlic with a small amount of water in heavy saucepan. Cook, covered, until vegetables are tender-crisp. Stir in ground beef, tomatoes, chili powder and cumin. Simmer for 1 hour or longer; skim. Place cornmeal in top of double boiler. Stir in cold water. Stir in boiling water and salt. Cook, covered, over boiling water for 45 minutes. Spread thin layer cornmeal mush in medium-sized baking dish coated with nonstick cooking spray. Spoon in ground beef mixture. Top with remaining cornmeal mush. Yield: 8 servings.

Approx Per Serving: Cal 382; Prot 25 g; Carbo 32 g; Fiber 4 g;
   T Fat 17 g; 40% Calories from Fat; Chol 74 mg; Sod 977 mg.

*Some people pay so much attention to their
reputation that they lose their character.*

Tater Tot Casserole

1 pound ground beef
1 small onion, chopped
1 16-ounce can chili with beans
1 10-ounce can Ro-Tel tomatoes

1 10-ounce can cream of mushroom
   soup
1 pound Cheddar cheese, shredded
1 16-ounce package Tater Tots

Brown ground beef with onion in skillet, stirring until ground beef is crumbly; drain. Stir in chili, tomatoes and soup. Simmer for 15 minutes. Spoon into 9x12-inch baking dish. Layer cheese and Tater Tots over top. Bake at 350 degrees for 30 minutes. Yield: 10 servings.

Approx Per Serving: Cal 464; Prot 25 g; Carbo 24 g; Fiber 3 g;
    T Fat 31 g; 59% Calories from Fat; Chol 85 mg; Sod 1225 mg.

Zucchini with Ground Beef

1 pound ground beef
1 large onion, chopped
1 clove of garlic, chopped
Salt and pepper to taste
Tabasco sauce to taste
1 large zucchini, sliced

1 tablespoon butter
1 cup cooked rice
1/2 cup grated Parmesan cheese
2 eggs, beaten
1 8-ounce can tomato sauce
1/4 cup grated Parmesan cheese

Brown ground beef with onion and garlic in skillet, stirring frequently; drain. Add salt, pepper and Tabasco sauce; mix well. Cook zucchini with butter and a very small amount of water in saucepan until tender. Add salt and pepper. Combine ground beef mixture, squash, rice, 1/2 cup Parmesan cheese and eggs in large bowl; mix well. Spoon into buttered baking dish. Top with tomato sauce. Sprinkle with remaining 1/4 cup Parmesan cheese. Bake at 350 degrees for 20 to 30 minutes. Yield: 6 servings.

Approx Per Serving: Cal 306; Prot 22 g; Carbo 15 g; Fiber 1 g;
    T Fat 18 g; 52% Calories from Fat; Chol 133 mg; Sod 501 mg.

Ham 'n Eggs Supper

1 8-ounce can whole kernel corn
1 cup (about) milk
1 12-ounce can luncheon meat,
   chopped

2 cups shredded Cheddar cheese
1 cup cracker crumbs
3 eggs, slightly beaten

Drain corn, reserving liquid. Add enough milk to reserved liquid to measure 1 1/4 cups. Combine with corn, luncheon meat, cheese, cracker crumbs and eggs in bowl; mix well. Spoon into greased 6x10-inch baking dish. Bake at 350 degrees for 40 to 45 minutes or until set. Yield: 6 servings.

Approx Per Serving: Cal 494; Prot 24 g; Carbo 19 g; Fiber 1 g;
    T Fat 36 g; 65% Calories from Fat; Chol 200 mg; Sod 1260 mg.

Ham Loaf

1 pound ground cured ham
1½ pounds lean ground pork
3 eggs, beaten
1 cup milk
1 cup bread crumbs

Salt and pepper to taste
1½ cups packed brown sugar
½ cup vinegar
1 tablespoon dry mustard
½ cup water

Combine ground ham, ground pork, eggs, milk, bread crumbs, salt and pepper in bowl; mix well. Shape into loaf. Place in loaf pan. Mix brown sugar, vinegar, dry mustard and water in saucepan. Cook over medium heat for 5 minutes. Pour over ham loaf. Bake at 325 degrees for 2 hours, basting frequently. Serve with any remaining sauce. Yield: 8 servings.

Approx Per Serving: Cal 533; Prot 40 g; Carbo 62 g; Fiber 1 g;
    T Fat 14 g; 24% Calories from Fat; Chol 179 mg; Sod 956 mg.

Ham and Rice Casserole

1 cup chopped onion
1 tablespoon oil
2 cups chopped ham

3 cups cooked rice
1   16-ounce can bean sprouts,
    drained

Brown onion in oil in skillet. Add ham. Cook until heated through. Stir in rice and bean sprouts. Cook until heated through. Yield: 6 servings.

Approx Per Serving: Cal 223; Prot 15 g; Carbo 28 g; Fiber 2 g;
    T Fat 5 g; 21% Calories from Fat; Chol 26 mg; Sod 628 mg.

Ham Balls

1 pound ground pork
1 pound ham, ground
2 slices white bread, crumbled
2 eggs, beaten
1 cup milk

¾ cup vinegar
¼ cup water
1½ cups packed brown sugar
1½ teaspoons dry mustard

Combine ground meat, bread crumbs, eggs and milk in bowl; mix well. Shape into balls. Place in baking dish. Mix vinegar, water, brown sugar and dry mustard in bowl. Pour over ham balls. Bake at 350 degrees for 1½ hours, basting every 15 minutes. May shape into small balls for cocktail-sized servings. Yield: 8 servings.

Approx Per Serving: Cal 442; Prot 31 g; Carbo 56 g; Fiber <1 g;
    T Fat 10 g; 21% Calories from Fat; Chol 130 mg; Sod 874 mg.

Skillet-Fried Corn and Ham

2 cups corn
1/2 cup chopped onion
1/2 cup chopped green bell pepper
1/2 cup chopped ham

2 tablespoons margarine
3 tablespoons milk
1/2 teaspoon salt
1/4 teaspoon pepper

Sauté corn, onion, green pepper and ham in hot margarine in skillet until onion and green pepper are tender-crisp. Stir in milk, salt and pepper. Cook until heated through. Yield: 4 servings.

Approx Per Serving: Cal 161; Prot 8 g; Carbo 17 g; Fiber 4 g;
 T Fat 8 g; 42% Calories from Fat; Chol 11 mg; Sod 583 mg.

Creole Pork Chops

2 cups tomato juice
1/2 cup chopped green bell pepper
1 1/2 tablespoons Worcestershire sauce
1 teaspoon lemon juice
Tabasco sauce to taste

1 teaspoon salt
1/2 teaspoon pepper
6 1-inch thick lean pork chops
Salt and pepper to taste

Combine tomato juice, green pepper, Worcestershire sauce, lemon juice, Tabasco sauce, 1 teaspoon salt and 1/2 teaspoon pepper in saucepan. Cook until heated through. Brown pork chops on both sides in hot skillet. Season with salt and pepper. Pour sauce over top. Simmer, covered, for 1 hour or until tender. Serve over hot cooked rice. Yield: 6 servings.

Approx Per Serving: Cal 248; Prot 33 g; Carbo 5 g; Fiber 1 g;
 T Fat 11 g; 39% Calories from Fat; Chol 98 mg; Sod 763 mg.

Pork Chop Casserole

4 thick pork chops
7 small potatoes, sliced
1 10-ounce can cream of mushroom soup

1 5-ounce can evaporated milk
1/2 cup water
Salt and pepper to taste

Brown pork chops on both sides in skillet. Layer pork chops, potatoes, soup, evaporated milk, water, salt and pepper in greased baking dish. Bake, covered, at 450 degrees for 1 hour. Remove cover. Bake for 20 minutes longer. Yield: 4 servings.

Approx Per Serving: Cal 539; Prot 39 g; Carbo 53 g; Fiber 3 g;
 T Fat 19 g; 31% Calories from Fat; Chol 109 mg; Sod 699 mg.

Pork Chop Skillet

4 pork chops
Salt and pepper to taste
2 tablespoons margarine

1 envelope onion soup mix
4 medium potatoes
4 carrots, cut into 2-inch pieces

Season pork chops with salt and pepper. Brown on both sides in margarine in skillet. Mix onion soup mix with 1 to 2 cups warm water. Pour over pork chops. Add potatoes and carrots. Simmer, covered, for 30 minutes or until meat and vegetables are tender. Yield: 4 servings.

Approx Per Serving: Cal 432; Prot 35 g; Carbo 35 g; Fiber 4 g;
   T Fat 17 g; 34% Calories from Fat; Chol 98 mg; Sod 333 mg.

Rice Chop-Chop

1 pound pork, cut into thin strips
1/4 cup butter
1 cup shredded carrot
1/2 cup sliced green onions
1/4 cup chopped parsley

3 cups chicken broth
1 cup uncooked rice
1/2 teaspoon salt
Pepper to taste

Stir-fry pork strips in butter in skillet until tender. Remove pork to warm plate. Sauté carrot, green onions and parsley in drippings in skillet until tender. Stir in broth, rice, salt and pepper. Add cooked pork. Cook, covered, over low heat for 30 minutes. Yield: 6 servings.

Approx Per Serving: Cal 318; Prot 20 g; Carbo 28 g; Fiber 1 g;
   T Fat 13 g; 39% Calories from Fat; Chol 67 mg; Sod 676 mg.

Marinated Pork Tenderloin

1/2 cup red wine
1/2 cup oil
2 or 3 cloves of garlic, cut into halves
1 teaspoon thyme
1 teaspoon rosemary

1 teaspoon marjoram
2 tablespoons chopped fresh parsley
1/4 cup chopped onion
Freshly ground pepper to taste
1   2-pound pork tenderloin

Mix wine, oil, garlic, thyme, rosemary, marjoram, parsley, onion and pepper in bowl. Place tenderloin in shallow dish. Pour marinade over top. Marinate, covered, in refrigerator for 4 hours to overnight, turning several times. Drain marinade. Grill tenderloin over hot coals for 30 minutes or until cooked through. Yield: 4 servings.

Approx Per Serving: Cal 593; Prot 45 g; Carbo 2 g; Fiber <1 g;
   T Fat 42 g; 67% Calories from Fat; Chol 139 mg; Sod 112 mg.

Breakfast Pizza

1 8-count package crescent rolls
1 12-ounce package bacon,
   crisp-fried, crumbled
1 medium onion, chopped

2 cups shredded Cheddar cheese
2 cups shredded mozzarella cheese
8 to 10 eggs, beaten

Press roll dough into 12-inch pizza pan. Spread bacon over dough. Layer onion and cheeses over bacon. Pour beaten eggs over top. Bake at 400 degrees for 12 to 15 minutes or until done to taste. May substitute 1 pound cooked sausage for bacon. Yield: 6 servings.

Approx Per Serving: Cal 630; Prot 34 g; Carbo 19 g; Fiber <1 g;
     T Fat 45 g; 66% Calories from Fat; Chol 438 mg; Sod 1068 mg.

Cajun's Feast

1 package shrimp and crab boil
3 to 4 pounds summer sausage, cut
   into chunks

8 to 10 baking potatoes, pierced with
   fork
10 to 12 ears of corn, cooked

Place shrimp and crab boil in large pan. Fill ¾ full with water. Simmer mixture for 20 minutes. Add sausage and unpeeled potatoes. Simmer until potatoes are nearly done. Add cooked corn on the cob. Cook for 5 minutes longer. Drain liquid. May serve with rice and corn bread. Yield: 12 servings.

Approx Per Serving: Cal 513; Prot 18 g; Carbo 63 g; Fiber 7 g;
     T Fat 23 g; 38% Calories from Fat; Chol 50 mg; Sod 1059 mg.
     Nutritional information does not include shrimp and crab boil.

Potato Crust Quiche

4 cups grated unpeeled new potatoes
¼ cup flour
1 egg
⅛ teaspoon salt
1 tablespoon oil
2 eggs
1 cup light cream
¼ teaspoon salt

Pepper to taste
¼ cup chopped onion
½ cup chopped ham
½ cup chopped broccoli
1½ cups shredded sharp Cheddar
   cheese
Paprika to taste

Mix potatoes, flour, 1 egg and salt in bowl. Press into greased glass pie plate. Brush with oil. Bake at 400 degrees for 20 minutes or until light brown. Set aside. Beat remaining 2 eggs with light cream, salt and pepper. Layer onion, ham and broccoli in baked crust. Pour egg mixture over top. Top with cheese; sprinkle with paprika. Bake at 350 degrees for 20 minutes or until set. Yield: 6 servings.

Approx Per Serving: Cal 458; Prot 19 g; Carbo 52 g; Fiber 4 g;
     T Fat 18 g; 35% Calories from Fat; Chol 157 mg; Sod 527 mg.

Potato and Sausage Casserole

1 pound sausage
1/4 cup flour
1 tablespoon salt
1 teaspoon pepper

8 medium potatoes, chopped
1 large onion, chopped
1 1/2 cups milk, scalded

Brown sausage in skillet, stirring until crumbly; drain. Mix flour, salt and pepper in bowl. Combine with potatoes and onion in bowl; mix well. Layer sausage and potato mixture 1/2 at a time into 9x12-inch baking dish. Pour hot milk over top. Bake, covered, at 325 degrees for 1 hour. Remove cover. Bake for 15 minutes longer. May add 1/4 to 1/2 pound ground beef or sausage to layers. Yield: 6 servings.

Approx Per Serving: Cal 390; Prot 14 g; Carbo 54 g; Fiber 4 g;
    T Fat 13 g; 31% Calories from Fat; Chol 37 mg; Sod 1562 mg.

Quick Sausage Dinner

1 pound sausage
1 green bell pepper, chopped
2 green onions, chopped
2 or 3 stalks celery, chopped

2 cups chicken broth
1 cup uncooked rice
1 tablespoon Worcestershire sauce
1/4 to 1/2 teaspoon salt

Brown sausage in skillet, stirring until crumbly; drain. Stir in green pepper, green onions, celery, broth, rice, Worcestershire sauce and salt. Simmer, covered, for 1 hour. Yield: 4 servings.

Approx Per Serving: Cal 398; Prot 17 g; Carbo 41 g; Fiber 2 g;
    T Fat 18 g; 41% Calories from Fat; Chol 44 mg; Sod 1409 mg.

Sausage-Stuffed Cabbage

8 large cabbage leaves
1 pound sausage
1 cup finely chopped onion
3/4 cup uncooked rice

1 to 2 teaspoons curry powder
Salt and pepper to taste
2   16-ounce cans tomatoes

Cook cabbage leaves in 1 inch boiling salted water in covered saucepan for 5 minutes; drain. Brown sausage in skillet, stirring until crumbly; drain. Combine sausage with onion, rice, curry powder, salt and pepper in bowl; mix well. Spoon mixture onto cabbage leaves. Roll up; secure with wooden picks. Place in skillet. Pour undrained tomatoes over top. Simmer, covered, for 1 to 1 1/2 hours, adding additional tomato juice if desired. Yield: 8 servings.

Approx Per Serving: Cal 194; Prot 7 g; Carbo 22 g; Fiber 2 g;
    T Fat 9 g; 42% Calories from Fat; Chol 22 mg; Sod 652 mg.

Sausage and Egg Scramble

This recipe is great to serve on Christmas morning as it can be baking while children are opening gifts. —Jean Prange

1 pound sausage
5 slices sandwich bread
8 eggs
2 cups milk

1 teaspoon prepared mustard
1 teaspoon salt
1 teaspoon pepper
1 cup shredded Cheddar cheese

Brown sausage in skillet, stirring until crumbly; drain. Break bread into small pieces. Place in greased 9x13-inch baking dish. Scatter sausage over top. Beat eggs with milk, prepared mustard, salt and pepper in bowl. Pour over sausage layer. Sprinkle with cheese. Chill, covered with foil, overnight. Bake at 325 degrees for 45 to 50 minutes. Yield: 8 servings.

Approx Per Serving: Cal 319; Prot 18 g; Carbo 13 g; Fiber <1 g;
    T Fat 21 g; 61% Calories from Fat; Chol 258 mg; Sod 891 mg.

Sausage-Cheese Lasagna

1 pound hot sausage
1   10-ounce can tomato soup
3 cloves of garlic, crushed
1$^{1}/_{2}$ teaspoons oregano
1$^{1}/_{2}$ teaspoons basil

1   8-ounce package lasagna noodles
2 cups shredded mozzarella cheese
2 cups cottage cheese
$^{3}/_{4}$ cup grated Parmesan cheese

Brown sausage in skillet, stirring until crumbly; drain. Stir in soup, garlic, oregano and basil. Cook lasagna noodles using package directions; drain. Place 3 noodles in lightly greased 9x13-inch baking dish. Layer sausage mixture, mozzarella cheese, cottage cheese and Parmesan cheese $^{1}/_{3}$ at time over noodles. Chill, covered, for 2 hours to overnight. Bake, uncovered, at 350 degrees for 30 minutes. Yield: 6 servings.

Approx Per Serving: Cal 532; Prot 33 g; Carbo 38 g; Fiber <1 g;
    T Fat 26 g; 45% Calories from Fat; Chol 76 mg; Sod 1403 mg.

Be what you wish others to become.

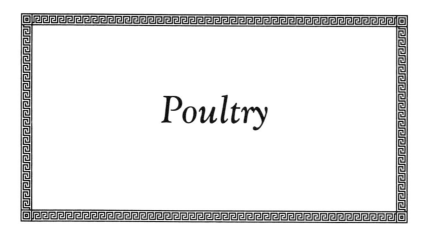

Poultry

Chicken with Honey Sauce

1 cup flour
1 teaspoon paprika
1 teaspoon salt
¹/₄ teaspoon pepper
4 chicken breasts, boned, skinned

¹/₂ cup melted butter
¹/₄ cup honey
¹/₄ cup lemon juice
¹/₄ cup melted butter

Combine flour, paprika, salt and pepper in plastic bag; shake to mix well. Rinse chicken and pat dry. Shake 2 pieces at a time in flour mixture, coating well. Dip in ¹/₂ cup melted butter. Arrange in 9x13-inch baking dish sprayed with nonstick cooking spray. Bake at 400 degrees for 25 minutes. Drain baking dish and turn chicken over. Combine honey, lemon juice and ¹/₄ cup melted butter in bowl; mix well. Pour over chicken. Bake for 25 minutes longer or until chicken is tender. Yield: 4 servings.

Approx Per Serving: Cal 627; Prot 30 g; Carbo 43 g; Fiber 1 g;
    T Fat 38 g; 54% Calories from Fat; Chol 165 mg; Sod 888 mg.

An immaculant home is a sign of a misspent life.

Mexicali Chicken

2 3-pound chickens, cut up
2 tablespoons butter
2 tablespoons olive oil
1 large onion, chopped
1 large green bell pepper, chopped
1 large red bell pepper, chopped
1 tablespoon chili powder

¹/₄ cup flour
1 32-ounce can stewed Italian
   tomatoes, chopped
1 teaspoon sugar
1 tablespoon salt
¹/₄ teaspoon pepper

Rinse chicken and pat dry. Brown several pieces at a time in butter and oil in heavy Dutch oven; remove browned chicken to platter. Add onion and green pepper to drippings in Dutch oven. Sauté until tender. Stir in chili powder. Cook for 1 minute. Sprinkle with flour. Add tomatoes, sugar, salt and pepper; mix well. Cook over medium-high heat until sauce boils for 1 minute and thickens, stirring constantly. Return chicken to Dutch oven, spooning sauce over each layer. Bake, covered, at 350 degrees for 1 hour. Bake, uncovered, for 30 minutes longer or until chicken is tender and sauce is of desired consistency. Garnish with additional green and red pepper rings and fresh parsley. Serve over rice or pasta. Yield: 10 servings.

Approx Per Serving: Cal 355; Prot 41 g; Carbo 12 g; Fiber 1 g;
   T Fat 15 g; 39% Calories from Fat; Chol 128 mg; Sod 1076 mg.

Chicken Breasts Reuben

4 chicken breasts, skinned
¹/₄ teaspoon salt
¹/₄ teaspoon pepper
1 16-ounce can sauerkraut, drained

4 4x6-inch slices Swiss cheese
1¹/₄ cups Thousand Island salad
   dressing
1 tablespoon chopped parsley

Rinse chicken and pat dry; arrange in shallow baking dish sprayed with nonstick cooking spray. Sprinkle with salt and pepper. Layer sauerkraut and cheese over chicken. Pour salad dressing evenly over top. Bake, covered, at 325 degrees for 1¹/₂ hours or until tender. Sprinkle with parsley. Yield: 4 servings.

Approx Per Serving: Cal 563; Prot 36 g; Carbo 18 g; Fiber 2 g;
   T Fat 39 g; 62% Calories from Fat; Chol 118 mg; Sod 1568 mg.

Who gossips with you will gossip of you.

Chicken Breast Casserole

1 4-ounce jar dried beef
6 boneless chicken breasts
6 slices bacon

1 10-ounce can cream of mushroom
   soup
1 cup sour cream

Spread dried beef in 9x13-inch baking dish. Rinse chicken and pat dry. Wrap each with 1 slice bacon; secure with wooden pick. Arrange in prepared dish. Combine soup and sour cream in bowl; mix well. Spread over chicken. Bake at 300 degrees for 3 hours. Serve with rice. Yield: 6 servings.

Approx Per Serving: Cal 339; Prot 36 g; Carbo 5 g; Fiber <1 g;
     T Fat 18 g; 50% Calories from Fat; Chol 126 mg; Sod 1222 mg.

Chicken Parmigiana

4 chicken breast filets
2 eggs, slightly beaten
1 teaspoon salt
$1/8$ teaspoon pepper
$3/4$ cup fine dry bread crumbs
$1/2$ cup oil

2 cups tomato sauce
$1/4$ teaspoon basil
$1/8$ teaspoon garlic powder
1 tablespoon butter
$1/2$ cup grated Parmesan cheese
8 ounces mozzarella cheese, sliced

Rinse chicken and pat dry. Pound with meat mallet or back of heavy knife to flatten to $1/4$ inch. Beat eggs with salt and pepper in bowl. Dip chicken in eggs; coat with bread crumbs. Brown on both sides in very hot oil in large skillet; remove to shallow baking dish. Drain excess oil from skillet. Add tomato sauce, basil and garlic powder. Bring to a boil; reduce heat. Simmer for 10 minutes or until of desired consistency. Stir in butter. Pour over chicken; sprinkle with Parmesan cheese. Bake, covered, at 350 degrees for 30 minutes. Top with mozzarella cheese. Bake for 10 minutes longer or until cheese melts. Yield: 4 servings.

Approx Per Serving: Cal 762; Prot 49 g; Carbo 24 g; Fiber 3 g;
     T Fat 52 g; 61% Calories from Fat; Chol 239 mg; Sod 1934 mg.
     Nutritional information includes entire amount of oil for browning chicken.

Chicken Breasts in Wine Sauce

1 pound mushrooms, sliced
$3/4$ cup white cooking wine
$1/4$ cup soy sauce
2 teaspoons brown sugar

1 clove of garlic, crushed
2 tablespoons cornstarch
$1/4$ cup water
4 boneless chicken breasts

Combine first 5 ingredients in bowl; mix well. Stir in mixture of cornstarch and water. Rinse chicken and pat dry. Combine with sauce in baking dish. Bake at 350 degrees for 1 hour. Store sauce in refrigerator overnight to enhance flavor. Yield: 4 servings.

Approx Per Serving: Cal 232; Prot 30 g; Carbo 13 g; Fiber 2 g;
     T Fat 3 g; 14% Calories from Fat; Chol 72 mg; Sod 1100 mg.

Dijon Chicken

8 boneless chicken breasts
1/4 teaspoon poultry seasoning
1/4 teaspoon MSG

1/2 cup orange marmalade
2 tablespoons Dijon mustard
1 10-ounce can cream of celery soup

Rinse chicken and pat dry. Sauté in skillet sprayed with nonstick cooking spray; remove to baking dish. Spoon mixture of remaining ingredients over chicken. Bake at 350 degrees for 15 minutes or until tender. Yield: 8 servings.

Approx Per Serving: Cal 224; Prot 27 g; Carbo 17 g; Fiber <1 g;
    T Fat 5 g; 21% Calories from Fat; Chol 76 mg; Sod 569 mg.

Glorified Chicken Breasts

1 cup sour cream
1/2 teaspoon chopped garlic
2 teaspoons Worcestershire sauce
1 teaspoon Tabasco sauce

1 teaspoon paprika
1 teaspoon salt
4 chicken breasts
1/2 cup bread crumbs

Mix first 6 ingredients in bowl. Rinse chicken; pat dry. Add to sour cream mixture, coating each piece well. Chill, covered, overnight. Coat chicken with bread crumbs; arrange in 9x13-inch baking dish. Bake at 325 degrees for 1 hour. Yield: 4 servings.

Approx Per Serving: Cal 315; Prot 30 g; Carbo 12 g; Fiber 1 g;
    T Fat 16 g; 45% Calories from Fat; Chol 98 mg; Sod 749 mg.

Stuffed Chicken Breasts

*This South Louisiana recipe can be used with wild geese,
duck, pork or beef. —John Le Maire*

2 slices bacon, chopped
1/4 cup chopped green onions
1 clove of garlic, finely chopped
4 chicken breast filets
2 tablespoons prepared mustard

2 tablespoons Worcestershire sauce
1/4 teaspoon sugar
1/4 teaspoon salt
1/4 teaspoon pepper

Combine bacon with green onions and garlic in bowl; mix well. Rinse chicken and pat dry. Cut pocket in each piece of chicken. Stuff with bacon mixture; secure with wooden picks. Spread with mixture of mustard and Worcestershire sauce. Sprinkle sugar, salt and pepper in cast-iron skillet. Cook over low heat until sugar melts. Add chicken. Cook for 25 to 30 minutes or until juices begin to make gravy, adding 1 tablespoon water every 2 minutes. Cook, covered, for 30 minutes longer, adding water as needed for desired consistency and turning chicken occasionally. Serve over rice. Yield: 4 servings.

Approx Per Serving: Cal 174; Prot 28 g; Carbo 3 g; Fiber <1 g;
    T Fat 5 g; 26% Calories from Fat; Chol 75 mg; Sod 409 mg.

Parmesan Chicken

1/2 cup grated Parmesan cheese
11/2 cups bread crumbs

8 chicken breasts
1/2 cup melted butter

Mix cheese and bread crumbs in bowl. Rinse chicken and pat dry. Dip in melted butter; coat with bread crumb mixture. Place in baking pan. Bake at 350 degrees for 45 to 60 minutes or until crisp and tender. Yield: 8 servings.

Approx Per Serving: Cal 338; Prot 31 g; Carbo 14 g; Fiber 1 g;
　　T Fat 17 g; 46% Calories from Fat; Chol 108 mg; Sod 392 mg.

Southern Fried Chicken

2 cups flour
11/2 cups cracker crumbs
Garlic salt and pepper to taste

4 medium chicken breasts
4 eggs, beaten
Shortening for frying

Mix flour, cracker crumbs, garlic salt and pepper in bowl. Rinse chicken and pat dry. Dip into eggs; coat with flour mixture. Place 1/2 inch apart on platter. Chill, covered with foil, for 30 minutes or longer. Heat about 2 cups shortening to 350 degrees in medium-large skillet. Add chicken. Fry until golden brown; remove to rack in baking pan. Bake at 375 degrees for 35 to 45 minutes or until tender. May change or add seasonings to suit individual taste. Yield: 4 servings.

Approx Per Serving: Cal 578; Prot 40 g; Carbo 71 g; Fiber 2 g;
　　T Fat 12 g; 20% Calories from Fat; Chol 296 mg; Sod 540 mg.
　　Nutritional information does not include shortening for frying.

Swiss Chicken

8 boneless chicken breasts
1　10-ounce can cream of chicken
　　soup
1/2 soup can water

8 slices Swiss cheese
1/2 cup melted margarine
1　8-ounce package herb-seasoned
　　stuffing mix

Rinse chicken and pat dry; arrange in 8x12-inch baking dish. Combine soup and water in bowl; mix well. Spoon over chicken. Top with cheese slices. Toss margarine with stuffing mix in bowl; sprinkle over cheese. Bake, covered, at 375 degrees for 1 hour. Yield: 8 servings.

Approx Per Serving: Cal 489; Prot 39 g; Carbo 24 g; Fiber <1 g;
　　T Fat 25 g; 47% Calories from Fat; Chol 101 mg; Sod 1037 mg.

Stir-Fry Chicken and Rice

4 chicken breast filets
1   4-ounce can sliced mushrooms
1 tablespoon cornstarch
1 cup water
2 tablespoons oil
2 tablespoons soy sauce
¹/₄ teaspoon pepper

1 chicken bouillon cube
1 cup chopped celery
1 cup chopped onion
1 tablespoon oil
1 tablespoon Greek seasoning
1   7-ounce can water chestnuts, drained
1 cup rice, cooked

Rinse chicken and pat dry; cut into bite-sized pieces. Drain mushrooms, reserving liquid. Combine reserved liquid with cornstarch and water in bowl. Stir-fry chicken in 2 tablespoons oil in wok or skillet. Stir in soy sauce, pepper, bouillon cube and cornstarch mixture. Simmer for 6 minutes, stirring frequently. Combine celery and onion with 1 tablespoon oil in glass bowl. Microwave on High for 4 minutes. Stir in Greek seasoning. Microwave for 1 minute longer. Add to chicken mixture. Add mushrooms and water chestnuts; mix well. Simmer until heated through. Serve over rice. Yield: 8 servings.

Approx Per Serving: Cal 231; Prot 16 g; Carbo 26 g; Fiber 2 g;
T Fat 7 g; 27% Calories from Fat; Chol 36 mg; Sod 510 mg.
Nutritional information does not include Greek seasoning.

Chicken and Artichoke Dish

4 whole chicken breasts
1 carrot
1 stalk celery
1 small onion
Salt and pepper to taste
2   16-ounce cans artichoke hearts,
    drained

1 cup mayonnaise
1   10-ounce can cream of mushroom
    soup
1   10-ounce can cream of chicken
    soup
1 teaspoon curry powder
1 cup shredded Cheddar cheese

Rinse chicken and cut into halves. Combine with carrot, celery, onion, salt, pepper and water to cover in saucepan. Simmer until chicken is tender. Cool in broth. Remove chicken from broth; discard skin and bones. Layer artichoke hearts and chicken in buttered baking dish. Combine mayonnaise, soups and curry powder in bowl. Spread evenly over chicken; top with cheese. Bake at 350 degrees for 30 minutes. May add first layer of cooked rice to make a heartier dish. Yield: 8 servings.

Approx Per Serving: Cal 509; Prot 34 g; Carbo 13 g; Fiber <1 g;
T Fat 35 g; 63% Calories from Fat; Chol 107 mg; Sod 1164 mg.

The best way to have a friend is to be a friend.

Chicken and Asparagus Casserole

This recipe received from a friend, always receives many compliments.
Serve at Christmas luncheons or increase the recipe and serve
at wedding rehearsal dinners. —Chris Shoemake

6 whole chicken breasts
1 medium onion, chopped
1/2 cup butter
1   8-ounce can mushrooms, drained
1   10-ounce can cream of mushroom
    soup
1   10-ounce can cream of chicken
    soup
1   5-ounce can evaporated milk
2 cups shredded sharp Cheddar
    cheese

1/4 teaspoon Tabasco sauce
2 teaspoons soy sauce
2 tablespoons chopped pimento
1 teaspoon MSG
1 teaspoon salt
1/2 teaspoon pepper
2   16-ounce cans asparagus spears,
    drained
1/2 cup slivered almonds

Rinse chicken and pat dry. Boil or bake until tender; cool. Cut into bite-sized pieces. Sauté onion in butter in saucepan. Add mushrooms, soups, evaporated milk, cheese, Tabasco sauce, soy sauce, pimento, MSG, salt and pepper; mix well. Simmer until cheese melts. Layer chicken, asparagus and cheese sauce 1/2 at a time in 9x13-inch baking dish. Top with almonds. Bake at 350 degrees for 30 to 40 minutes or until bubbly. May substitute broccoli for asparagus. Yield: 12 servings.

Approx Per Serving: Cal 399; Prot 36 g; Carbo 10 g; Fiber 3 g;
    T Fat 25 g; 54% Calories from Fat; Chol 118 mg; Sod 1485 mg.

Chicken and Broccoli Casserole

2 1/2 cups chopped celery
1 1/2 cups chopped onion
1/2 cup chopped green bell pepper
12 ounces fresh mushrooms, sliced
1 1/2 pounds fresh broccoli, chopped

3/4 cup butter
2 pounds chicken, cooked, chopped
1/4 teaspoon garlic salt
Salt and pepper to taste
20 ounces cream cheese

Sauté celery, onion, green pepper, mushrooms and broccoli in butter in skillet until tender. Add chicken, garlic salt, salt and pepper; mix well. Add cream cheese. Cook over low heat until cream cheese melts, stirring constantly. Spoon into buttered 9x13-inch baking dish. Bake at 350 degrees until golden brown. Yield: 10 servings.

Approx Per Serving: Cal 447; Prot 21 g; Carbo 10 g; Fiber 4 g;
    T Fat 37 g; 73% Calories from Fat; Chol 140 mg; Sod 421 mg.

Happiness is a state of mind, not a state of finance.

Chicken and Almond Casserole

3 cups chopped cooked chicken
4 hard-boiled eggs, chopped
2 cups cooked rice
1½ cups chopped celery
1 small onion, chopped
1 cup mayonnaise
1 10-ounce can cream of chicken soup

1 10-ounce can cream of mushroom soup
1 3-ounce package slivered almonds
2 teaspoons lemon juice
1 teaspoon salt
1 cup bread crumbs
2 tablespoons melted butter

Combine first 11 ingredients in bowl; mix well. Spoon into 9x13-inch baking dish. Top with mixture of bread crumbs and melted butter. Chill, covered with foil, overnight. Let stand at room temperature for 1 hour. Bake, covered, at 350 degrees for 45 minutes. Yield: 12 servings.

Approx Per Serving: Cal 405; Prot 17 g; Carbo 21 g; Fiber 2 g;
     T Fat 28 g; 63% Calories from Fat; Chol 121 mg; Sod 802 mg.

Easy Chicken Casserole

2 10-ounce cans cream of chicken and mushroom soup
1 cup light mayonnaise
5 chicken breasts, cooked, chopped

1 8-ounce can sliced water chestnuts, drained
2 hard-boiled eggs, chopped
2 cups stuffing mix

Combine soup and mayonnaise in bowl; mix well. Add chicken and water chestnuts; mix well. Fold in eggs. Spoon into greased rectangular baking dish. Sprinkle evenly with stuffing mix. Bake at 350 degrees for 40 minutes. Yield: 10 servings.

Approx Per Serving: Cal 249; Prot 18 g; Carbo 16 g; Fiber <1 g;
     T Fat 12 g; 44% Calories from Fat; Chol 90 mg; Sod 353 mg.

Crunchy Chicken Casserole

1 envelope sour cream mix
2 cups chopped cooked chicken
1 10-ounce can cream of chicken soup
1 2-ounce jar chopped pimento
1 8-ounce can water chestnuts, drained, chopped

1 medium onion, finely chopped
½ cup melted margarine
1 16-ounce package herb-seasoned corn bread stuffing mix
2 tablespoons butter

Prepare sour cream mix using package directions. Combine with chicken, soup, pimento, water chestnuts and onion in bowl; mix well. Toss ½ cup melted margarine with stuffing mix in bowl. Layer half the stuffing, chicken mixture and remaining stuffing in 2½-quart baking dish. Dot with 2 tablespoons butter. Bake at 350 degrees for 30 minutes or until golden brown. Yield: 8 servings.

Approx Per Serving: Cal 524; Prot 22 g; Carbo 55 g; Fiber 1 g;
     T Fat 25 g; 42% Calories from Fat; Chol 53 mg; Sod 1350 mg.

Chicken Casserole

15 ounces chopped cooked chicken
1   10-ounce can cream of chicken
   soup
1 cup chopped celery
2/3 cup mushroom pieces
2 teaspoons minced onion
1/2 cup slivered almonds
3 hard-boiled eggs, chopped

1   8-ounce can sliced water
   chestnuts, drained
1 tablespoon lemon juice
3/4 cup mayonnaise
1/2 teaspoon salt
1/4 teaspoon pepper
1 cup crushed potato chips

Combine chicken, soup, celery, mushrooms, onion, almonds, eggs, water chestnuts, lemon juice, mayonnaise, salt and pepper in bowl; mix well. Spoon into 2-quart baking dish. Top with crushed potato chips. Bake at 350 degrees for 30 minutes. Yield: 8 servings.

Approx Per Serving: Cal 411; Prot 21 g; Carbo 12 g; Fiber 2 g;
   T Fat 32 g; 68% Calories from Fat; Chol 142 mg; Sod 648 mg.

Ten-Can Chicken Casserole

1   3-pound chicken, cooked, chopped
1   10-ounce can cream of mushroom
   soup
1   5-ounce can evaporated milk
1   16-ounce can asparagus tips,
   drained
1   16-ounce can French-style green
   beans, drained

1   4-ounce can sliced mushrooms,
   drained
1   2-ounce jar chopped pimento
1   7-ounce can sliced water
   chestnuts, drained
1   3-ounce can chow mein noodles
Salt and pepper to taste
2   3-ounce cans French-fried onions

Combine chicken, soup, evaporated milk, asparagus, green beans, mushrooms, pimento, water chestnuts, chow mein noodles, salt and pepper in bowl; mix well. Spoon into greased baking dish. Top with French-fried onions. Bake at 350 degrees for 20 minutes or until heated through. Yield: 15 servings.

Approx Per Serving: Cal 235; Prot 17 g; Carbo 14 g; Fiber 2 g;
   T Fat 12 g; 47% Calories from Fat; Chol 44 mg; Sod 513 mg.

Have the guts to say no, or go forth pleasantly.

Chicken Chow Mein

2 cups chopped cooked chicken
2 tablespoons butter
2 cups thinly sliced celery
1¹/₂ cups sliced onions
¹/₄ teaspoon pepper
2 cups chicken broth

1 16-ounce can chow mein
   vegetables, drained
¹/₂ cup drained canned mushrooms
2 tablespoons cornstarch
3 tablespoons soy sauce
1 5-ounce can chow mein noodles

Sauté chicken in butter in saucepan. Add celery, onions, pepper and chicken broth. Simmer, covered, until vegetables are tender. Add chow mein vegetables and mushrooms. Bring to a boil. Stir in mixture of cornstarch and soy sauce. Cook for 2 minutes or until slightly thickened, stirring constantly. Spoon onto deep platter; top with chow mein noodles. Yield: 6 servings.

Approx Per Serving: Cal 339; Prot 21 g; Carbo 27 g; Fiber 2 g;
    T Fat 17 g; 44% Calories from Fat; Chol 55 mg; Sod 1411 mg.

Chicken and Dumplings

1 3-pound chicken
1 10-ounce can cream of chicken
   soup

1 10-ounce can cream of celery soup
1 12-count package flour tortillas,
   cut into strips

Rinse chicken well. Cook in water to cover in saucepan until tender. Remove chicken from saucepan, reserving broth. Chop chicken, discarding skin and bones. Skim reserved broth. Stir in soups. Bring to a boil. Add tortillas a few at a time. Cook for 10 to 15 minutes or until tortillas are tender, stirring frequently. Add chicken. Let stand, covered, for several minutes. Yield: 8 servings.

Approx Per Serving: Cal 382; Prot 31 g; Carbo 34 g; Fiber 2 g;
    T Fat 14 g; 33% Calories from Fat; Chol 83 mg; Sod 918 mg.

Microwave Chicken Enchilada Casserole

2 cups crushed corn chips
2 cups chopped cooked chicken
1 10-ounce can cream of chicken
   soup
1 4-ounce can chopped green chilies
2 green onions, chopped

¹/₂ cup chicken broth
1 15-ounce can tomatoes, drained,
   chopped
¹/₂ teaspoon salt
1 cup shredded Cheddar cheese

Layer corn chips and chicken in 2-quart glass dish. Combine soup, green chilies, green onions, chicken broth, tomatoes and salt in bowl; mix well. Spoon over chicken. Microwave, covered with waxed paper, on High for 10 minutes. Top with cheese. Microwave on Medium for 2 minutes. May add sour cream if desired. Yield: 6 servings.

Approx Per Serving: Cal 334; Prot 22 g; Carbo 19 g; Fiber 2 g;
    T Fat 19 g; 51% Calories from Fat; Chol 65 mg; Sod 1175 mg.

Easy Chicken Enchiladas

1 7-ounce can chicken chunks
2 10-ounce cans cream of chicken soup
1/2 cup shredded Cheddar cheese
1 4-ounce can chopped green chilies

1 small onion, chopped
2 cups sour cream
12 flour tortillas
1/2 cup shredded Cheddar cheese

Combine chicken, soup, 1/2 cup cheese, green chilies, onion and sour cream in bowl; mix well. Spoon 2 to 3 tablespoons mixture onto each tortilla; roll tortillas to enclose filling. Place seam side down in 9x13-inch baking dish. Top with remaining chicken mixture and 1/2 cup cheese. Bake at 350 degrees for 30 minutes. Yield: 6 servings.

Approx Per Serving: Cal 588; Prot 23 g; Carbo 52 g; Fiber 2 g;
    T Fat 34 g; 51% Calories from Fat; Chol 61 mg; Sod 1420 mg.

Chicken Potpie

1 3-pound chicken, cooked, chopped
2 or 3 stalks celery, chopped
1 12-ounce package frozen mixed
   vegetables, cooked
1 cup chicken broth

1 10-ounce can cream of chicken soup
Salt and pepper to taste
1/2 cup melted margarine
1 cup milk
1 cup baking mix

Layer chicken, celery and mixed vegetables in 2-quart baking dish. Pour chicken broth over layers. Spread soup over top; sprinkle with salt and pepper. Combine margarine, milk and baking mix in bowl; mix just until moistened. Spread over layers. Bake at 400 degrees for 20 minutes or until top is brown. Yield: 8 servings.

Approx Per Serving: Cal 415; Prot 30 g; Carbo 21 g; Fiber 2 g;
    T Fat 23 g; 51% Calories from Fat; Chol 83 mg; Sod 821 mg.

Chicken Salad Pies

Serve at luncheons with fruit cup, banana-nut bread,
zucchini bread and pumpkin bread. —Bobbie Stigall

2 unbaked 9-inch deep-dish pie shells
2 chicken breasts, cooked, chopped
3 hard-boiled eggs, chopped
1 cup chopped celery
1/2 7-ounce can water chestnuts,
   drained, chopped

1/2 cup mayonnaise
1 10-ounce can cream of chicken soup
Juice of 1/2 lemon
Salt and pepper to taste
1 cup shredded Cheddar cheese
51/2 ounces potato chips, crushed

Bake pie shells at 350 degrees for 10 minutes. Combine next 9 ingredients in bowl; mix well. Spoon into pie shells. Top with cheese and potato chips. Bake for 30 minutes. Yield: 16 servings.

Approx Per Serving: Cal 306; Prot 9 g; Carbo 19 g; Fiber 1 g;
    T Fat 22 g; 65% Calories from Fat; Chol 62 mg; Sod 446 mg.

Mexican Chicken Pie

This recipe was the end result of an act of desperation when we
had surprise guests once and no food in the refrigerator. —Elizabeth Horn

1 pound chicken pieces
Greek seasoning, salt and pepper to
  taste
1 16-ounce can mixed vegetables,
  drained
1 10-ounce can (or less) tomatoes
  with green chilies, chopped

1 10-ounce can cream of chicken
  soup
1 5-ounce can (or less) evaporated
  milk
1 recipe 2-crust pie pastry
1 cup shredded Cheddar cheese
1 tablespoon melted butter

Rinse chicken well. Combine with Greek seasoning, salt, pepper and water to cover
in saucepan. Cook until chicken is tender; drain. Cool and chop chicken, discarding
any skin and bones. Combine with mixed vegetables, tomatoes with chilies, soup
and evaporated milk in bowl; mix well. Spoon into pastry-lined 9-inch pie plate;
sprinkle with cheese. Top with remaining pastry; brush with butter. Trim edge and
cut vents. Bake at 350 degrees for 30 minutes or until golden brown. Yield: 6 servings.

Approx Per Serving: Cal 553; Prot 24 g; Carbo 38 g; Fiber 4 g;
    T Fat 34 g; 55% Calories from Fat; Chol 70 mg; Sod 1231 mg.

Chicken Quiche

3 eggs, slightly beaten
1 cup sour cream
1 small onion, chopped
1½ teaspoons Worcestershire sauce
Salt to taste

1 5-ounce can chicken, drained,
  flaked
1 cup shredded mozzarella cheese
1 3-ounce can French-fried onions
1 unbaked 9-inch deep-dish pie shell

Combine eggs, sour cream, chopped onion, Worcestershire sauce, salt, chicken, half
the cheese and ½ cup French-fried onions in bowl; mix well. Spoon into pie shell.
Top with remaining cheese and French-fried onions. Bake at 400 degrees for 1 hour.
Let stand for 10 minutes before serving. Yield: 6 servings.

Approx Per Serving: Cal 448; Prot 17 g; Carbo 23 g; Fiber 1 g;
    T Fat 32 g; 64% Calories from Fat; Chol 138 mg; Sod 498 mg.

The greatest thing a father can do for his
children is to love their mother.

South-of-the-Border Chicken and Rice

1 medium onion, finely chopped
1/2 cup chopped green bell pepper
1 tablespoon margarine
1   10-ounce can cream of chicken
    and mushroom soup
1   10-ounce can tomato soup

1/2 cup mild chunky salsa
1 teaspoon cumin
1 teaspoon chili powder
3 cups chopped cooked chicken
3 cups cooked rice
1 cup shredded Cheddar cheese

Sauté onion and green pepper in margarine in skillet just until tender. Combine soups, salsa, cumin and chili powder in large saucepan. Heat until bubbly, stirring to mix well. Stir in onion mixture, chicken and rice. Spoon into 9x13-inch baking dish; sprinkle with cheese. Bake at 350 degrees for 45 minutes. Yield: 8 servings.

Approx Per Serving: Cal 319; Prot 22 g; Carbo 27 g; Fiber 1 g;
    T Fat 13 g; 38% Calories from Fat; Chol 65 mg; Sod 485 mg.

Chicken and Rice Spectacular

3 whole chicken breasts
1   10-ounce can cream of celery soup
1 cup mayonnaise
1   6-ounce package long grain and
    wild rice mix, cooked
1 cup long grain rice, cooked
1   2-ounce jar chopped pimento
1   8-ounce can water chestnuts,
    drained, chopped
1   4-ounce can mushrooms, drained,
    chopped

1 cup chopped onion
1   16-ounce can French-style green
    beans, drained
Salt and pepper to taste
1   10-ounce can cream of chicken
    soup
1 cup sour cream
30 butter crackers
1/2 cup melted margarine
Poppy seed to taste

Rinse chicken well. Combine with water to cover in saucepan. Cook until tender. Drain, reserving 2 1/2 cups broth. Chop chicken, discarding skin and bones. Spread in 1 greased 9x13-inch baking dish and 1 greased 9x9-inch baking dish. Combine celery soup, mayonnaise and reserved broth in bowl; beat until smooth. Add rice, pimento, water chestnuts, mushrooms, onion, beans, salt and pepper; mix well. Spoon over chicken. Combine chicken soup with sour cream in bowl; mix well. Spread over casseroles. Sprinkle with cracker crumbs; drizzle with margarine. Top with poppy seed. Bake at 350 degrees for 30 to 40 minutes or until heated through. Yield: 20 servings.

Approx Per Serving: Cal 315; Prot 12 g; Carbo 24 g; Fiber 1 g;
    T Fat 20 g; 56% Calories from Fat; Chol 36 mg; Sod 719 mg.

Chicken Spaghetti

1 3-pound chicken
1 bay leaf
1 stalk celery
1/4 onion
3 to 4 quarts water
10 ounces uncooked spaghetti

1 10-ounce can tomato soup
1 cup chopped celery
1 cup chopped onion
1 5-ounce can mushrooms
Salt and pepper to taste
1 pound American cheese, shredded

Rinse chicken well. Combine with bay leaf, 1 stalk celery, 1/4 onion and water in saucepan. Cook until chicken is tender. Strain and reserve broth. Chop chicken into bite-sized pieces, discarding skin and bone. Cook spaghetti in reserved broth, using package directions; drain. Combine soup, 1 cup celery, 1 cup onion, and undrained mushrooms in saucepan; mix well. Simmer for 10 minutes. Season with salt and pepper. Layer spaghetti, chicken, soup mixture and cheese 1/2 at a time in buttered 9x13-inch baking dish. Bake at 350 degrees for 30 minutes. Yield: 8 servings.

Approx Per Serving: Cal 549; Prot 44 g; Carbo 36 g; Fiber 3 g;
    T Fat 25 g; 42% Calories from Fat; Chol 130 mg; Sod 1321 mg.

Easy Chicken Tetrazzini

1 4-pound chicken, rinsed
12 ounces uncooked spaghetti
1 16-ounce can mushrooms, drained
1/4 cup butter
2 10-ounce cans cream of chicken soup

1 cup sour cream
1 tablespoon parsley flakes
Salt and pepper to taste
1/2 cup Parmesan cheese

Cook chicken in water to cover in saucepan until tender; drain, reserving broth. Chop into bite-sized pieces, discarding skin and bones. Cook spaghetti in reserved broth, using package directions; drain. Sauté mushrooms in butter in skillet for 10 minutes. Stir in soup, sour cream, parsley flakes, salt and pepper. Add chicken and spaghetti; mix gently. Spoon into baking dish. Sprinkle with cheese. Bake at 300 degrees until bubbly. Yield: 10 servings.

Approx Per Serving: Cal 474; Prot 36 g; Carbo 33 g; Fiber 3 g;
    T Fat 20 g; 38% Calories from Fat; Chol 111 mg; Sod 939 mg.

A smooth sea never produced a skilled sailor.

Creamed Chicken

2/3 cup margarine
2/3 cup flour
1 teaspoon salt
1 teaspoon pepper
3 cups chicken broth
2 cups milk
2¹/₂ cups chopped cooked chicken

1 tablespoon lemon juice
1 egg
2/3 cup milk
3 tablespoons oil
1 tablespoon sugar
1 cup white self-rising cornmeal

Melt margarine in saucepan over low heat. Stir in flour, salt and pepper gradually. Cook over low heat until bubbly. Stir in chicken broth and 2 cups milk. Bring to a boil. Boil for 1 minute, stirring constantly; reduce heat. Stir in chicken and lemon juice. Spoon into baking dish. Combine egg, 2/3 cup milk, oil, sugar and cornmeal in bowl; mix well. Spoon evenly over chicken. Bake at 400 degrees for 25 minutes. May substitute bacon drippings for oil. Yield: 6 servings.

Approx Per Serving: Cal 609; Prot 28 g; Carbo 40 g; Fiber <1 g;
    T Fat 37 g; 55% Calories from Fat; Chol 103 mg; Sod 1469 mg.

Huntington Chicken

1 3-pound chicken, cut up
1 cup chopped celery
1 cup chopped onion
1 cup chopped green onions
1 12-ounce package noodles

1 10-ounce can cream of mushroom
    soup
1 pound Cheddar cheese, shredded
Salt and pepper to taste

Rinse chicken well. Cook in water to cover until tender; drain, reserving broth. Chop chicken into bite-sized pieces, discarding skin and bones. Combine celery, onion and green onions with reserved broth in saucepan. Cook until tender; drain, reserving broth. Cook noodles in reserved broth in saucepan until tender; drain. Combine soup and cheese in bowl; mix well. Fold in chicken, noodles, vegetables, salt and pepper. Spoon into large baking dish. Bake at 400 degrees until bubbly. May top with additional cheese, add mushrooms or serve in pastry shells if preferred. Yield: 10 servings.

Approx Per Serving: Cal 483; Prot 37 g; Carbo 29 g; Fiber 1 g;
    T Fat 24 g; 45% Calories from Fat; Chol 171 mg; Sod 657 mg.

Act as if it is impossible to fail.

Chicken Vino

1 14-ounce can artichoke hearts,
   drained, chopped
4 large onions, chopped
1/4 cup butter
1/2 cup semidry liebfraumilch

1 tablespoon basil
1/2 teaspoon salt
1/2 teaspoon pepper
1 41/2-pound chicken, cooked,
   chopped

Combine artichokes, onions, butter, wine, basil, salt and pepper in skillet. Simmer until onions are tender-crisp. Add chicken; toss lightly. Spoon into greased 9x13-inch baking pan. Bake at 325 degrees for 1 hour. Yield: 8 servings.

Approx Per Serving: Cal 349; Prot 39 g; Carbo 9 g; Fiber 1 g;
   T Fat 16 g; 43% Calories from Fat; Chol 129 mg; Sod 417 mg.

Poppy Seed Chicken

4 cups chopped cooked chicken
1 cup sour cream
1 10-ounce can cream of chicken
   soup

36 butter crackers, crushed
1/2 cup melted margarine
Poppy seed to taste

Spread chicken in lightly greased rectangular 2-quart baking dish. Combine sour cream and soup in bowl; mix well. Spread over chicken. Sprinkle with cracker crumbs; drizzle with margarine. Top with poppy seed. Bake at 350 degrees for 30 minutes. Yield: 6 servings.

Approx Per Serving: Cal 529; Prot 31 g; Carbo 18 g; Fiber <1 g;
   T Fat 39 g; 64% Calories from Fat; Chol 104 mg; Sod 830 mg.

Cornish Hens with Wild Rice

1 5-ounce package long grain and
   wild rice mix
1 10-ounce can cream of chicken soup
2 soup cans water

1/2 large onion, chopped
1 8-ounce jar sliced mushrooms
Salt and pepper to taste
2 Cornish game hens

Sprinkle rice and seasoning packet in buttered 9x13-inch baking pan. Spread mixture of soup and water over rice. Sprinkle with onion and mushrooms; mix lightly. Season with salt and pepper. Rinse game hens and pat dry. Place in center of baking dish. Bake, covered, for 1 hour. Bake, uncovered, for 30 minutes longer or until hens are golden brown. Yield: 4 servings.

Approx Per Serving: Cal 450; Prot 40 g; Carbo 36 g; Fiber 2 g;
   T Fat 16 g; 33% Calories from Fat; Chol 107 mg; Sod 1651 mg.

Duck and Rice Casserole

2 whole duck breasts, cut into halves
1 cup chopped onion
1 cup chopped celery
2 tablespoons butter

½ cup rice, cooked
1 10-ounce can cream of chicken
  soup
1 cup shredded Cheddar cheese

Rinse duck well. Cook in water to cover in saucepan until tender; drain, reserving broth. Chop duck into bite-sized pieces, discarding skin and bones. Sauté onion and celery in butter in skillet. Add rice, soup, cheese and duck; mix well. Add enough reserved broth to make of desired consistency. Spoon into buttered baking dish. Bake at 350 degrees for 1 hour. Yield: 6 servings.

Approx Per Serving: Cal 263; Prot 14 g; Carbo 19 g; Fiber 1 g;
    T Fat 14 g; 50% Calories from Fat; Chol 55 mg; Sod 685 mg.

Turkey Roll-Ups

8 slices Swiss cheese
8 slices lean ham
8 thin slices turkey breast
2 tablespoons flour
2 tablespoons oil
1 14-ounce can chicken broth

1 10-ounce can cream of chicken
  soup
½ teaspoon garlic powder
Salt and pepper to taste
3 cups hot cooked rice

Layer 1 slice cheese and 1 slice ham on each turkey slice. Roll up and secure with wooden picks. Arrange rolls in 9x13-inch baking dish. Stir flour into oil in skillet. Cook until light brown, stirring constantly. Stir in chicken broth, soup, garlic powder, salt and pepper. Cook until thickened, stirring constantly. Spoon over turkey roll-ups. Bake at 350 degrees for 10 minutes. Serve roll-ups on bed of rice; spoon sauce over top. Yield: 8 servings.

Approx Per Serving: Cal 357; Prot 27 g; Carbo 24 g; Fiber <1 g;
    T Fat 16 g; 41% Calories from Fat; Chol 64 mg; Sod 905 mg.

Life is not a rehearsal.

Seafood

Fish Patties

2 pounds ground fish, clams or crab
  meat
1 16-ounce can peas and carrots,
  drained
1¹/₂ teaspoons salt
1 teaspoon pepper

1 egg
¹/₄ cup oil
1 cup instant potato flakes
¹/₂ cup flour
Oil for frying

Combine fish, peas and carrots, salt, pepper, egg, ¹/₄ cup oil, potato flakes and flour in bowl; mix well. Shape into patties using 1 tablespoon mixture per patty. Cook in oil in skillet until brown, turning once. Yield: 8 servings.

Approx Per Serving: Cal 316; Prot 27 g; Carbo 32 g; Fiber 4 g;
    T Fat 9 g; 26% Calories from Fat; Chol 89 mg; Sod 685 mg.
    Nutritional information does not include oil for frying.

Flounder au Gratin

1 pound flounder filets
Salt to taste
Juice of 1 lemon
¹/₄ cup fine bread crumbs

¹/₄ cup shredded Cheddar cheese
¹/₂ cup minced onion
3 tablespoons margarine

Arrange filets in greased shallow baking dish. Sprinkle with salt and lemon juice. Cover with bread crumbs, cheese and onion. Dot with margarine. Bake at 375 degrees for 20 to 30 minutes or until fish flakes easily. Yield: 4 servings.

Approx Per Serving: Cal 244; Prot 25 g; Carbo 7 g; Fiber 1 g;
    T Fat 13 g; 47% Calories from Fat; Chol 70 mg; Sod 286 mg.

Salmon Mousse

1 envelope unflavored gelatin
1/4 cup cold water
1/2 cup boiling water
1/2 cup mayonnaise
1 tablespoon lemon juice
1 tablespoon finely grated onion

1/8 teaspoon Tabasco sauce
1/4 teaspoon paprika
1 teaspoon salt
2 tablespoons finely chopped dill
2 cups flaked salmon
1 cup whipping cream, whipped

Soften gelatin in cold water. Stir in boiling water until dissolved. Cool. Add next 7 ingredients; mix well. Chill for 20 minutes. Stir in salmon. Fold in whipped cream. Spoon into 8-cup mold. Chill, covered, for 4 hours or longer. Unmold onto serving plate. Serve with Melba toast or crackers. Yield: 12 servings.

Approx Per Serving: Cal 210; Prot 10 g; Carbo 1 g; Fiber <1 g;
T Fat 18 g; 78% Calories from Fat; Chol 62 mg; Sod 261 mg.

Salmon with Spinach Pasta

1 pound spinach pasta
2 tablespoons salt
2 tablespoons butter
2 cups chicken broth
2 tablespoons each flour and butter

1 teaspoon salt
1/8 teaspoon nutmeg
1 tablespoon grated Parmesan cheese
1 1/2 to 2 cups flaked salmon
1/3 cup fresh dill

Cook pasta with 2 tablespoons salt using package directions; drain. Return to pan; toss with 2 tablespoons butter. Combine broth, flour and 2 tablespoons butter in saucepan. Stir in salt and nutmeg. Cook until slightly thickened. Add cheese, salmon and dill; mix well. Spoon pasta onto heated plates. Top with sauce. Yield: 6 servings.

Approx Per Serving: Cal 526; Prot 36 g; Carbo 54 g; Fiber <1 g;
T Fat 17 g; 30% Calories from Fat; Chol 81 mg; Sod 2886 mg.
Nutritional information includes entire amount of salt used in cooking pasta.

Salmon Timbales

1   16-ounce can salmon, drained
1/2 cup evaporated milk
1/2 teaspoon salt
1/8 teaspoon pepper
1/4 cup chopped onion

1/2 teaspoon lemon juice
1 tablespoon chopped parsley
4 egg yolks, beaten
4 egg whites, beaten

Remove bone from salmon; mash. Combine with next 6 ingredients in bowl; mix well. Stir in egg yolks. Fold in egg whites. Spoon into 6 greased ramekins. Place ramekins in pan of hot water. Bake at 400 degrees for 30 minutes or until firm and brown. Invert onto serving plates. Yield: 6 servings.

Approx Per Serving: Cal 189; Prot 21 g; Carbo 3 g; Fiber <1 g;
T Fat 10 g; 49% Calories from Fat; Chol 186 mg; Sod 658 mg.

Filet of Sole Valencia

1 teaspoon salt
1/8 teaspoon pepper
1/8 teaspoon mace
1/8 teaspoon thyme
6 sole filets

1/2 cup dry vermouth
2 tablespoons lemon juice
2 tablespoons melted margarine
1 tablespoon minced chives
2 tablespoons minced onion

Mix salt, pepper, mace and thyme in bowl. Sprinkle over both sides of filets. Place fish in buttered ovenproof skillet. Mix next 3 ingredients in bowl. Pour over fish. Sprinkle with chives and onion. Cover skillet. Bring to a boil over low heat. Uncover skillet; place in oven. Bake at 325 degrees for 15 minutes or until fish flakes easily. Garnish with chopped parsley and lemon wedges. Yield: 6 servings.

Approx Per Serving: Cal 166; Prot 22 g; Carbo 2 g; Fiber <1 g;
T Fat 5 g; 28% Calories from Fat; Chol 62 mg; Sod 498 mg.

Herb-Baked Sole

1/2 cup margarine
2/3 cup cracker crumbs
1/4 cup grated Parmesan cheese
1/2 teaspoon basil

1/2 teaspoon salt
1/2 teaspoon oregano
1/4 teaspoon garlic powder
1 pound sole filets

Melt margarine in 9x13-inch baking dish in 350-degree oven. Mix next 6 ingredients in bowl. Dip filets into margarine. Coat with crumb mixture. Arrange in prepared dish. Bake for 25 minutes or until fish flakes easily. Serve with lemon wedges. Yield: 4 servings.

Approx Per Serving: Cal 391; Prot 25 g; Carbo 11 g; Fiber <1 g;
T Fat 27 g; 63% Calories from Fat; Chol 71 mg; Sod 904 mg.

Baked Trout J & M

My daughter-in-law and I wanted to do something different with trout, and we put this recipe together. My husband and my son say it's the best ever! —Mary Ella DuBois

3 tablespoons butter
Juice of 1/2 lemon
1 tablespoon Worcestershire sauce
1 tablespoon soy sauce

1 teaspoon Tabasco sauce
1 clove of garlic, minced
1/2 lemon, sliced
3 fresh trout

Melt butter in saucepan. Add lemon juice, Worcestershire sauce, soy sauce, Tabasco sauce and garlic; mix well. Baste trout with a small amount of garlic mixture. Arrange in 9x13-inch baking dish. Pour remaining garlic mixture over fish. Place 2 lemon slices on each fish. Bake, covered with foil, at 350 degrees for 40 minutes or until fish flakes easily. May grill on foil in covered grill. Yield: 3 servings.

Approx Per Serving: Cal 373; Prot 45 g; Carbo 4 g; Fiber <1 g;
T Fat 19 g; 46% Calories from Fat; Chol 155 mg; Sod 555 mg.

Steamed Trout

3 dressed whole trout
2 tablespoons oil
2 tablespoons minced fresh chives

2 tablespoons chopped peeled
  gingerroot

Rub cavities of trout with oil. Stuff with chives and gingerroot. Place fish in steamer over boiling water. Steam for 15 minutes or until cooked through. Remove stuffing from fish then filet. Chill before removing stuffing to serve cold. Yield: 6 servings.

Approx Per Serving: Cal 173; Prot 23 g; Carbo 1 g; Fiber <1 g;
    T Fat 8 g; 44% Calories from Fat; Chol 62 mg; Sod 29 mg.

Tuna Casserole

1 16-ounce package macaroni, cooked
1 6-ounce can tuna
1 10-ounce can cream of mushroom
   soup

1 4-ounce can sliced mushrooms
2 tablespoons margarine
1½ cups cornflakes

Combine macaroni, tuna, soup and mushrooms in casserole; mix well. Melt margarine in skillet. Add cornflakes. Cook until brown. Sprinkle over tuna mixture. Bake at 325 degrees for 30 minutes. Serve with green salad. Yield: 4 servings.

Approx Per Serving: Cal 703; Prot 31 g; Carbo 114 g; Fiber 6 g;
    T Fat 13 g; 17% Calories from Fat; Chol 25 mg; Sod 1231 mg.

Crab Meat Quiche

1½ cups crab meat
½ cup shredded Gruyère or Swiss
   cheese
1 unbaked 9-inch pie shell
2 tablespoons chopped parsley
2 tablespoons dry vermouth

2 tablespoons grated onion
Salt and black pepper to taste
5 eggs, lightly beaten
1½ cups milk
⅛ teaspoon cayenne pepper
⅛ teaspoon paprika

Drain crab meat; remove shells. Sprinkle cheese in pie shell. Mix crab meat, parsley, vermouth, onion, salt and black pepper in bowl. Spread in prepared pie shell. Mix eggs, milk and cayenne pepper in bowl. Pour over crab meat mixture. Sprinkle with paprika. Bake at 450 degrees for 10 minutes. Reduce oven temperature to 350 degrees. Bake for 20 minutes or until knife inserted near center comes out clean. Yield: 6 servings.

Approx Per Serving: Cal 334; Prot 19 g; Carbo 17 g; Fiber 1 g;
    T Fat 20 g; 56% Calories from Fat; Chol 230 mg; Sod 393 mg.

Crab-Stuffed Potatoes

This is delicious with steak—our non-traditional Christmas dinner! —Marjie Hart

4 medium potatoes, baked
1/2 cup butter
1/2 cup sour cream
1 teaspoon salt
4 teaspoons grated onion

1 cup shredded Cheddar cheese
1 6-ounce can crab meat, rinsed,
   drained
2 tablespoons paprika

Cut potatoes into halves. Scoop out pulp, reserving shells. Combine with butter, sour cream, salt, onion and cheese in mixer bowl; beat well. Stir in crab meat. Spoon into reserved potato shells. Sprinkle with paprika. Bake at 450 degrees for 15 minutes. Yield: 8 servings.

Approx Per Serving: Cal 326; Prot 11 g; Carbo 27 g; Fiber 3 g;
   T Fat 20 g; 54% Calories from Fat; Chol 71 mg; Sod 538 mg.

Fettucini and Shrimp

1 16-ounce package fettucini
1/4 cup butter
2 cups whipping cream
1 envelope onion-mushroom soup mix

1 cup shredded mozzarella cheese
1/4 cup chopped parsley
1 pound cooked shrimp
1 6-ounce can mushrooms

Cook fettucini using package directions; drain. Melt butter in saucepan. Stir in whipping cream and soup mix. Cook until heated through; do not boil. Mix with remaining ingredients in bowl. Toss fettucini with shrimp mixture. Yield: 6 servings.

Approx Per Serving: Cal 744; Prot 28 g; Carbo 62 g; Fiber 4 g;
   T Fat 43 g; 52% Calories from Fat; Chol 262 mg; Sod 528 mg.

Shrimp Belhaven

3 tablespoons butter
12 large shrimp, peeled, deveined
1/4 cup chopped onion
1/2 cup chopped green bell pepper
1/2 cup chopped tomato
2 large mushrooms, sliced

1/8 teaspoon rosemary
1/8 teaspoon basil
1/8 teaspoon thyme
1/4 cup Italian dressing
2 cups cooked rice

Melt butter in 10-inch sauté pan. Add shrimp, stirring to coat. Add onion. Sauté until tender. Add green pepper, tomato and mushrooms; mix well. Stir in rosemary, basil and thyme. Sauté until shrimp turn pink. Remove from heat. Stir in dressing. Serve over hot cooked rice. Yield: 2 servings.

Approx Per Serving: Cal 671; Prot 34 g; Carbo 58 g; Fiber 3 g;
   T Fat 37 g; 47% Calories from Fat; Chol 307 mg; Sod 593 mg.

Shrimp and Cheese Casserole

6 slices white bread, torn
1 pound cooked shrimp
1/2 pound English cheese, cubed
1/4 cup melted margarine

3 eggs, beaten
1/2 teaspoon dry mustard
Salt to taste
2 cups milk

Layer bread, shrimp and cheese in 3-quart casserole. Pour melted margarine over all. Add mixture of remaining ingredients. Chill for 3 hours to overnight. Bake, covered, at 350 degrees for 1 hour. Yield: 4 servings.

Approx Per Serving: Cal 691; Prot 50 g; Carbo 28 g; Fiber 1 g;
    T Fat 42 g; 55% Calories from Fat; Chol 457 mg; Sod 1058 mg.

Shrimp de Jonghe

1/2 cup margarine, softened
1 cup fine bread crumbs
2 cloves of garlic, minced
1/3 teaspoon tarragon
2/3 teaspoon each parsley, grated onion

Salt and pepper to taste
1/8 teaspoon each nutmeg, mace and
    thyme
1/2 cup sherry
2 pounds shrimp, peeled, deveined

Combine first 12 ingredients in bowl; mix well. Layer alternately with shrimp in 6 buttered casseroles. Bake at 400 degrees for 15 minutes or until shrimp turn pink. Yield: 6 servings.

Approx Per Serving: Cal 346; Prot 28 g; Carbo 13 g; Fiber 1 g;
    T Fat 17 g; 45% Calories from Fat; Chol 237 mg; Sod 574 mg.

Shrimp Marengo

8 slices bacon, cut into small pieces
3 to 4 pounds shrimp, peeled
2 cloves of garlic
1 pound fresh mushrooms
1 onion, chopped
5 tablespoons flour
2 16-ounce cans tomatoes
1 6-ounce can tomato paste
1/2 cup sherry

2 cups chicken or beef stock
3/8 teaspoon Tabasco sauce
1 1/2 teaspoons each oregano and basil
1/2 teaspoon thyme
2 bay leaves
1 teaspoon sugar
Salt and pepper to taste
8 teaspoons spicy mustard
1/4 cup chopped shallots

Fry bacon in skillet. Remove bacon. Sauté shrimp in drippings for 5 minutes. Add next 3 ingredients. Cook for several minutes. Stir in flour, tomatoes, tomato paste, bacon, sherry and stock. Bring to a boil. Stir in seasonings and mustard. Simmer for 15 minutes. Add shallots. Cook for several minutes. Let stand for 10 minutes. Remove garlic and bay leaves. Serve over rice. Yield: 10 servings.

Approx Per Serving: Cal 270; Prot 36 g; Carbo 15 g; Fiber 3 g;
    T Fat 6 g; 19% Calories from Fat; Chol 288 mg; Sod 831 mg.

Vegetables

Pott's Tavern

Pott's Tavern

One of the best-preserved stagecoach stations on the Butterfield Overland mail route between Memphis and Fort Smith is the Potts home in Pottsville, Arkansas. This fine example of antebellum architecture, built in 1850, occupies a large block in the town of Pottsville. The Potts family lived in the home from the time it was finished in 1858 until it was sold to Pope County in 1970. It is under the direction of the Pope County Historical Foundation.

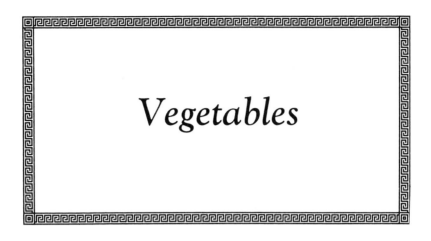

Vegetables

Artichoke Willie

³/₄ cup chopped onion
¹/₂ cup butter
2   14-ounce cans stewed tomatoes
2   16-ounce cans artichoke hearts,
    drained, cut into quarters

3 green onions with tops, chopped
2 teaspoons sugar
¹/₂ teaspoon basil
¹/₂ teaspoon salt
¹/₄ teaspoon pepper

Cook onion in butter in skillet over low heat until tender. Add tomatoes, artichoke hearts, green onions, sugar, basil, salt and pepper; mix well. Simmer for 20 minutes or until mixture thickens. May be cooked and reheated in oven at 350 degrees or may be reheated in microwave. Yield: 6 servings.

Approx Per Serving: Cal 245; Prot 4 g; Carbo 22 g; Fiber <1 g;
    T Fat 17 g; 58% Calories from Fat; Chol 41 mg; Sod 1111 mg.

Blanche's Baked Beans

1   29-ounce can pork and beans
1 medium onion, chopped
3 or 4 slices bacon, chopped
¹/₄ cup packed brown sugar
¹/₄ cup catsup

2 tablespoons molasses
2 teaspoons prepared mustard
1 teaspoon Worcestershire sauce
Pepper to taste

Combine pork and beans, onion, bacon, brown sugar, catsup, molasses, prepared mustard, Worcestershire sauce and pepper in bowl; mix well. Spoon into 9x9-inch baking dish. Bake at 400 degrees for 30 to 35 minutes. Yield: 10 servings.

Approx Per Serving: Cal 154; Prot 6 g; Carbo 29 g; Fiber 5 g;
    T Fat 3 g; 14% Calories from Fat; Chol 8 mg; Sod 409 mg.

Chuck Wagon Beans

³/₄ pound ground beef
¹/₄ cup chopped green bell pepper
¹/₂ cup chopped onion
3 16-ounce cans pork and beans

1 16-ounce can chili beans
1 cup packed brown sugar
2 tablespoons chili powder

Brown ground beef with green pepper and onion in skillet, stirring frequently; drain. Combine with pork and beans, chili beans, brown sugar and chili powder in bowl; mix well. Spoon into slow cooker. Cook on Low for 3 hours. Yield: 10 servings.

Approx Per Serving: Cal 365; Prot 16 g; Carbo 63 g; Fiber 8 g;
     T Fat 7 g; 17% Calories from Fat; Chol 31 mg; Sod 675 mg.

Delicious Green Beans

2 16-ounce cans Blue Lake whole
   green beans, drained
1 16-ounce can chopped artichoke
   hearts, drained

1 8-ounce bottle of Italian salad
   dressing
¹/₂ cup bread crumbs
¹/₄ cup grated Parmesan cheese

Combine green beans and artichoke hearts in bowl. Pour salad dressing over top; toss. Chill for 2 hours; drain. Spoon green bean mixture into 9x12-inch baking dish. Sprinkle with mixture of bread crumbs and Parmesan cheese. Bake at 350 degrees for 30 minutes. Yield: 6 servings.

Approx Per Serving: Cal 281; Prot 6 g; Carbo 21 g; Fiber 2 g;
     T Fat 25 g; 68% Calories from Fat; Chol 3 mg; Sod 878 mg.
     Nutritional information includes entire amount of salad dressing.

Green Beans Greek-Style

*For a main dish meal add cooked lamb or beef near
end of cooking time. —Barbara Skouras*

1 onion, chopped
2 tablespoons olive oil
3 to 5 cloves of garlic, crushed
1 16-ounce package frozen cut green
   beans

2 28-ounce cans crushed undrained
   tomatoes
¹/₂ teaspoon oregano
Salt to taste

Sauté onion in olive oil in skillet until golden brown. Remove from heat. Stir in garlic. Combine with green beans, tomatoes, oregano and salt in large saucepan. Cook, covered, over low heat for several hours. Remove cover. Cook until liquid is reduced to desired thickness. Yield: 10 servings.

Approx Per Serving: Cal 75; Prot 2 g; Carbo 11 g; Fiber 3 g;
     T Fat 3 g; 35% Calories from Fat; Chol 0 mg; Sod 264 mg.

Marinated Beans

1 16-ounce can each green beans,
   lima beans and Mexicorn
1 large sweet onion, sliced
1 cup (scant) vinegar

1 cup (scant) oil
1 cup sugar
Garlic to taste
1/2 teaspoon salt

Mix vegetables in bowl. Add mixture of vinegar and remaining ingredients; mix well. Marinate in refrigerator overnight. Drain. Spoon into serving dish. Yield: 10 servings.

Approx Per Serving: Cal 356; Prot 4 g; Carbo 39 g; Fiber 4 g;
   T Fat 22 g; 54% Calories from Fat; Chol 0 mg; Sod 573 mg.

Mexican Baked Beans

1 pound ground beef
2 slices bacon, chopped
1 medium onion, chopped
2 16-ounce cans pork and beans
1/2 cup light corn syrup

1/2 cup catsup
1/2 teaspoon Worcestershire sauce
2 teaspoons brown sugar
2 teaspoons chili powder

Brown ground beef with bacon and onion in skillet, stirring until ground beef is crumbly; drain. Stir in remaining ingredients. Spoon into medium-sized baking dish. Bake at 375 degrees for 35 minutes. Yield: 7 servings.

Approx Per Serving: Cal 385; Prot 20 g; Carbo 53 g; Fiber 8 g;
   T Fat 12 g; 27% Calories from Fat; Chol 53 mg; Sod 719 mg.

Oriental Green Beans

1 10-ounce package frozen green
   beans, slightly thawed
1 cup diagonally sliced celery
1 green bell pepper, chopped
1/4 cup oil
8 ounces fresh mushrooms, sliced
1 tablespoon butter
2 tablespoons cornstarch

1 cup chicken stock
1 2-ounce jar chopped pimento,
   drained
1 6-ounce can sliced water
   chestnuts, drained
1 1/2 teaspoons salt
1/4 teaspoon garlic salt
1 1-ounce package slivered almonds

Simmer first 4 ingredients in saucepan for 10 minutes; drain. Sauté mushrooms in butter in skillet. Combine cornstarch and 1/4 cup chicken stock in saucepan. Bring remaining stock to a boil in small saucepan. Stir into cornstarch mixture. Cook over medium heat until thickened, stirring constantly. Combine green bean mixture, mushrooms, sauce, pimento, water chestnuts, salt, garlic salt and half the almonds in bowl; mix well. Spoon into 2-quart baking dish. Bake at 350 degrees for 15 to 25 minutes or until heated through. Top with remaining almonds. Yield: 6 servings.

Approx Per Serving: Cal 106; Prot 4 g; Carbo 14 g; Fiber 4 g;
   T Fat 5 g; 39% Calories from Fat; Chol 5 mg; Sod 792 mg.

Sesame Green Beans

1 pound fresh green beans
2 teaspoons instant bouillon
1¹/₂ cups water
1 tablespoon margarine

2 teaspoons soy sauce
2 teaspoons sesame seed
1 tablespoon water

Cut tip ends from beans; wash and drain. Simmer green beans with bouillon powder and 1¹/₂ cups water in saucepan for 10 minutes; drain. Add remaining ingredients. Cook over low heat for 1 minute, stirring constantly. Turn off heat. Place cover on saucepan. Let stand for several minutes. Serve warm. Yield: 4 servings.

Approx Per Serving: Cal 76; Prot 3 g; Carbo 9 g; Fiber 3 g;
T Fat 4 g; 42% Calories from Fat; Chol 1 mg; Sod 788 mg.

Spiked Beans

1 16-ounce package dry pinto beans
Salt to taste
1 onion, chopped
1 large green bell pepper, chopped
2 to 3 tablespoons shortening
1¹/₂ pounds ground chuck

1 8-ounce can tomato sauce
3 tablespoons catsup
¹/₂ cup mild picante sauce
Tabasco sauce to taste
Pepper to taste

Soak beans in water overnight. Cook beans with salt using package directions. Sauté onion and green pepper in shortening in skillet. Add ground beef. Cook until ground beef is brown and crumbly, stirring constantly. Stir into beans. Add tomato sauce, catsup, picante sauce, Tabasco sauce, salt and pepper; mix well. Simmer for 15 to 20 minutes. Spoon into serving dish. Yield: 20 servings.

Approx Per Serving: Cal 174; Prot 12 g; Carbo 16 g; Fiber 5 g;
T Fat 7 g; 36% Calories from Fat; Chol 22 mg; Sod 152 mg.

Texas Beans

2 pounds dry pinto beans
2 pounds ground beef
1 large onion, chopped
2 6-ounce cans taco sauce
1 4-ounce can chopped green chilies

2 16-ounce cans tomatoes
1 tablespoon garlic powder
1 teaspoon cumin
Salt to taste
1 tablespoon pepper

Cook pinto beans using package directions. Brown ground beef with onion in skillet, stirring until ground beef is crumbly; drain. Combine beans, ground beef mixture, taco sauce, green chilies, tomatoes, garlic powder, cumin, salt and pepper in large saucepan. Simmer for 45 minutes. Serve with corn bread. Yield: 12 servings.

Approx Per Serving: Cal 446; Prot 34 g; Carbo 54 g; Fiber 17 g;
T Fat 13 g; 25% Calories from Fat; Chol 49 mg; Sod 478 mg.

Broccoli Casserole

1 20-ounce package frozen chopped
 broccoli
2 eggs
2 tablespoons flour

8 ounces shredded Cheddar cheese
3/4 cup cottage cheese
2 tablespoons margarine

Cook broccoli using package directions. Beat eggs with flour, Cheddar cheese and cottage cheese in large bowl. Stir in broccoli. Melt margarine in 1 1/2-quart baking dish; spread to coat. Spoon in broccoli mixture. Bake at 350 degrees for 25 to 30 minutes. Yield: 8 servings.

Approx Per Serving: Cal 206; Prot 14 g; Carbo 6 g; Fiber 2 g;
 T Fat 15 g; 62% Calories from Fat; Chol 86 mg; Sod 323 mg.

Broccoli-Onion Bake

1 bunch fresh broccoli
4 large onions, cut into quarters
Salt to taste
3 ounces cream cheese, softened

1/2 cup butter
2 tablespoons flour
1 cup milk
Pepper to taste

Separate broccoli into flowerets. Peel stems; cut into strips. Cook stems and onions in salted water in saucepan for 10 minutes. Add flowerets. Cook for 10 minutes longer; drain. Place broccoli in shallow baking dish. Combine cream cheese and butter in saucepan. Cook over low heat until smooth, stirring constantly. Stir in flour, milk, salt and pepper. Cook until thickened, stirring constantly. Pour over broccoli; toss lightly. Bake at 325 degrees for 30 to 45 minutes or until top is lightly browned. Yield: 6 servings.

Approx Per Serving: Cal 287; Prot 8 g; Carbo 18 g; Fiber 6 g;
 T Fat 22 g; 66% Calories from Fat; Chol 62 mg; Sod 222 mg.

Sautéed Broccoli

2 pounds fresh broccoli
2 cloves of garlic, minced
1/2 cup olive oil

Juice of 1/2 lemon
Salt to taste

Cut broccoli stalks into halves lengthwise. Cook broccoli in 1 inch of boiling water in saucepan for 8 minutes or until tender; drain. Sauté garlic in olive oil in large skillet for 2 minutes. Add broccoli. Sauté for 6 to 8 minutes or until tender. Sprinkle with lemon juice and salt. Place in serving dish. Serve immediately. Yield: 6 servings.

Approx Per Serving: Cal 203; Prot 5 g; Carbo 9 g; Fiber 5 g;
 T Fat 19 g; 76% Calories from Fat; Chol 0 mg; Sod 41 mg.

Cajun Cabbage

1 medium onion, chopped
1 green bell pepper, chopped
1 large head cabbage, chopped
1 10-ounce can Ro-Tel tomatoes

¹/₂ cup vinegar
¹/₄ cup sugar
Salt and pepper to taste

Combine onion, green pepper, cabbage and tomatoes in large deep skillet; mix well. Mix vinegar, sugar, salt and pepper in small bowl. Pour over vegetables. Simmer, covered, for 45 to 50 minutes. Yield: 8 servings.

Approx Per Serving: Cal 48; Prot 1 g; Carbo 12 g; Fiber 1 g;
    T Fat <1 g; 3% Calories from Fat; Chol 0 mg; Sod 149 mg.

German Red Cabbage

2 tablespoons bacon drippings
4 cups chopped red cabbage
2 cups chopped tart apples
1 small onion, chopped
¹/₄ cup packed brown sugar

¹/₄ cup red wine vinegar
¹/₂ teaspoon caraway seed
1 teaspoon salt
Pepper to taste
¹/₂ cup water

Heat bacon drippings in large saucepan. Add cabbage, apples, onion, brown sugar, vinegar, caraway seed, salt, pepper and water; mix well. Simmer, covered, for 25 to 30 minutes, stirring occasionally. Yield: 6 servings.

Approx Per Serving: Cal 127; Prot 1 g; Carbo 22 g; Fiber 2 g;
    T Fat 5 g; 33% Calories from Fat; Chol 28 mg; Sod 416 mg.

Mexican Cabbage

2 pounds ground beef
1 medium onion, chopped
1 green bell pepper
1 large head cabbage, chopped

1 10-ounce can Ro-Tel tomatoes
1 10-ounce can Cheddar cheese soup
Salt and pepper to taste

Brown ground beef with onion and green pepper in skillet, stirring until ground beef is crumbly; drain. Stir in cabbage, tomatoes, soup, salt and pepper. Simmer for 50 to 60 minutes. Yield: 8 servings.

Approx Per Serving: Cal 295; Prot 24 g; Carbo 8 g; Fiber 1 g;
    T Fat 19 g; 58% Calories from Fat; Chol 82 mg; Sod 478 mg.

Carrot Soufflé

1 pound carrots, cooked, mashed
1 cup packed brown sugar
3 tablespoons flour
1 teaspoon baking powder

½ cup melted margarine
3 eggs, beaten
¼ teaspoon cinnamon

Place mashed carrots in mixer bowl. Add brown sugar, flour, baking powder, margarine, eggs and cinnamon in order listed, mixing well after each addition. Spoon into baking dish. Bake at 400 degrees for 15 minutes. Reduce oven temperature to 350 degrees. Bake for 45 minutes. May substitute equivalent amount of egg substitute for eggs. Yield: 6 servings.

Approx Per Serving: Cal 394; Prot 4 g; Carbo 55 g; Fiber 3 g;
  T Fat 18 g; 41% Calories from Fat; Chol 106 mg; Sod 314 mg.

Corn Pudding

1 16-ounce can whole kernel corn
1 17-ounce can cream-style corn
1 cup sour cream

1 6-ounce package corn bread mix
1 egg
½ cup melted butter

Combine corns, sour cream, corn bread mix, egg and butter in bowl; mix well. Spoon into greased baking dish. Bake at 400 degrees for 25 to 30 minutes or until golden. May sprinkle cheese on top before serving. Yield: 8 servings.

Approx Per Serving: Cal 294; Prot 5 g; Carbo 28 g; Fiber 2 g;
  T Fat 20 g; 57% Calories from Fat; Chol 70 mg; Sod 542 mg.

Bessie's Corn Casserole

My mother-in-law gave this recipe to me. Each time she would serve it, I would eat more of it than any other dish. —Diann Yarber

1 16-ounce can whole kernel corn,
  drained
1 16-ounce can tomatoes, crushed
1 cup cracker crumbs

1 tablespoon bacon drippings, melted
Salt to taste
¼ cup saltine cracker crumbs
1 tablespoon butter

Combine corn and tomatoes in buttered 8x8-inch baking dish. Add 1 cup cracker crumbs, bacon drippings and salt; mix well. Top with ¼ cup cracker crumbs; dot with butter. Bake at 350 degrees for 1 hour. Yield: 6 servings.

Approx Per Serving: Cal 187; Prot 3 g; Carbo 30 g; Fiber 2 g;
  T Fat 7 g; 31% Calories from Fat; Chol 25 mg; Sod 564 mg.

Corn Casserole

1 17-ounce can cream-style corn
1 16-ounce can whole kernel corn
1 cup French onion dip
1/2 cup melted butter
1/2 cup water

2 eggs, stiffly beaten
1 6-ounce package corn muffin mix
1/2 teaspoon sage
Salt to taste

Combine corns, onion dip, butter, water, eggs, corn muffin mix, sage and salt in bowl; mix well. Spoon into large baking dish. Bake at 350 degrees for 20 to 30 minutes. May top hot casserole with shredded cheese if desired. Yield: 12 servings.

Approx Per Serving: Cal 201; Prot 4 g; Carbo 20 g; Fiber 1 g;
    T Fat 12 g; 53% Calories from Fat; Chol 56 mg; Sod 517 mg.

Corn and Oyster Casserole

1 16-ounce can cream-style corn
1 10-ounce can oyster stew
1 3/4 cups cracker crumbs
1 cup milk
1/4 cup chopped celery

2 tablespoons melted butter
2 eggs, beaten
1 tablespoon pimento
1/4 teaspoon salt
1 8-ounce can oysters

Combine corn, oyster stew, cracker crumbs, milk, celery, butter, eggs, pimento and salt in bowl; mix well. Spoon into greased 2-quart baking dish. Bake at 350 degrees for 45 minutes. Place oysters in center of casserole. Bake for 15 minutes longer. Yield: 8 servings.

Approx Per Serving: Cal 219; Prot 7 g; Carbo 28 g; Fiber 2 g;
    T Fat 9 g; 37% Calories from Fat; Chol 91 mg; Sod 838 mg.

Green Chilies and Corn

8 ounces cream cheese
2 tablespoons margarine
3 10-ounce cans Shoe Peg corn, drained
1 4-ounce can chopped mild green chilies

Garlic powder to taste
Cayenne pepper to taste
Salt and pepper to taste

Melt cream cheese and margarine in saucepan over low heat, stirring constantly. Combine with corn, green chilies, garlic powder, cayenne pepper, salt and pepper in bowl; mix well. Spoon into 1 3/4-quart baking dish. Bake at 350 degrees for 30 to 45 minutes or until bubbly. Yield: 8 servings.

Approx Per Serving: Cal 193; Prot 4 g; Carbo 17 g; Fiber 1 g;
    T Fat 13 g; 58% Calories from Fat; Chol 31 mg; Sod 487 mg.

Margland II Bed and Breakfast Corn Fritters

Grated kernels of 7 ears of corn
1/2 cup flour
1/4 teaspoon salt
2 teaspoons baking powder

2 eggs
Oil for deep frying
1/2 cup confectioners' sugar, sifted

Combine grated corn, flour, salt, baking powder and eggs in bowl; mix well. Shape into balls. Deep-fry in oil heated to 375 degrees until golden brown; drain. Roll in confectioners' sugar. Serve immediately. Yield: 12 servings.

Approx Per Serving: Cal 101; Prot 3 g; Carbo 21 g; Fiber 2 g;
    T Fat 2 g; 13% Calories from Fat; Chol 36 mg; Sod 118 mg.
    Nutritional information does not include oil for frying.

Santa Fe Corn

8 ounces cream cheese
1/2 cup milk
2 tablespoons margarine
2 cups drained whole kernel corn
1   4-ounce can chopped green chilies

1/2 teaspoon cumin
1/2 teaspoon cayenne pepper
1 teaspoon salt
1/2 teaspoon black pepper

Combine cream cheese, milk and margarine in saucepan. Cook over low heat until smooth, stirring constantly. Stir in corn, chilies, cumin, cayenne pepper, salt and black pepper. Spoon into baking dish. Bake at 325 degrees for 30 minutes. Yield: 8 servings.

Approx Per Serving: Cal 170; Prot 4 g; Carbo 10 g; Fiber 1 g;
    T Fat 14 g; 69% Calories from Fat; Chol 33 mg; Sod 586 mg.

Scalloped Corn

This recipe came from one of the best cooks in western Iowa. —Alice D. Reinsch

1   17-ounce can cream-style corn,
    drained
1   16-ounce can whole kernel corn,
    drained
1/2 cup milk
2 tablespoons flour
3 tablespoons sugar

1 tablespoon melted butter
2 eggs, beaten
Salt and pepper to taste
2 cups soda cracker crumbs
2   10-ounce cans cream of mushroom
    soup

Mix corns, milk, flour, sugar, butter, eggs, salt and pepper in bowl. Spoon into 9x13-inch baking dish. Sprinkle with half the cracker crumbs. Spread soup over cracker crumb layer. Top with remaining cracker crumbs. Bake at 350 degrees for 45 minutes. May adjust amount of cracker crumbs to suit personal taste. Yield: 12 servings.

Approx Per Serving: Cal 211; Prot 4 g; Carbo 33 g; Fiber 2 g;
    T Fat 8 g; 32% Calories from Fat; Chol 45 mg; Sod 789 mg.

Shoe Peg Corn

2   16-ounce cans Shoe Peg corn,
    drained
1/2 cup half and half

1/2 cup melted butter
2 teaspoons flour
1/2 teaspoon white pepper

Combine corn, half and half, butter, flour and pepper in bowl; mix well. Spoon into baking dish. Bake at 350 degrees for 30 minutes. Yield: 4 servings.

Approx Per Serving: Cal 430; Prot 7 g; Carbo 44 g; Fiber 3 g;
    T Fat 29 g; 56% Calories from Fat; Chol 73 mg; Sod 731 mg.

Skillet Corn

1 green bell pepper, chopped
1 onion, chopped
3 tablespoons margarine

2   16-ounce cans whole kernel corn
2 tablespoons cornstarch
Salt and pepper to taste

Cook green pepper and onion in margarine in skillet until tender. Drain corn, reserving liquid. Stir cornstarch into reserved liquid. Add corn to green pepper mixture. Simmer for 5 minutes. Stir in cornstarch mixture. Bring to a boil, stirring constantly; reduce heat. Cook until thickened, stirring constantly. Stir in salt and pepper. Spoon into serving dish. Yield: 6 servings.

Approx Per Serving: Cal 166; Prot 3 g; Carbo 27 g; Fiber 2 g;
    T Fat 7 g; 32% Calories from Fat; Chol 0 mg; Sod 450 mg.

Southern-Style Scalloped Corn

1   17-ounce can cream-style corn
1 cup cracker crumbs
1/2 cup chopped celery
1/4 cup chopped onion
2/3 cup shredded American cheese

2 eggs, beaten
2 tablespoons melted butter
1 cup milk
1/4 teaspoon paprika
1 teaspoon salt

Combine corn, cracker crumbs, celery, onion, cheese, eggs, butter, milk, paprika and salt in bowl; mix well. Spoon into greased 1 1/2-quart round baking dish. Bake at 350 degrees for 50 to 55 minutes. Yield: 6 servings.

Approx Per Serving: Cal 253; Prot 8 g; Carbo 28 g; Fiber 3 g;
    T Fat 13 g; 44% Calories from Fat; Chol 104 mg; Sod 1027 mg.

What goes around comes around.

Eggplant Casserole

1 medium onion, chopped
2 tablespoons butter
1 eggplant, chopped, cooked, drained
1 20-ounce can tomatoes, drained

4 eggs, lightly beaten
1¹/₂ cups fresh bread crumbs
2 tablespoons melted butter
1¹/₂ cups shredded Cheddar cheese

Sauté onion in butter in skillet. Mash eggplant slightly. Add to onion with tomatoes. Simmer for 5 to 8 minutes, stirring frequently. Add eggs, stirring until mixture resembles scrambled eggs. Remove from heat. Toss crumbs with melted butter. Stir cheese and half the crumb mixture into eggs. Spoon into greased 1¹/₂-quart baking dish. Top with remaining crumb mixture. Bake at 350 degrees for 20 to 25 minutes. May substitute 1 chopped tomato for canned tomatoes. May prepare and chill overnight before baking to enhance flavor. Yield: 6 servings.

Approx Per Serving: Cal 329; Prot 15 g; Carbo 16 g; Fiber 5 g;
T Fat 22 g; 60% Calories from Fat; Chol 185 mg; Sod 542 mg.

Ratatouille

2¹/₂ medium onions, chopped
¹/₂ cup oil
5 seeded peeled tomatoes, chopped

2 small zucchini, thinly sliced
1 peeled eggplant, chopped
Salt and pepper to taste

Sauté onions in oil in heavy saucepan. Add tomatoes. Simmer for 15 minutes. Stir in zucchini, eggplant, salt and pepper. Simmer for 3 to 4 hours. Yield: 8 servings.

Approx Per Serving: Cal 167; Prot 2 g; Carbo 10 g; Fiber 4 g;
T Fat 15 g; 72% Calories from Fat; Chol 0 mg; Sod 9 mg.

Okra and Rice

3 or 4 slices bacon
2 cups chopped okra
1 cup uncooked long grain rice
2 cups chicken broth

1¹/₂ teaspoons dried basil
¹/₈ teaspoon hot pepper sauce
Salt and pepper to taste

Fry bacon in skillet until crisp. Drain bacon on paper towels. Cook okra in pan drippings in skillet for 1 minute. Stir in rice, broth, basil, hot pepper sauce, salt and pepper. Bring to a boil. Reduce heat to low. Cook, covered, for 25 minutes or until rice is tender. Remove cover. Cook until most of liquid is absorbed. May substitute 1 heaping tablespoon fresh basil for dried basil. Yield: 6 servings.

Approx Per Serving: Cal 172; Prot 6 g; Carbo 30 g; Fiber 2 g;
T Fat 3 g; 15% Calories from Fat; Chol 4 mg; Sod 329 mg.

Onion Pie

1 cup finely crushed cracker crumbs
1/4 cup melted butter
2 cups finely sliced onions
2 tablespoons butter
2 eggs

3/4 cup milk
3/4 teaspoon salt
Pepper to taste
1/4 cup Cheddar cheese
Paprika to taste

Mix cracker crumbs and butter in bowl. Press into 8-inch pie plate. Sauté onions in butter in skillet just until transparent. Spoon into prepared pie plate. Combine eggs, milk, salt and pepper in bowl; mix well. Pour over onions. Sprinkle with cheese and paprika. Bake at 350 degrees for 30 minutes or until set. Garnish with parsley. Serve immediately. Yield: 8 servings.

Approx Per Serving: Cal 178; Prot 4 g; Carbo 11 g; Fiber 1 g;
     T Fat 13 g; 66% Calories from Fat; Chol 87 mg; Sod 457 mg.

Margland II Vidalia Onion Casserole

4 large Vidalia onions, sliced into
     rings
1/2 cup unsalted butter, at room
     temperature
50 butter crackers, crushed

8 ounces Cheddar cheese, shredded
Salt to taste
Paprika to taste
3 eggs, beaten
1 cup milk

Sauté onions in 1/4 cup butter in skillet. Combine remaining 1/4 cup butter with cracker crumbs. Reserve 1/4 of the crumb mixture for topping. Spread remaining crumb mixture in bottom of greased 9x13-inch baking dish. Layer onions and cheese over top. Sprinkle with salt and paprika. Mix eggs and milk in bowl. Pour over layers. Sprinkle with reserved crumb mixture. Bake at 350 degrees for 35 to 40 minutes. Yield: 10 servings.

Approx Per Serving: Cal 308; Prot 10 g; Carbo 17 g; Fiber 1 g;
     T Fat 24 g; 67% Calories from Fat; Chol 116 mg; Sod 324 mg.

Cheddar Cheese Potatoes

1 10-ounce can Cheddar cheese soup
1/2 cup milk
1/2 teaspoon pepper
4 cups sliced peeled potatoes

1 large onion, sliced
2 tablespoons margarine
Paprika to taste

Combine soup, milk and pepper in bowl; mix well. Alternate layers of potatoes, onion and soup mixture in 3-quart baking dish until all ingredients are used. Dot with margarine; sprinkle with paprika. Bake, covered, at 375 degrees for 1 hour. Bake, uncovered, for 15 minutes longer or until brown. Yield: 6 servings.

Approx Per Serving: Cal 190; Prot 5 g; Carbo 25 g; Fiber 2 g;
     T Fat 8 g; 39% Calories from Fat; Chol 14 mg; Sod 411 mg.

Easy Oven-Baked Potatoes and Onions

6 medium potatoes
6 medium onions
1/2 cup melted butter
1 clove of garlic, crushed

1/4 teaspoon celery seed
3/4 teaspoon salt
3/4 teaspoon pepper
1/4 teaspoon paprika

Slice unpeeled potatoes and onions 1/4 inch thick. Arrange potatoes in slightly overlapping single layer in 9x13-inch baking dish. Arrange onions over potatoes. Combine butter, garlic, celery seed, salt and pepper in bowl; mix well. Spoon over layers. Bake, covered, at 400 degrees for 40 minutes. Sprinkle with paprika. Bake, uncovered, for 20 minutes longer. Yield: 8 servings.

Approx Per Serving: Cal 308; Prot 5 g; Carbo 47 g; Fiber 5 g;
    T Fat 12 g; 34% Calories from Fat; Chol 31 mg; Sod 311 mg.

Hashed Brown Potato Casserole

1/4 cup butter
1 medium onion, chopped
1   10-ounce can cream of chicken
    soup
1 cup sour cream
1 cup shredded American cheese

1 teaspoon salt
1/4 teaspoon pepper
1   32-ounce package frozen hashed
    brown potatoes, thawed
2 cups crushed cornflakes
1/4 cup melted butter

Combine 1/4 cup butter, onion, soup, sour cream, cheese, salt and pepper in bowl; mix well. Fold in potatoes. Spoon into 9x13-inch baking dish sprayed with nonstick cooking spray. Top with cornflakes; drizzle with 1/4 cup butter. Bake at 350 degrees for 45 minutes. Yield: 10 servings.

Approx Per Serving: Cal 455; Prot 8 g; Carbo 42 g; Fiber 2 g;
    T Fat 30 g; 57% Calories from Fat; Chol 48 mg; Sod 887 mg.

Hoover Hash

*This recipe is from the Depression Era and was given
to me by my mother-in-law. —Mrs. Bill Koen*

3 medium potatoes, chopped
3 large carrots, sliced
1 medium onion, chopped

Salt and pepper to taste
3 tablespoons shortening

Combine potatoes, carrots and onion with salt and pepper in melted shortening in skillet. Cook, covered, over medium heat until tender. Yield: 4 servings.

Approx Per Serving: Cal 287; Prot 5 g; Carbo 47 g; Fiber 6 g;
    T Fat 10 g; 30% Calories from Fat; Chol 0 mg; Sod 32 mg.

Onion-Roasted Potatoes

1 envelope onion soup mix
2 pounds potatoes, coarsely chopped

¹/₃ cup olive oil
Italian seasoning to taste

Combine soup mix, potatoes and olive oil in large plastic bag; mix to coat potatoes well. Pour into 9x13-inch baking dish. Bake at 450 degrees for 30 minutes, stirring occasionally. Sprinkle with Italian seasoning. Bake for 10 minutes longer or until potatoes are tender and golden brown. May substitute parsley for Italian seasoning. Yield: 8 servings.

Approx Per Serving: Cal 187; Prot 2 g; Carbo 25 g; Fiber 2 g;
T Fat 9 g; 43% Calories from Fat; Chol 0 mg; Sod 84 mg.

Marinated Potatoes and Mushrooms

¹/₃ cup oil
¹/₄ cup lemon juice
1¹/₂ teaspoons Dijon mustard
1 teaspoon sugar
1 teaspoon instant chicken bouillon

4 cups chopped, cooked small new
  potatoes
1 cup sliced fresh mushrooms
¹/₃ cup sliced celery
¹/₄ cup sliced green onions

Combine oil, lemon juice, mustard, sugar and bouillon in shallow dish. Add potatoes, mushrooms, celery and green onions; mix well. Marinate, covered, in refrigerator, for several hours to overnight, stirring occasionally. Yield: 6 servings.

Approx Per Serving: Cal 197; Prot 2 g; Carbo 21 g; Fiber 2 g;
T Fat 12 g; 55% Calories from Fat; Chol <1 mg; Sod 237 mg.

Microwave Fried Potatoes

6 large potatoes
Salt and pepper to taste

3 tablespoons butter

Peel and slice potatoes as for frying; place in glass dish. Sprinkle with salt and pepper; dot with butter. Microwave, covered, on High for 12 to 15 minutes; mix well. Microwave, covered, for 12 to 15 minutes longer or until tender. May add onion and squash if desired. Yield: 6 servings.

Approx Per Serving: Cal 207; Prot 3 g; Carbo 36 g; Fiber 2 g;
T Fat 6 g; 25% Calories from Fat; Chol 16 mg; Sod 59 mg.

Mississippi Potatoes

8 cups cooked chopped potatoes
1 cup mayonnaise
1 teaspoon salt
¹/₂ teaspoon pepper
1 pound American cheese, shredded

¹/₂ onion, chopped
6 slices bacon, crisp-fried, crumbled
¹/₄ cup green olives
¹/₄ cup black olives

Spread potatoes in 9x13-inch greased baking dish. Top with mayonnaise, salt, pepper, cheese, onion, bacon and olives. Bake at 325 degrees for 1 hour. Yield: 8 servings.

Approx Per Serving: Cal 570; Prot 17 g; Carbo 30 g; Fiber 3 g;
    T Fat 44 g; 68% Calories from Fat; Chol 74 mg; Sod 1484 mg.

Parslied Potatoes

5 medium red potatoes
Salt to taste

¹/₂ cup melted margarine
1 tablespoon chopped parsley

Peel potatoes and cut into halves lengthwise. Cook in salted water in saucepan for 5 minutes; drain well. Place cut side down in 9x13-inch baking dish. Drizzle with mixture of margarine and parsley. Bake at 400 degrees for 45 minutes, turning once to brown evenly. Yield: 5 servings.

Approx Per Serving: Cal 308; Prot 3 g; Carbo 34 g; Fiber 2 g;
    T Fat 18 g; 53% Calories from Fat; Chol 0 mg; Sod 222 mg.

Potato Casserole

1 32-ounce package frozen hashed
    brown potatoes, thawed
1 10-ounce can cream of celery soup
1 10-ounce can potato soup
1 cup sour cream

1 onion, chopped
1 cup shredded sharp Cheddar cheese
Salt and pepper to taste
2 tablespoons margarine
Paprika to taste

Spread potatoes in 3-quart baking dish. Microwave on High for 5 minutes. Combine soups, sour cream, onion, cheese, salt and pepper in bowl; mix well. Spoon over potatoes. Dot with margarine; sprinkle with paprika. Bake at 350 degrees for 1¹/₂ hours. Spoon from bottom of dish to serve. Yield: 12 servings.

Approx Per Serving: Cal 296; Prot 6 g; Carbo 27 g; Fiber 2 g;
    T Fat 19 g; 57% Calories from Fat; Chol 22 mg; Sod 484 mg.

Potatoes Grande

5 or 6 medium potatoes
Seasoning salt to taste
1/2 cup butter
1   16-ounce bottle of ranch salad
    dressing

1/2 cup shredded mozzarella cheese
1/2 cup shredded Cheddar cheese

Cut potatoes into quarters; place in baking dish. Sprinkle with seasoning salt; dot with butter. Bake, covered, at 350 degrees for 40 minutes or until tender. Drizzle with salad dressing; sprinkle with cheeses. Bake for 5 minutes longer or until cheese melts. Yield: 6 servings.

Approx Per Serving: Cal 621; Prot 10 g; Carbo 37 g; Fiber 2 g;
    T Fat 49 g; 70% Calories from Fat; Chol 88 mg; Sod 562 mg.

Ranch Potatoes

6 medium red potatoes, peeled, sliced
1 medium onion, sliced
1 envelope ranch salad dressing mix

1 cup mayonnaise
1 cup buttermilk
1 cup shredded Cheddar cheese

Cook potatoes and onion in water in saucepan until tender; drain. Combine salad dressing mix, mayonnaise and buttermilk in bowl; mix well. Layer potato mixture, salad dressing mixture and cheese 1/2 at a time in lightly greased 9x13-inch baking dish. Bake at 350 degrees for 30 minutes or until heated through. Yield: 8 servings.

Approx Per Serving: Cal 368; Prot 7 g; Carbo 26 g; Fiber 2 g;
    T Fat 27 g; 65% Calories from Fat; Chol 32 mg; Sod 525 mg.

Scalloped Potatoes

1   10-ounce can cream of mushroom
    soup
1/2 cup milk
Salt and pepper to taste
4 cups thinly sliced potatoes

1/2 cup thinly sliced onion
1 cup shredded Cheddar cheese
1 tablespoon butter
Paprika to taste

Combine soup, milk, salt and pepper in bowl; mix well. Alternate layers of potatoes, onion, soup mixture and cheese in 1 1/2-quart baking dish. Dot with butter; sprinkle with paprika. Bake, covered, at 375 degrees for 1 hour. Bake, uncovered, for 15 minutes longer or until tender. Yield: 6 servings.

Approx Per Serving: Cal 254; Prot 8 g; Carbo 28 g; Fiber 2 g;
    T Fat 13 g; 44% Calories from Fat; Chol 28 mg; Sod 530 mg.

Shake 'n Bake Potatoes

12 small potatoes
1 package Shake 'n Bake coating mix

1 cup melted butter

Peel potatoes and cut into quarters. Rinse, but do not dry. Combine with coating mix in bag; shake to coat well. Place in large baking dish; drizzle with butter. Bake at 350 degrees for 30 to 45 minutes or until tender. Yield: 6 servings.

Approx Per Serving: Cal 538; Prot 6 g; Carbo 59 g; Fiber 4 g;
    T Fat 32 g; 52% Calories from Fat; Chol 83 mg; Sod 563 mg.

Spinach and Artichoke Casserole

3 10-ounce packages frozen
    chopped spinach
1/2 cup finely chopped onion
1/2 cup butter
2 cups sour cream

1 12-ounce can artichoke hearts, cut
    into quarters
1/2 cup grated Parmesan cheese
Salt and pepper to taste

Cook spinach using package directions; drain well. Sauté onion in butter in skillet until tender. Combine with spinach, sour cream, artichoke hearts, cheese, salt and pepper in bowl; mix well. Spoon into 2 1/2-quart baking dish. Bake at 350 degrees for 20 to 30 minutes or until heated through. Yield: 8 servings.

Approx Per Serving: Cal 296; Prot 8 g; Carbo 11 g; Fiber 3 g;
    T Fat 26 g; 75% Calories from Fat; Chol 61 mg; Sod 420 mg.

Spinach Casserole

2 10-ounce packages frozen
    chopped spinach
2 eggs, beaten
1 cup chopped onion
1 cup shredded Cheddar cheese

1 10-ounce can cream of mushroom
    soup
1/2 cup mayonnaise
3/4 cup bread crumbs

Cook spinach using package directions; drain well. Combine with eggs, onion, cheese, soup and mayonnaise in bowl; mix well. Spoon into 2-quart baking dish. Top with bread crumbs. Bake at 350 degrees for 45 minutes. May substitute cracker crumbs for bread crumbs. Yield: 6 servings.

Approx Per Serving: Cal 366; Prot 13 g; Carbo 21 g; Fiber 4 g;
    T Fat 27 g; 65% Calories from Fat; Chol 103 mg; Sod 800 mg.

Spinach Pies

1 16-ounce package frozen chopped spinach, thawed
1½ cups small-curd cottage cheese
6 eggs, beaten
6 tablespoons margarine, chopped

10 ounces Cheddar cheese, coarsely shredded
½ teaspoon salt
½ teaspoon pepper

Drain spinach well. Combine with cottage cheese, eggs, margarine, cheese, salt and pepper in bowl; mix well. Spoon into 2 greased pie plates. Bake at 350 degrees for 45 to 60 minutes or until set. Yield: 12 servings.

Approx Per Serving: Cal 223; Prot 13 g; Carbo 3 g; Fiber 1 g;
    T Fat 18 g; 70% Calories from Fat; Chol 135 mg; Sod 475 mg.

Spinach Strata

54 butter crackers
2 10-ounce packages frozen chopped spinach, thawed, drained
2½ cups shredded Muenster cheese
2½ cups milk

5 eggs
2 tablespoons Dijon mustard
½ teaspoon hot pepper sauce
2 cloves of garlic, minced

Arrange 18 crackers in 3 rows in shallow 2-quart baking dish. Combine spinach and 2 cups cheese in bowl. Layer spinach mixture and remaining crackers ½ at a time in prepared dish. Sprinkle with remaining cheese. Combine milk, eggs, mustard, pepper sauce and garlic in bowl; mix well. Spoon evenly over layers. Chill for 1 hour. Bake at 350 degrees for 1 hour or until puffed and golden brown. Cut into squares to serve. Yield: 12 servings.

Approx Per Serving: Cal 236; Prot 12 g; Carbo 15 g; Fiber 1 g;
    T Fat 16 g; 56% Calories from Fat; Chol 118 mg; Sod 441 mg.

Spinach and Zucchini Strata

3 medium zucchini, shredded
Salt to taste
2 tablespoons butter

2 tablespoons oil
1 bunch spinach

Sprinkle shredded zucchini with salt in sieve. Let stand to drain. Heat 1 tablespoon butter and 1 tablespoon oil in wok or skillet. Add spinach. Cook for 5 minutes or until wilted; remove to bowl. Press zucchini to remove moisture. Add to wok with remaining butter and oil. Sauté for 2 to 3 minutes or until tender-crisp. Add spinach. Cook just until heated through. Sprinkle with salt. Yield: 6 servings.

Approx Per Serving: Cal 92; Prot 2 g; Carbo 3 g; Fiber 2 g;
    T Fat 9 g; 79% Calories from Fat; Chol 10 mg; Sod 63 mg.

Baked Squash Casserole

10 yellow squash, sliced
1 cup chopped onion
¼ cup margarine
2 eggs, beaten
1 cup shredded Cheddar cheese

1 10-ounce can cream of mushroom
   soup
¼ teaspoon salt
¼ teaspoon pepper
¼ cup bread crumbs

Sauté squash and onion in margarine in skillet. Combine eggs, cheese, soup, salt and pepper in bowl; mix well. Add to skillet. Cook until heated through, stirring constantly. Spoon into buttered 2-quart baking dish. Top with bread crumbs. Bake at 350 degrees for 20 minutes. Yield: 8 servings.

Approx Per Serving: Cal 215; Prot 8 g; Carbo 14 g; Fiber 3 g;
    T Fat 15 g; 61% Calories from Fat; Chol 69 mg; Sod 552 mg.

Squash Casserole

1¼ pounds small yellow squash,
   chopped
1 medium onion, chopped
⅓ cup milk
3 tablespoons melted margarine
1 tablespoon sugar

1 egg
⅔ cup shredded Cheddar cheese
16 to 20 saltine crackers, crushed
1 teaspoon salt
½ teaspoon pepper

Cook squash and onion in water in saucepan until tender; drain. Mash until smooth. Add milk, margarine, sugar, egg, cheese, cracker crumbs, salt and pepper; mix well. Spoon into buttered 9x9-inch baking dish. Bake at 350 degrees for 25 minutes. Yield: 8 servings.

Approx Per Serving: Cal 150; Prot 5 g; Carbo 12 g; Fiber 2 g;
    T Fat 9 g; 55% Calories from Fat; Chol 40 mg; Sod 487 mg.

Summer Squash Casserole

2 pounds summer squash
½ cup chopped onion
1 10-ounce can cream of chicken soup
1 cup sour cream

1 cup shredded carrot
1 8-ounce package herb-seasoned
   stuffing mix
½ cup melted margarine

Peel squash and slice ¼ inch thick. Cook with onion in a small amount of water in saucepan just until tender; drain. Combine soup and sour cream in bowl; mix well. Stir in carrot. Fold in squash mixture. Toss stuffing mix with melted margarine in bowl. Layer half the stuffing, squash mixture and remaining stuffing in 8x12-inch baking dish. Bake at 350 degrees for 30 minutes. May substitute cream of mushroom soup for chicken soup. Yield: 4 servings.

Approx Per Serving: Cal 670; Prot 14 g; Carbo 64 g; Fiber 6 g;
    T Fat 42 g; 56% Calories from Fat; Chol 32 mg; Sod 1844 mg.

Squash Stir-Fry

3 cups chopped squash
1/2 cup chopped onion

6 slices bacon, chopped
1/4 cup grated Parmesan cheese

Cook squash in water in saucepan until tender; drain and mash slightly. Fry onion with bacon in skillet until bacon is crisp; drain off excess bacon drippings. Add squash to skillet. Stir-fry until flavors blend. Stir in Parmesan cheese. Yield: 4 servings.

Approx Per Serving: Cal 104; Prot 6 g; Carbo 6 g; Fiber 2 g;
    T Fat 6 g; 54% Calories from Fat; Chol 12 mg; Sod 248 mg.

Sweet Potato and Apricot Casserole

6 medium sweet potatoes, peeled
1 1/4 cups packed brown sugar
1 1/2 tablespoons cornstarch
1 cup apricot juice
1 teaspoon grated orange rind

1/8 teaspoon cinnamon
1 cup drained apricots
2 tablespoons butter
1/2 cup chopped pecans

Cook sweet potatoes in water in saucepan just until tender; drain and cut into thick slices. Place in baking dish. Combine brown sugar, cornstarch, apricot juice, orange rind and cinnamon in saucepan; mix well. Cook until thickened, stirring constantly. Stir in apricots, butter and pecans. Spoon over sweet potatoes. Bake at 375 degrees for 25 minutes or until bubbly. Yield: 8 servings.

Approx Per Serving: Cal 399; Prot 2 g; Carbo 82 g; Fiber 4 g;
    T Fat 8 g; 18% Calories from Fat; Chol 8 mg; Sod 61 mg.

Sweet Potato Casserole

2 cups mashed cooked sweet potatoes
1/3 cup sugar
1/2 cup milk
2 eggs, beaten
1/4 cup margarine
1/2 teaspoon cinnamon

1/2 teaspoon nutmeg
Salt to taste
2/3 cup packed brown sugar
1/4 cup flour
1/4 cup margarine
1 cup chopped pecans

Combine sweet potatoes, sugar, milk, eggs, 1/4 cup margarine, cinnamon, nutmeg and salt in bowl; mix well. Spoon into 9x13-inch baking dish. Mix brown sugar, flour, 1/4 cup margarine and pecans in bowl until crumbly. Sprinkle over casserole. Bake at 350 degrees for 45 minutes. Yield: 10 servings.

Approx Per Serving: Cal 359; Prot 4 g; Carbo 46 g; Fiber 1 g;
    T Fat 19 g; 46% Calories from Fat; Chol 44 mg; Sod 143 mg.

Sweet Potatoes in Orange Sauce

1 cup sugar
3 cups water
1/4 teaspoon allspice
4 large sweet potatoes, peeled, sliced
1 cup sugar

1 tablespoon cornstarch
1 cup orange juice
1/2 teaspoon cinnamon
1 teaspoon salt

Bring 1 cup sugar, water and allspice to a boil in saucepan. Add sweet potatoes. Cook until tender; drain. Place sweet potatoes in baking dish. Combine 1 cup sugar, cornstarch, orange juice, cinnamon and salt in saucepan. Cook for 3 minutes or until thickened, stirring constantly. Spoon over sweet potatoes. Bake at 350 degrees for 30 minutes. Yield: 6 servings.

Approx Per Serving: Cal 387; Prot 2 g; Carbo 97 g; Fiber 3 g;
T Fat <1 g; 1% Calories from Fat; Chol 0 mg; Sod 371 mg.

Fried Green Tomatoes

2 medium green tomatoes
Seasoning salt and pepper to taste
1 cup milk

1/2 cup self-rising flour
1/2 cup self-rising yellow cornmeal
Oil for deep frying

Slice tomatoes 1/3 inch thick; place in bowl. Sprinkle with seasoning salt and pepper; pour milk over top. Let stand for 5 minutes. Mix flour and cornmeal in bowl. Remove tomatoes from milk; coat with flour mixture. Deep-fry in hot oil until golden brown. Yield: 4 servings.

Approx Per Serving: Cal 181; Prot 6 g; Carbo 33 g; Fiber <1 g;
T Fat 3 g; 13% Calories from Fat; Chol 8 mg; Sod 487 mg.
Nutritional information does not include oil for deep frying.

Scalloped Tomatoes

3 1/2 cups canned tomatoes
2 tablespoons chopped onion
1 tablespoon chopped green bell
  pepper
3 tablespoons chopped celery
3 tablespoons flour

4 teaspoons sugar
1 teaspoon salt
1/4 teaspoon pepper
1/2 cup soft bread crumbs
2 tablespoons margarine

Combine tomatoes, onion, green pepper and celery in bowl. Mix flour, sugar, salt and pepper in small bowl. Add to vegetables; mix well. Spoon into greased 1 1/2-quart baking dish. Sprinkle with bread crumbs; dot with margarine. Bake at 350 degrees for 45 minutes. Yield: 6 servings.

Approx Per Serving: Cal 98; Prot 2 g; Carbo 14 g; Fiber 2 g;
T Fat 4 g; 38% Calories from Fat; Chol 0 mg; Sod 650 mg.

Baked Cherry Tomatoes

1 1-pint carton cherry tomatoes
2 tablespoons butter

1 tablespoon (or more) sugar
Basil to taste

Place tomatoes in baking dish. Dot with butter; sprinkle with sugar and basil. Bake at 350 degrees for 8 to 10 minutes or until done to taste. Yield: 4 servings.

Approx Per Serving: Cal 87; Prot 1 g; Carbo 8 g; Fiber 2 g;
    T Fat 6 g; 58% Calories from Fat; Chol 16 mg; Sod 59 mg.

Marinated Vegetables

1 16-ounce can French-style green
    beans
1 16-ounce can whole kernel corn
1 16-ounce can tiny green peas
1 7-ounce can sliced water chestnuts
1 2-ounce jar sliced pimento

1 small red onion, chopped
1/2 green bell pepper, chopped
3 stalks celery, chopped
3/4 cup vinegar
1/2 cup oil
3/4 cup sugar

Drain green beans, corn, peas, water chestnuts and pimento. Combine with onion, green pepper and celery in large bowl. Bring vinegar, oil and sugar to a boil in saucepan. Add to vegetables; mix well. Marinate, covered, in refrigerator overnight, stirring several times. May store in refrigerator for up to 2 weeks. Yield: 15 servings.

Approx Per Serving: Cal 168; Prot 3 g; Carbo 24 g; Fiber 3 g;
    T Fat 8 g; 39% Calories from Fat; Chol 0 mg; Sod 221 mg.

Steamed Vegetables with Cheese

4 cups cauliflowerets
4 cups broccoli flowerets
6 large carrots, sliced lengthwise into
    thick sticks
1/4 cup butter
1/4 cup flour

2 1/2 cups milk
2 teaspoons Dijon mustard
1/4 teaspoon white pepper
1/8 teaspoon red pepper
10 ounces Cheddar cheese, shredded

Cook cauliflower in 8 cups boiling water in saucepan for 3 minutes or until tender-crisp; drain. Remove to bowl of ice water with slotted spoon; drain. Repeat process with broccoli and carrots. Combine vegetables in 8x11-inch baking dish. Melt butter in saucepan over medium heat. Stir in flour. Add milk, mustard and peppers. Cook for 5 minutes, stirring constantly. Stir in cheese until melted. Spoon over vegetables. Bake at 350 degrees for 20 to 25 minutes or until heated through. Yield: 8 servings.

Approx Per Serving: Cal 304; Prot 15 g; Carbo 17 g; Fiber 5 g;
    T Fat 21 g; 59% Calories from Fat; Chol 63 mg; Sod 371 mg.

Poached Vegetable Bundles in Sauce

6 cups water
1 teaspoon onion flakes
2 tablespoons instant chicken
 bouillon
6 large romaine lettuce leaves
2 medium carrots, cut into 4-inch sticks
1 10-ounce package frozen
 asparagus spears, thawed

18 whole green beans
4 egg yolks, beaten
1/3 cup water
3 tablespoons lemon juice
3 tablespoons nondairy creamer
1/2 cup margarine
1/4 teaspoon salt
Pepper to taste

Combine 6 cups water, onion flakes and bouillon in skillet. Bring to a boil, stirring to dissolve bouillon. Remove heavy stem portion of lettuce leaves. Poach in bouillon mixture just until wilted; remove from broth and drain. Fold each leaf into thirds. Arrange carrot sticks, asparagus spears and green beans into 6 bundles on lettuce leaves. Wrap lettuce around bundles; secure with wooden picks. Place in simmering broth in skillet. Simmer for 12 minutes or just until vegetables are tender-crisp. Combine egg yolks, 1/3 cup water, lemon juice, creamer, margarine, salt and pepper in double boiler. Cook until thickened to desired consistency, beating constantly. Lift vegetable bundles onto serving platter with slotted spoon. Spoon Hollandaise sauce over bundles. Serve immediately. May substitute spinach for romaine lettuce. Yield: 6 servings.

Approx Per Serving: Cal 233; Prot 7 g; Carbo 10 g; Fiber 2 g;
 T Fat 21 g; 74% Calories from Fat; Chol 143 mg; Sod 1442 mg.

Stir-Fry Vegetables

1 green bell pepper, sliced
2 medium carrots, sliced
2 stalks celery, sliced

1 small zucchini, sliced
2 tablespoons olive oil

Stir-fry green pepper, carrots, celery and zucchini in olive oil in skillet until tender-crisp. Serve immediately. May substitute yellow squash for zucchini. Yield: 4 servings.

Approx Per Serving: Cal 86; Prot 1 g; Carbo 6 g; Fiber 2 g;
 T Fat 7 g; 69% Calories from Fat; Chol 0 mg; Sod 31 mg.

It's better to be over the hill than under it.

Side Dishes

Hot Fruit Compote

1 21-ounce can cherry pie filling
1 21-ounce can peach pie filling
1 16-ounce can spiced apple rings,
   drained
1 16-ounce can apricots, drained

1 16-ounce can green grapes, drained
1 16-ounce can plums, drained
1/2 cup margarine
Nutmeg and cinnamon to taste

Combine pie fillings and fruits in bowl; mix well. Pour into 9x13-inch baking dish.
Dot with margarine; sprinkle with nutmeg and cinnamon. Bake at 350 degrees for
30 minutes or until bubbly. Serve warm. Yield: 12 servings.

Approx Per Serving: Cal 266; Prot 1 g; Carbo 52 g; Fiber 3 g;
    T Fat 8 g; 25% Calories from Fat; Chol 0 mg; Sod 130 mg.

Baked Pineapple Salad

1/2 cup each flour and sugar
2 tablespoons melted butter
1 egg, beaten

1 29-ounce can sliced pineapple
4 ounces American cheese, shredded
2 cups miniature marshmallows

Combine flour, sugar, butter and egg in double boiler; mix well. Drain pineapple,
pouring juice into flour mixture. Cook over hot water until thickened, stirring
constantly. Add pineapple, cheese and 1 cup marshmallows. Cook until cheese and
marshmallows are partially melted. Pour into 2-quart casserole. Sprinkle with
remaining marshmallows. Bake at 350 degrees for 10 minutes or until marshmallows
are brown. May substitute crushed pineapple for sliced. Yield: 6 servings.

Approx Per Serving: Cal 387; Prot 7 g; Carbo 68 g; Fiber 2 g;
    T Fat 11 g; 25% Calories from Fat; Chol 64 mg; Sod 333 mg.

Rice Dressing

8 ounces ground beef
4 ounces chicken gizzards, cooked,
 ground
4 ounces chicken livers, cooked,
 ground
1 medium green bell pepper, chopped

1 medium onion, chopped
1 teaspoon salt
1 teaspoon black pepper
1/8 teaspoon red pepper
3/4 cup water
3 cups cooked rice

Brown ground beef in 9-inch skillet, stirring until crumbly. Add chicken, green pepper, onion, salt and peppers; mix well. Stir in water. Bring to a boil. Cook over low heat for 15 minutes. Combine with rice in bowl; mix well. Yield: 8 servings.

Approx Per Serving: Cal 177; Prot 12 g; Carbo 21 g; Fiber 1 g;
 T Fat 5 g; 26% Calories from Fat; Chol 89 mg; Sod 294 mg.

Yellow Squash Dressing

3 cups (about) chopped squash
1 small onion, chopped
1 egg
1 10-ounce can cream of mushroom
 soup

2 cups corn bread crumbs
Salt, pepper and sage to taste
1/3 cup melted margarine
1/2 cup shredded Cheddar cheese

Cook enough squash to yield 2 cups with onion in skillet until tender; drain. Beat egg in bowl. Add soup, bread crumbs, seasonings and melted margarine. Stir into squash mixture. Spoon into greased shallow baking dish. Bake at 350 degrees for 30 minutes. Sprinkle with cheese. Bake for 5 minutes longer. Yield: 6 servings.

Approx Per Serving: Cal 303; Prot 7 g; Carbo 23 g; Fiber 1 g;
 T Fat 21 g; 61% Calories from Fat; Chol 59 mg; Sod 733 mg.

Surprise Hominy Casserole

3 15-ounce cans hominy, drained
1 4-ounce can green chilies

1 cup sour cream
1 8-ounce jar jalapeño Cheez Whiz

Combine hominy, chilies, sour cream and Cheez Whiz in bowl; mix well. Spoon into casserole. Bake at 350 degrees for 30 to 45 minutes or until heated through. Yield: 8 servings.

Approx Per Serving: Cal 242; Prot 8 g; Carbo 23 g; Fiber 0 g;
 T Fat 13 g; 49% Calories from Fat; Chol 31 mg; Sod 914 mg.

In every marriage there are disagreements.

Healthy Vegetable Lasagna

9 lasagna noodles
2 10-ounce packages frozen spinach,
   thawed, drained
1/2 cup chopped onion
1 tablespoon oil
1 pound mushrooms, sliced

1 16-ounce jar spaghetti sauce
8 ounces part-skim ricotta cheese
4 ounces part-skim mozzarella
   cheese, shredded
3 tablespoons grated Parmesan
   cheese

Cook lasagna noodles using package directions and omitting salt; drain. Sauté spinach in large skillet sprayed with nonstick cooking spray. Remove spinach to bowl; set aside. Cook onion in hot oil in same skillet for 3 minutes, stirring occasionally. Add mushrooms. Cook for 5 to 7 minutes or until tender, stirring frequently. Spoon 1/4 cup spaghetti sauce into 9x13-inch baking dish. Layer noodles, ricotta cheese, mushroom mixture, mozzarella cheese, spinach, remaining spaghetti sauce and Parmesan cheese 1/3 at a time in prepared dish. Bake, covered, at 350 degrees for 30 to 40 minutes or until heated through. Yield: 8 servings.

Approx Per Serving: Cal 318; Prot 17 g; Carbo 42 g; Fiber 4 g;
   T Fat 11 g; 29% Calories from Fat; Chol 18 mg; Sod 483 mg.

Twice-as-Good Macaroni and Cheese

8 ounces elbow macaroni
16 ounces cream-style cottage cheese
3/4 cup sour cream
1 egg, slightly beaten
1 teaspoon salt

1/8 teaspoon pepper
2 teaspoons grated onion
8 ounces shredded sharp Cheddar
   cheese

Cook macaroni using package directions; drain. Combine with cottage cheese, sour cream, egg, salt, pepper, onion and cheese in large bowl; mix well. Stir in macaroni. Spoon into 9x9-inch baking dish. Bake at 350 degrees for 45 minutes or until bubbly. Yield: 6 servings.

Approx Per Serving: Cal 444; Prot 26 g; Carbo 32 g; Fiber 2 g;
   T Fat 23 g; 47% Calories from Fat; Chol 99 mg; Sod 923 mg.

You can only make <u>one</u> <u>first</u> impression.

Veggie Pizza

2 8-count cans crescent rolls
²/₃ cup mayonnaise
¹/₂ cup sour cream
8 ounces cream cheese, softened
1 envelope ranch salad dressing mix
¹/₃ cup finely chopped broccoli

¹/₃ cup finely chopped cauliflower
¹/₃ cup finely chopped green onions
¹/₃ cup finely chopped green bell pepper
¹/₃ cup finely shredded carrots
1 cup shredded Cheddar cheese
¹/₃ cup sliced black olives

Unroll roll dough. Press dough into 11x15-inch baking pan; seal perforations. Bake at 350 degrees for 10 to 15 minutes or until lightly browned. Mix mayonnaise, sour cream, cream cheese and salad dressing mix in bowl. Spread over baked layer. Press vegetables into pizza. Sprinkle with cheese and olives. Chill overnight. Yield: 8 servings.

Approx Per Serving: Cal 544; Prot 10 g; Carbo 28 g; Fiber 1 g;
    T Fat 45 g; 73% Calories from Fat; Chol 63 mg; Sod 1043 mg.

Arkansas County Rice

2 cups cooked rice
1 16-ounce can chopped tomatoes
¹/₂ 10-ounce can chopped Ro-Tel
    tomatoes
1 4-ounce can sliced mushrooms

1 green bell pepper, chopped
1¹/₂ cups shredded Cheddar cheese
Salt, pepper, garlic salt, onion salt
    and celery salt to taste

Combine rice, tomatoes, mushrooms, green pepper, half the cheese and seasonings in 9x13-inch baking dish; mix well. Top with remaining cheese. Bake, covered, at 350 degrees for 30 minutes or until cheese is melted and mixture is heated through and bubbly. Yield: 10 servings.

Approx Per Serving: Cal 128; Prot 6 g; Carbo 14 g; Fiber 1 g;
    T Fat 6 g; 40% Calories from Fat; Chol 18 mg; Sod 284 mg.

Baked Rice

This recipe is from my good friend's grandmother. It is always well received. —Nancy Stiles

1 cup canned chopped pimentos
1 cup canned mushroom pieces
1 cup uncooked rice

¹/₂ cup margarine
2 medium onions, chopped
2 10-ounce cans onion soup

Drain pimentos and mushrooms, reserving liquid. Cook rice in margarine in skillet until lightly browned. Add onions. Cook until mixture is golden. Add soup, mushrooms, pimenos and reserved liquids; mix well. Spoon into 9x13-inch baking dish. Cook, covered, with foil, at 400 degrees for 45 minutes. Turn off oven. Let stand for 15 minutes. Yield: 12 servings.

Approx Per Serving: Cal 163; Prot 3 g; Carbo 19 g; Fiber 2 g;
    T Fat 9 g; 46% Calories from Fat; Chol 0 mg; Sod 552 mg.

Chinese-Style Fried Rice

1 cup water
1¹/₃ cups uncooked minute rice
1 egg, beaten
3 tablespoons butter

¹/₃ cup chopped onion
2 to 3 tablespoons soy sauce
¹/₃ cup water

Bring 1 cup water to a boil in saucepan. Stir in rice; remove from heat. Let stand, covered, for 5 minutes. Cook egg in butter in 10-inch skillet until set. Add onion and rice. Cook over medium heat for 5 minutes or until lightly browned, stirring frequently. Stir in mixture of soy sauce and ¹/₃ cup water. Yield: 4 servings.

Approx Per Serving: Cal 226; Prot 5 g; Carbo 28 g; Fiber 1 g;
    T Fat 10 g; 41% Calories from Fat; Chol 77 mg; Sod 862 mg.

Gourmet Rice

1 cup chopped onion
1 cup chopped celery
1 cup chopped celery leaves
1   4-ounce can sliced mushrooms,
    drained
1 cup uncooked rice

3 tablespoons butter
2 cups boiling chicken broth
1 teaspoon salt
³/₄ teaspoon poultry seasoning
¹/₂ cup toasted sliced almonds

Sauté onion, celery, celery leaves, mushrooms and rice in butter in skillet until vegetables are tender and rice is golden. Spoon into buttered 2-quart casserole. Stir in chicken broth, salt and poultry seasoning. Bake, covered, at 350 degrees for 30 minutes. Fluff with fork. Sprinkle with almonds. Yield: 8 servings.

Approx Per Serving: Cal 179; Prot 5 g; Carbo 23 g; Fiber 2 g;
    T Fat 8 g; 39% Calories from Fat; Chol 12 mg; Sod 573 mg.
    Nutritional information does not include celery leaves.

Consommé Rice

¹/₄ cup margarine
1 cup uncooked rice
2 tablespoons onion flakes

2   10-ounce cans condensed beef
    consommé

Melt margarine in skillet. Add rice. Cook over medium-high heat until rice is browned, stirring constantly. Stir in onion flakes and consommé. Spoon into 2-quart baking dish. Bake, covered, at 350 degrees for 1 hour. Yield: 8 servings.

Approx Per Serving: Cal 154; Prot 5 g; Carbo 20 g; Fiber <1 g;
    T Fat 6 g; 34% Calories from Fat; Chol 0 mg; Sod 437 mg.

Mandarin Rice

1 cup chopped onion
1 cup chopped celery
3 tablespoons butter
2 cups cooked rice

3 tablespoons soy sauce
1   4-ounce can chopped mushrooms
1   8-ounce can sliced water chestnuts

Sauté onion and celery in butter in 12-inch skillet. Add rice, soy sauce, mushrooms and water chestnuts; mix well. Simmer, covered, for 15 minutes. Yield: 4 servings.

Approx Per Serving: Cal 248; Prot 5 g; Carbo 38 g; Fiber 3 g;
    T Fat 9 g; 32% Calories from Fat; Chol 23 mg; Sod 997 mg.

Brown Rice Pilaf

3 tablespoons butter
1 cup chopped pecans
1 tablespoon butter
1/4 cup chopped onion
1 cup uncooked brown rice

2 1/2 cups chicken broth
1 teaspoon salt
1/4 teaspoon thyme
1/8 teaspoon pepper
2 tablespoons chopped parsley

Melt 3 tablespoons butter in skillet. Add pecans. Sauté for 10 minutes or until lightly browned. Remove to bowl; cover and set aside. Melt 1 tablespoon butter in skillet. Add onion. Sauté until tender. Stir in rice. Combine rice mixture, chicken broth, salt, thyme and pepper in heavy 2 1/2-quart saucepan; mix well. Simmer, covered, for 45 minutes or until rice is tender and all liquid is absorbed. Remove from heat. Stir in pecans and parsley. Serve warm. Yield: 6 servings.

Approx Per Serving: Cal 330; Prot 6 g; Carbo 28 g; Fiber 3 g;
    T Fat 22 g; 59% Calories from Fat; Chol 21 mg; Sod 747 mg.

Rice Pilaf

1/4 cup butter
1 onion, chopped
1 1/2 cups uncooked rice

3 cups chicken stock
Salt and pepper to taste
Chopped parsley to taste

Melt butter in heavy 2-quart saucepan. Add onion. Sauté over high heat until transparent. Stir in rice. Add chicken stock, salt and pepper; mix well. Bring to a boil over high heat; reduce heat. Simmer, covered, for 23 minutes; do not remove cover while cooking. Fluff rice with 2 forks. Sprinkle with parsley. May use brown rice and simmer for 30 to 40 minutes. Yield: 8 servings.

Approx Per Serving: Cal 198; Prot 4 g; Carbo 30 g; Fiber 1 g;
    T Fat 6 g; 30% Calories from Fat; Chol 16 mg; Sod 341 mg.

Rice with Tomatoes and Cheese

1 green bell pepper, chopped
$^1/_4$ cup margarine
8 ounces Cheddar cheese, cut into
    small pieces

3 cups cooked rice
1 pint tomatoes, chopped

Sauté green pepper in margarine in skillet until tender. Combine with cheese, rice and tomatoes in 1$^1/_2$-quart casserole; mix well. Bake at 350 degrees for 25 to 30 minutes or until bubbly. Yield: 8 servings.

Approx Per Serving: Cal 260; Prot 9 g; Carbo 22 g; Fiber 1 g;
    T Fat 15 g; 53% Calories from Fat; Chol 30 mg; Sod 247 mg.

Wild Rice

1 cup uncooked wild rice
2 quarts water
1 medium onion, chopped

1 medium green bell pepper, chopped
1 cup sliced mushrooms
$^1/_2$ cup melted margarine

Cook rice in water in saucepan until tender; drain. Sauté onion, green pepper and mushrooms in melted margarine in electric skillet. Add rice; mix well. Cook until heated through. Yield: 10 servings.

Approx Per Serving: Cal 147; Prot 3 g; Carbo 14 g; Fiber <1 g;
    T Fat 9 g; 55% Calories from Fat; Chol 0 mg; Sod 109 mg.

*A good hostess is like a duck—calm, serene and
unruffled on the surface—but paddling
like crazy underneath.*

Breads

The William H. H. Clayton House

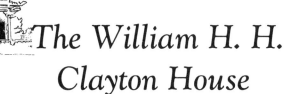

The William H. H. Clayton House

The William H. H. Clayton House in Fort Smith was originally built by the Bruce Sutton family, who fled before its occupation by federal troops.

William Clayton came to Fort Smith in 1874 after having been appointed by President Grant to serve as District Attorney of the U.S. for the Western District of Arkansas. He bought the house in 1882 and made many changes and additions during its restoration. There is little remaining of the original house.

In 1969, the house was bought by the Fort Smith Heritage Foundation, and its second restoration was begun. It was entered in the National Register of Historic Places in 1970, and is now open to the public.

Biscuits

3 cups flour
1½ tablespoons baking powder
¾ teaspoon baking soda
¼ teaspoon salt

½ cup butter
1½ cups buttermilk
2 tablespoons melted butter

Mix flour, baking powder, baking soda and salt in bowl. Cut in ½ cup butter with pastry blender until crumbly. Add buttermilk, mixing just until moistened. Knead lightly 4 or 5 times on floured surface. Roll ½ inch thick; cut with 2-inch heart-shaped cutter. Place on lightly greased baking sheet. Bake at 450 degrees for 10 to 12 minutes or until golden brown. Brush with melted butter. Yield: 24 servings.

Approx Per Serving: Cal 106; Prot 2 g; Carbo 13 g; Fiber <1 g;
    T Fat 5 g; 43% Calories from Fat; Chol 14 mg; Sod 166 mg.

Margland II Bed and Breakfast Biscuits

These are great for brunches, luncheons or
graduation parties. —Wanda Bateman, Innkeeper

2 cups flour
1 tablespoon baking powder
¼ teaspoon baking soda
½ cup sugar
1 teaspoon salt
⅓ cup shortening
1 egg, beaten

¾ cup buttermilk
½ cup blueberries, drained
3 tablespoons melted unsalted butter
3 tablespoons sugar
¼ teaspoon cinnamon
⅛ teaspoon nutmeg

Mix flour, baking powder, baking soda, ½ cup sugar and salt in medium bowl. Cut in shortening until crumbly. Stir in mixture of egg and buttermilk. Fold in blueberries. Knead 4 or 5 times on lightly floured surface. Roll or pat ½ inch thick; cut with 2½-inch cutter. Place on lightly greased baking sheet. Bake at 400 degrees for 15 minutes or until golden brown. Combine butter, 3 tablespoons sugar, cinnamon and nutmeg in bowl; mix well. Brush on warm biscuits. Yield: 15 servings.

Approx Per Serving: Cal 170; Prot 3 g; Carbo 23 g; Fiber 1 g;
    T Fat 7 g; 39% Calories from Fat; Chol 21 mg; Sod 240 mg.

Dress up to go shopping—you'll get better service.

Breakfast Loaf

1/2 cup sugar	1/2 cup margarine
1/2 teaspoon cinnamon	3/4 cup sugar
3 10-count cans buttermilk biscuits	3/4 teaspoon cinnamon

Mix 1/2 cup sugar and 1/2 teaspoon cinnamon in bowl. Cut each biscuit into quarters. Coat well with cinnamon and sugar mixture. Place in greased bundt pan. Melt margarine with 3/4 cup sugar and 3/4 teaspoon cinnamon in saucepan. Pour over biscuits. Bake at 350 degrees for 30 to 35 minutes or until golden brown. Cool in pan for 15 minutes. Invert onto serving plate. Yield: 16 servings.

Approx Per Serving: Cal 291; Prot 4 g; Carbo 45 g; Fiber 0 g;
 T Fat 12 g; 37% Calories from Fat; Chol 0 mg; Sod 612 mg.

Cranberry Coffee Cake

1/2 cup butter, softened	1/2 teaspoon salt
1 cup sugar	1 cup sour cream
2 eggs	1 teaspoon almond extract
2 cups flour	1 7-ounce can whole cranberry sauce
1 teaspoon baking soda	1/2 cup chopped walnuts

Cream butter in mixer bowl until light. Add sugar, beating until fluffy. Beat in eggs 1 at a time. Add mixture of flour, baking soda and salt alternately with sour cream, mixing well after each addition. Stir in almond extract. Layer batter and cranberry sauce 1/2 at a time in greased and floured tube pan. Sprinkle with walnuts. Bake at 350 degrees for 55 minutes. Cool in pan on wire rack. Remove to serving plate. Yield: 12 servings.

Approx Per Serving: Cal 319; Prot 5 g; Carbo 41 g; Fiber 1 g;
 T Fat 16 g; 44% Calories from Fat; Chol 65 mg; Sod 250 mg.

Crescent Coffee Cake

8 ounces cream cheese, softened	1 teaspoon vanilla extract
1/2 cup sugar	2 8-count cans crescent rolls
1 egg yolk	1 egg white, slightly beaten

Combine cream cheese, sugar, egg yolk and vanilla in bowl; mix well. Spread 1 package roll dough in greased and floured 9x13-inch baking pan, pressing perforations to seal. Spread with cream cheese mixture. Top with remaining roll dough, pressing perforations and edges to seal. Brush with egg white. Bake at 325 degrees for 30 minutes or until golden brown. Yield: 12 servings.

Approx Per Serving: Cal 238; Prot 4 g; Carbo 24 g; Fiber 0 g;
 T Fat 14 g; 54% Calories from Fat; Chol 38 mg; Sod 368 mg.

Sunday Morning Coffee Cake

1 cup sugar
¼ cup butter, softened
2 egg yolks
½ cup milk
1¼ cups flour
2 teaspoons baking powder

½ teaspoon salt
2 egg whites, stiffly beaten
¼ cup sugar
½ teaspoon cinnamon
¼ cup chopped pecans

Cream 1 cup sugar and butter in mixer bowl until light and fluffy. Beat egg yolks with milk in bowl. Add to creamed mixture. Sift in flour, baking powder and salt; mix well. Fold in stiffly beaten egg whites. Spoon into greased 8x8-inch baking pan. Mix ¼ cup sugar, cinnamon and pecans in bowl. Sprinkle over batter. Bake at 350 degrees for 30 minutes. Yield: 6 servings.

Approx Per Serving: Cal 397; Prot 6 g; Carbo 64 g; Fiber 1 g;
    T Fat 14 g; 31% Calories from Fat; Chol 95 mg; Sod 381 mg.

Broccoli Corn Bread

2 7-ounce packages corn muffin mix
4 eggs, beaten
1 cup melted margarine
1 cup cottage cheese

1 cup chopped onion
16 ounces fresh or frozen broccoli,
    cooked

Combine corn muffin mix, eggs, margarine, cottage cheese and onion in bowl; mix well. Stir in broccoli. Spoon into 9x13-inch baking pan sprayed with nonstick cooking spray. Bake at 400 degrees for 45 minutes. Yield: 6 servings.

Approx Per Serving: Cal 520; Prot 13 g; Carbo 31 g; Fiber 3 g;
    T Fat 39 g; 67% Calories from Fat; Chol 147 mg; Sod 861 mg.

Broccoli and Cheese Corn Bread

½ cup butter
4 eggs, beaten
1 medium onion, chopped
1 10-ounce package frozen broccoli,
    thawed

1 7-ounce package corn bread mix
2 cups shredded Cheddar cheese
Garlic salt to taste

Melt butter in 9x9-inch baking pan in 400-degree oven. Combine eggs, onion, broccoli, corn bread mix, cheese and garlic salt in bowl; mix well. Spoon evenly into prepared baking pan. Bake at 400 degrees for 30 minutes. Yield: 9 servings.

Approx Per Serving: Cal 285; Prot 11 g; Carbo 12 g; Fiber 1 g;
    T Fat 22 g; 69% Calories from Fat; Chol 149 mg; Sod 391 mg.

The Best Mexican Corn Bread Ever

Mrs. Frances Buckman makes this recipe for chili suppers at the
DeWitt First Christian Church. It is wonderful! —Pattie Hornbeck

2 onions, chopped
6 tablespoons margarine
2 eggs
2 tablespoons milk

2 7-ounce packages corn bread mix
2 15-ounce cans cream-style corn
1 cup sour cream
2 cups shredded Cheddar cheese

Sauté onions in margarine in skillet. Beat eggs and milk in 3-quart mixer bowl. Add corn bread mix and corn; mix well. Spread in greased 9x13-inch baking pan; sprinkle with onions. Spread sour cream evenly over onions; sprinkle with cheese. Bake at 425 degrees for 35 minutes or until puffed and golden brown. Yield: 12 servings.

Approx Per Serving: Cal 308; Prot 9 g; Carbo 28 g; Fiber 2 g;
      T Fat 19 g; 53% Calories from Fat; Chol 64 mg; Sod 575 mg.

Small Skillet Corn Bread

³/₄ cup cornmeal
2 teaspoons (scant) baking powder
¹/₈ teaspoon baking soda
¹/₂ teaspoon salt

¹/₂ cup buttermilk
1 egg
2 tablespoons hot melted shortening
1 tablespoon cornmeal

Mix ³/₄ cup cornmeal, baking powder, baking soda and salt in bowl. Add buttermilk and egg; mix well. Stir in shortening. Heat skillet until hot; sprinkle with 1 tablespoon cornmeal. Spoon batter into hot skillet. Bake at 425 degrees for 15 to 20 minutes or until golden brown. Yield: 4 servings.

Approx Per Serving: Cal 193; Prot 5 g; Carbo 24 g; Fiber 2 g;
      T Fat 8 g; 40% Calories from Fat; Chol 54 mg; Sod 506 mg.

Hush Puppies

¹/₄ cup flour
³/₄ cup cornmeal mix
1 tablespoon baking powder
1 tablespoon sugar
Salt to taste

¹/₄ cup chopped onion
1 egg
¹/₂ cup (or more) milk
Oil for frying

Mix flour, cornmeal mix, baking powder, sugar and salt in bowl. Add onion, egg and enough milk to make of desired consistency. Drop by teaspoonfuls into hot oil in skillet. Fry until golden brown on both sides. Yield: 6 servings.

Approx Per Serving: Cal 132; Prot 4 g; Carbo 24 g; Fiber <1 g;
      T Fat 2 g; 15% Calories from Fat; Chol 38 mg; Sod 437 mg.
      Nutritional information does not include oil for frying.

Jalapeño Corn Muffins

1 cup flour
1 cup yellow cornmeal
1 tablespoon baking powder
1/2 teaspoon salt
1 egg, beaten

1 cup buttermilk
2 tablespoons honey
1/4 cup canned whole kernel corn
1 jalapeño pepper, seeded, minced

Mix flour, cornmeal, baking powder and salt in bowl. Combine egg, buttermilk and honey in medium bowl; whisk until smooth. Add honey, corn and jalapeño pepper; mix well. Add to mixture of dry ingredients; stir to moisten well. Spoon into lightly oiled muffin cups. Bake at 375 degrees for 20 to 25 minutes or until golden brown. Yield: 12 servings.

Approx Per Serving: Cal 111; Prot 3 g; Carbo 22 g; Fiber 1 g;
    T Fat 1 g; 8% Calories from Fat; Chol 19 mg; Sod 199 mg.

Sour Cream Corn Muffins

1 cup cornmeal
1 cup flour
1/4 cup sugar
2 teaspoons baking powder
1/2 teaspoon baking soda

1 teaspoon salt
1 cup sour cream
2 eggs, slightly beaten
1/4 cup melted butter

Mix cornmeal, flour, sugar, baking powder, baking soda and salt in bowl. Combine sour cream, eggs and butter in bowl; mix well. Add dry ingredients; mix just until moistened. Spoon into greased muffin cups. Bake at 425 degrees for 15 to 20 minutes or until golden brown. May bake in 24 miniature muffin cups for 10 to 15 minutes if preferred. Yield: 12 servings.

Approx Per Serving: Cal 185; Prot 4 g; Carbo 22 g; Fiber 1 g;
    T Fat 9 g; 44% Calories from Fat; Chol 54 mg; Sod 321 mg.

Blackberry Jam Muffins

2 1/4 cups flour
1/2 cup packed brown sugar
1 tablespoon baking powder
1/2 teaspoon cinnamon
1/2 teaspoon salt

1 cup milk
1 cup blackberry jam
1/4 cup butter
2 eggs, slightly beaten
1/2 cup raisins

Mix flour, brown sugar, baking powder, cinnamon and salt in bowl. Combine milk, jam, butter, eggs and raisins in bowl; mix well. Add to dry ingredients; mix just until moistened. Fill greased muffin cups 2/3 full. Bake at 350 degrees for 25 minutes or until golden brown. Yield: 24 servings.

Approx Per Serving: Cal 141; Prot 2 g; Carbo 27 g; Fiber 1 g;
    T Fat 3 g; 18% Calories from Fat; Chol 24 mg; Sod 116 mg.

Bran Muffins

5 cups flour
3 cups sugar
1 12-ounce package Raisin Bran
1 tablespoon (or more) baking soda

2 teaspoons salt
1 cup oil
4 eggs, slightly beaten
4 cups buttermilk

Combine flour, sugar, cereal, baking soda and salt in bowl. Add oil, eggs and buttermilk; mix well to form thick batter. Fill greased muffin cups ⅔ full. Bake at 400 degrees for 15 to 20 minutes or until golden brown. May store, covered, in refrigerator and bake as needed. To avoid danger of salmonella, use egg substitute instead of fresh eggs if planning to store batter in refrigerator. Yield: 60 servings.

Approx Per Serving: Cal 139; Prot 3 g; Carbo 23 g; Fiber 1 g;
    T Fat 4 g; 27% Calories from Fat; Chol 15 mg; Sod 168 mg.

Bran and Molasses Muffins

1½ cups Bran Buds cereal
½ cup apple juice
⅓ cup raisins
1 cup flour
1½ teaspoons baking soda

1 egg, beaten
1 cup lemon yogurt
¼ cup molasses
¼ cup safflower oil

Combine cereal, apple juice and raisins in medium bowl; mix well. Let stand for 10 minutes. Sift in flour and baking soda; mix well. Combine egg, yogurt, molasses and oil in bowl; mix well. Add to cereal mixture; beat with rubber spatula for 20 strokes. Fill greased muffin cups ¾ full. Bake at 400 degrees for 20 minutes.
Yield: 12 servings.

Approx Per Serving: Cal 161; Prot 4 g; Carbo 27 g; Fiber 3 g;
    T Fat 6 g; 29% Calories from Fat; Chol 19 mg; Sod 187 mg.

Oatbran-Honey Muffins

1½ cups oatbran
1½ cups wheat flour
1½ teaspoons baking powder
¼ teaspoon baking soda
½ cup chopped walnuts

2 eggs, beaten
1 cup buttermilk
2½ tablespoons canola oil
½ cup honey
1 banana, sliced

Mix oatbran, wheat flour, baking powder, baking soda and walnuts in bowl. Combine eggs, buttermilk, oil and honey in bowl; mix well. Add dry ingredients; mix until moistened. Fold in banana. Spoon into lightly oiled muffin cups. Bake at 400 degrees for 10 to 15 minutes or until golden brown. Yield: 12 servings.

Approx Per Serving: Cal 208; Prot 7 g; Carbo 35 g; Fiber 4 g;
    T Fat 8 g; 30% Calories from Fat; Chol 36 mg; Sod 96 mg.

Refrigerator Bran Muffins

1/2 cup shortening	2 cups buttermilk
1 1/2 cups sugar	2 1/2 cups flour
1 cup 100% bran cereal	2 1/2 teaspoons baking soda
1 cup boiling water	1/2 teaspoon salt
2 eggs, beaten	2 cups All-Bran cereal

Cream shortening and sugar in mixer bowl until light. Add mixture of 100% bran cereal and water; mix well. Add eggs and buttermilk; mix well. Sift flour, baking soda and salt together. Add with All-Bran cereal to batter; mix just until moistened. Chill for 24 hours or longer. Spoon into greased muffin cups. Bake at 400 degrees for 20 minutes. To avoid danger of salmonella, use egg substitute instead of fresh eggs if planning to store in refrigerator. Yield: 60 servings.

Approx Per Serving: Cal 69; Prot 2 g; Carbo 12 g; Fiber 1 g;
    T Fat 2 g; 26% Calories from Fat; Chol 7 mg; Sod 103 mg.

Applesauce Bread

1 egg, beaten	1 teaspoon cinnamon
1/2 cup oil	1/2 teaspoon salt
1 cup sugar	1 teaspoon baking soda
1 teaspoon vanilla extract	1 cup applesauce
1 1/2 cups flour	1/2 cup chopped walnuts

Beat first 7 ingredients in bowl until smooth. Dissolve baking soda in a small amount of warm water. Add to batter with applesauce and walnuts; mix well. Spoon into greased loaf pan. Bake at 350 degrees for 1 hour. Cool on wire rack. Yield: 10 servings.

Approx Per Serving: Cal 307; Prot 3 g; Carbo 40 g; Fiber 1 g;
    T Fat 15 g; 44% Calories from Fat; Chol 21 mg; Sod 198 mg.

Chocolate-Banana Bread

1 1/2 cups flour	1/2 teaspoon salt
1/2 cup baking cocoa	1/2 cup shortening
2/3 cup sugar	1 cup mashed bananas
1 teaspoon baking powder	2 eggs, slightly beaten
1 teaspoon baking soda	

Mix flour, cocoa, sugar, baking powder, baking soda and salt in large bowl. Cut in shortening until crumbly. Add bananas and eggs; stir with fork to mix well. Spread evenly in greased and floured 5x9-inch loaf pan. Bake at 350 degrees for 50 to 55 minutes or until loaf tests done. Cool in pan for 10 minutes. Remove to wire rack to cool completely. Garnish with confectioners' sugar. Yield: 12 servings.

Approx Per Serving: Cal 215; Prot 3 g; Carbo 29 g; Fiber 2 g;
    T Fat 10 g; 42% Calories from Fat; Chol 36 mg; Sod 198 mg.

Easy Beer Bread

2 cups self-rising flour	**12 ounces warm beer**
3 tablespoons sugar	**1 tablespoon melted butter**

Combine flour, sugar and beer in bowl; mix just until moistened. Spoon into greased loaf pan. Bake at 375 degrees for 30 to 35 minutes or until loaf tests done. Brush with butter. Remove to wire rack to cool. Yield: 12 servings.

Approx Per Serving: Cal 105; Prot 2 g; Carbo 20 g; Fiber 1 g;
    T Fat 1 g; 10% Calories from Fat; Chol 3 mg; Sod 234 mg.

Italian Parmesan Bread

1 envelope dry yeast	**$1/2$ teaspoon Italian seasoning**
1 cup 110 to 115-degree water	**$1/2$ teaspoon garlic salt**
$1/4$ cup butter, softened	**1 teaspoon salt**
1 egg, beaten	**3 cups flour**
2 tablespoons sugar	**$1/2$ cup grated Parmesan cheese**
$1^1/2$ teaspoons onion flakes	**1 tablespoon melted butter**

Dissolve yeast in warm water in large bowl. Add $1/4$ cup butter, egg, sugar, onion flakes, Italian seasoning, garlic salt, salt and 2 cups flour; mix well at low speed for 30 seconds. Beat at medium speed for 2 minutes. Stir in remaining 1 cup flour and $1/3$ cup cheese. Let rise, covered, in warm place for 1 hour or until doubled in bulk. Stir batter 25 strokes. Spread in greased $1^1/2$-quart baking dish. Brush with 1 tablespoon melted butter; sprinkle with remaining cheese. Let rise for 30 minutes. Bake at 350 degrees for 35 minutes or until golden brown. Cool in baking dish for 10 minutes. Remove to wire rack to cool completely. Yield: 12 servings.

Approx Per Serving: Cal 188; Prot 5 g; Carbo 26 g; Fiber 1 g;
    T Fat 7 g; 32% Calories from Fat; Chol 33 mg; Sod 373 mg.

Life is uncertain; eat desserts first.

Lemon Bread

½ cup shortening
1 cup sugar
2 eggs
1½ cups flour
1 teaspoon baking powder

Grated rind of 1 lemon
⅛ teaspoon salt
½ cup milk
¼ cup sugar
Juice of 1 lemon

Cream shortening and 1 cup sugar in mixer bowl until light and fluffy. Beat in eggs. Mix flour, baking powder, lemon rind and salt. Add to batter alternately with milk, mixing well after each addition. Spoon into greased loaf pan. Bake at 350 degrees for 50 to 55 minutes or until loaf tests done. Mix ¼ cup sugar and lemon juice in small bowl. Spoon over hot loaf. Let stand in pan for several minutes. Remove to wire rack to cool. Yield: 12 servings.

Approx Per Serving: Cal 234; Prot 3 g; Carbo 34 g; Fiber <1 g;
    T Fat 10 g; 38% Calories from Fat; Chol 37 mg; Sod 66 mg.

Grandmother Lee's Graham-Pecan Bread

This recipe was given to me by my grandmother, Mary Josephine Lee.
She also baked very delicious pies. —Joyce Hartnett

2 cups all-purpose flour
2 cups graham flour
2 cups sour milk
1 cup (scant) sugar

1 teaspoon baking soda
1 teaspoon baking powder
½ teaspoon salt
½ cup (or more) chopped pecans

Combine all-purpose flour, graham flour, sour milk, sugar, baking soda, baking powder and salt in bowl in order listed; mix well. Stir in pecans. Spoon into greased loaf pan. Let stand for 20 to 30 minutes. Bake at 350 degrees for 1 hour or until loaf tests done. Remove to wire rack to cool. May substitute raisins for pecans if desired. Yield: 12 servings.

Approx Per Serving: Cal 265; Prot 7 g; Carbo 50 g; Fiber 3 g;
    T Fat 5 g; 18% Calories from Fat; Chol 6 mg; Sod 203 mg.

Good taste is something you grow up with.

Pumpkin Bread

3¹/₂ cups flour
3 cups sugar
1 teaspoon baking powder
2 teaspoons baking soda
1 teaspoon each nutmeg, allspice and
   cinnamon

¹/₂ teaspoon ground cloves
2 teaspoons salt
1 16-ounce can pumpkin
4 eggs, beaten
1 cup oil
²/₃ cup water

Sift flour, sugar, baking powder, baking soda, nutmeg, allspice, cinnamon, cloves and salt in large bowl. Combine pumpkin, eggs and oil in bowl; mix well. Add to dry ingredients alternately with water, mixing well after each addition. Spoon into 2 greased and floured 6x10-inch loaf pans. Bake at 350 degrees for 1¹/₂ hours. Remove to wire rack to cool. Yield: 24 servings.

Approx Per Serving: Cal 263; Prot 3 g; Carbo 40 g; Fiber 1 g;
    T Fat 10 g; 35% Calories from Fat; Chol 36 mg; Sod 273 mg.

Brown Rice Sally Lunn Bread

²/₃ cup milk
¹/₃ cup water
¹/₂ cup margarine, chopped
4 cups (about) flour
¹/₄ cup sugar

1 envelope dry yeast
1 teaspoon salt
3 eggs, at room temperature
1¹/₂ cups cooked brown rice

Combine milk, water and margarine in small saucepan. Heat to 120 to 130 degrees. Mix 1¹/₄ cups flour, sugar, yeast and salt in large bowl. Add warm mixture gradually, beating constantly for 2 minutes. Beat in eggs. Add remaining flour gradually, beating constantly. Beat in rice. Let rise, covered, in warm place for 1 hour or until doubled in bulk. Stir dough well. Spoon into greased 10-inch bundt pan. Let rise, covered, for 30 to 40 minutes or until doubled in bulk. Bake at 375 degrees for 30 to 40 minutes or until golden brown. Cool in pan on wire rack for 5 minutes. Remove to wire rack to cool completely. Yield: 12 servings.

Approx Per Serving: Cal 294; Prot 7 g; Carbo 43 g; Fiber 2 g;
    T Fat 10 g; 31% Calories from Fat; Chol 55 mg; Sod 291 mg.

A friend is one who comes to you when all others leave.

Whole Wheat Bread

1 envelope dry yeast
1½ cups warm water
2½ cups whole wheat flour
1 cup bread flour

2 tablespoons honey
2 tablespoons margarine
3 tablespoons nonfat dry milk
  powder

Dissolve yeast in warm water in mixer bowl. Add whole wheat flour, bread flour, honey, margarine and dry milk powder; mix well. Knead until smooth and elastic. Place in greased bowl, turning to coat surface. Let rise, covered, in warm place for 1½ hours or until doubled in bulk. Punch dough down; divide into 2 portions. Shape into loaves in 2 greased 4x8-inch loaf pans. Let rise until doubled in bulk. Bake at 350 degrees for 40 to 45 minutes or until loaves test done. Remove to wire rack to cool. Yield: 24 servings.

Approx Per Serving: Cal 77; Prot 3 g; Carbo 15 g; Fiber 2 g;
    T Fat 1 g; 14% Calories from Fat; Chol <1 mg; Sod 15 mg.

Zucchini Bread

3 cups flour
¼ teaspoon baking powder
1 teaspoon baking soda
1 teaspoon salt
3 eggs
1 cup oil

2½ cups sugar
1 teaspoon vanilla extract
1 teaspoon cinnamon
2 cups grated zucchini
1 cup chopped pecans

Sift flour, baking powder, baking soda and salt together. Combine eggs, oil, sugar, vanilla and cinnamon in mixer bowl; mix well. Add dry ingredients; mix well. Stir in zucchini and pecans. Spoon into 2 greased loaf pans. Bake at 350 degrees for 1 hour. Remove to wire rack to cool. Yield: 24 servings.

Approx Per Serving: Cal 264; Prot 3 g; Carbo 34 g; Fiber 1 g;
    T Fat 13 g; 45% Calories from Fat; Chol 27 mg; Sod 136 mg.

Mayonnaise-Parmesan Bread

¼ cup grated Parmesan cheese
¼ cup mayonnaise

1 tablespoon chopped chives
1 loaf French bread

Combine cheese, mayonnaise and chives in bowl. Cut bread into halves horizontally. Spread with cheese mixture; place cut side up on baking sheet. Broil until golden brown. Yield: 8 servings.

Approx Per Serving: Cal 223; Prot 6 g; Carbo 29 g; Fiber 1 g;
    T Fat 8 g; 35% Calories from Fat; Chol 6 mg; Sod 415 mg.

Dinner Rolls

1 cup milk
2/3 cup water
1/4 cup shortening
2 envelopes dry yeast

1/2 cup sugar
2 eggs
Salt to taste
5 to 6 cups flour

Combine milk, water and shortening in saucepan. Heat just until warm. Add yeast; stir to dissolve well. Add sugar, eggs and salt; mix well. Stir in flour gradually until dough pulls from side of pan. Knead on floured surface for 5 to 10 minutes or until smooth and elastic. Let rise, covered, for 20 minutes. Roll on floured surface; cut with round cutter. Place in 9x13-inch baking pan . Chill for 2 to 24 hours. Let rise, uncovered, for 20 to 30 minutes. Bake at 375 degrees for 10 to 20 minutes or until golden brown. Yield: 24 servings.

Approx Per Serving: Cal 163; Prot 4 g; Carbo 29 g; Fiber 1 g;
    T Fat 3 g; 18% Calories from Fat; Chol 19 mg; Sod 11 mg.

Make-and-Store Snowflakes

5 cups flour, sifted
5 teaspoons baking powder
1 teaspoon baking soda
3 tablespoons sugar
2 teaspoons salt

3/4 cup margarine
1 envelope dry yeast
5 tablespoons warm water
2 cups buttermilk

Sift flour, baking powder, baking soda, sugar and salt together. Cut in margarine until crumbly. Dissolve yeast in warm water in large bowl. Stir in buttermilk. Add dry ingredients gradually, mixing to form stiff dough. Store, covered, in refrigerator. Pinch off biscuit-sized pieces. Shape into balls; flatten on greased baking sheet. Place in cold oven. Set oven temperature at 450 degrees. Bake for 15 minutes or until golden brown. Yield: 60 servings.

Approx Per Serving: Cal 64; Prot 1 g; Carbo 9 g; Fiber <1 g;
    T Fat 2 g; 31% Calories from Fat; Chol <1 mg; Sod 140 mg.

All people smile in the same language.

Mashed Potato Rolls

1 envelope dry yeast
1/2 cup lukewarm water
1 cup mashed potatoes
1/2 cup sugar
2 eggs

2/3 cup oil
1 cup milk, scalded
1 teaspoon salt
5 to 6 cups flour

Dissolve yeast in lukewarm water. Combine potatoes, sugar, eggs, oil, milk and salt in large bowl; mix well. Add yeast mixture and enough flour to form a stiff dough, mixing well. Place in greased bowl, turning to coat surface. Chill, covered, for up to 4 days. Knead lightly on floured surface. Shape into rolls; place in baking pan. Let rise for 1½ hours or until doubled in bulk. Bake at 400 degrees for 8 to 10 minutes or until golden brown. Yield: 42 servings.

Approx Per Serving: Cal 116; Prot 3 g; Carbo 17 g; Fiber 1 g;
    T Fat 4 g; 32% Calories from Fat; Chol 11 mg; Sod 72 mg.

Red Apple Inn Rolls

1 cup butter
2/3 cup sugar
2 teaspoons salt
1 cup boiling water
2½ envelopes dry yeast

1 cup warm water
2 eggs
6 cups flour
2 tablespoons melted butter
Poppy seed to taste

Combine 1 cup butter, sugar and salt in large bowl. Add 1 cup boiling water. Cool to lukewarm. Dissolve yeast in 1 cup warm water in bowl. Beat in eggs. Add to butter mixture. Add flour; mix well. Chill, covered, in refrigerator overnight. Roll on floured surface; cut out as desired. Place in greased baking pan. Let rise for 2 hours. Brush with 2 tablespoons melted butter; sprinkle with poppy seed. Bake at 425 degrees for 12 minutes. Yield: 60 servings.

Approx Per Serving: Cal 88; Prot 2 g; Carbo 12 g; Fiber <1 g;
    T Fat 4 g; 39% Calories from Fat; Chol 16 mg; Sod 103 mg.

*The largest room in the world is the room
for self-improvement.*

Mom's Simple Never-Fail Yeast Rolls

This recipe was given to me by my mother, Clara McDonald Bryant of Harrison, Arkansas, over 50 years ago. —Priscilla Bryant Baker

1 envelope dry yeast	**¹/₂ cup oil**
2 cups lukewarm water	**1 teaspoon salt**
¹/₂ cup sugar	**5 to 6 cups flour**
2 eggs, beaten	**2 tablespoons oil**

Dissolve yeast in lukewarm water in bowl. Stir in sugar, eggs, ¹/₂ cup oil and salt. Add flour 2 cups at time, mixing to form stiff dough. Place in oiled bowl, turning to oil surface. Let rise, covered with damp cloth, until doubled in bulk. Knead on floured surface until smooth and elastic. Shape into rolls; place in greased baking pan or muffin cups. Brush with oil. Let rise until doubled in bulk. Bake at 350 degrees for 17 to 20 minutes or until golden brown. May glaze or brush with melted margarine. Yield: 36 servings.

Bear Claws: Divide dough into 2 portions. Roll each into ¹/₃ to ¹/₂-inch thick circle. Spread with melted margarine; sprinkle with cinnamon, brown sugar and chopped pecans. Roll as for jelly roll. Shape as for horseshoe on greased baking sheet. Cut with scissors from outer edge to but not through inner edge at 1¹/₂-inch intervals. Twist to turn cut sides up and overlap slightly. Bring ends of roll together to form "claw." Brush with oil. Let rise until doubled in bulk. Bake at 350 degrees for 20 to 24 minutes or until golden brown. Spread with favorite confectioners' sugar glaze if desired. Yield: 2 bear claws.

Cinnamon Rolls: Prepare, fill and roll dough as for Bear Claws. Cut into slices; arrange in greased baking pan. Bake as above. Yield: 3 dozen rolls.

Approx Per Serving: Cal 125; Prot 3 g; Carbo 19 g; Fiber 1 g;
    T Fat 5 g; 36% Calories from Fat; Chol 12 mg; Sod 64 mg.
    Nutritional information is for basic recipe only.

*It is difficult to see the picture when
you are inside the frame.*

Desserts

Boone County Courthouse

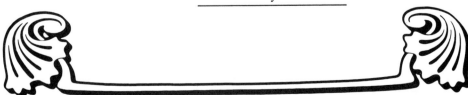

Boone County Courthouse

Re-built in 1909 after a fire destroyed the original building, the Boone County Courthouse in Harrison was designed by Arkansas Architect, Charles L. Thompson of Little Rock. It is also on the National Register of Historic Places.

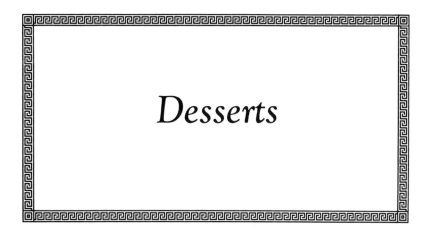

Desserts

Apple Cobbler

3 cups water
1¹/₂ cups sugar
¹/₂ cup margarine
¹/₂ cup shortening
2 cups self-rising flour

²/₃ cup milk
2 cups finely chopped apples
1 teaspoon cinnamon
¹/₂ teaspoon nutmeg

Combine water and sugar in saucepan. Heat over medium heat until sugar is dissolved, stirring frequently. Melt margarine in 9x13-inch baking dish in 350-degree oven. Cut shortening into flour in bowl until crumbly. Add milk gradually, stirring until well mixed. Roll dough into ¹/₄-inch rectangle on floured surface. Spread chopped apples over dough; sprinkle with cinnamon and nutmeg. Roll dough to enclose filling as for jelly roll, pressing ends together to seal. Cut into 1¹/₂-inch slices; place cut side down in melted margarine in baking dish. Pour sugar water around slices. Bake at 350 degrees for 55 to 60 minutes or until apples are tender and cobbler is brown. Yield: 12 servings.

Approx Per Serving: Cal 333; Prot 3 g; Carbo 44 g; Fiber 1 g;
    T Fat 17 g; 45% Calories from Fat; Chol 2 mg; Sod 320 mg.

Adell's Delight

¹/₂ cup butter
1 cup flour
³/₄ cup chopped pecans
9 ounces whipped topping
1 cup confectioners' sugar
8 ounces cream cheese, softened
1 cup sugar

3 tablespoons cornstarch
Salt to taste
3 tablespoons baking cocoa
1 12-ounce can evaporated milk
2 egg yolks, beaten
1 teaspoon butter
1 teaspoon vanilla extract

Cut ¹/₂ cup butter into flour in bowl until crumbly. Stir in pecans. Press mixture into greased 9x13-inch baking dish. Bake at 250 degrees for 25 minutes or until brown. Cool. Reserve 1 cup whipped topping. Combine remaining whipped topping, confectioners' sugar and cream cheese in bowl; mix well. Spread over cooled crust. Chill in refrigerator. Combine sugar, cornstarch, salt and baking cocoa in microwave-safe bowl. Add enough water to evaporated milk to measure 2 cups. Add milk mixture to cocoa mixture. Microwave, covered, on High until mixture boils. Add a small amount of hot mixture to egg yolks. Stir egg yolks into hot mixture. Microwave, covered, until mixture thickens to pie filling consistency, stirring occasionally. Stir in 1 teaspoon butter and vanilla. Pour over cream cheese layer; top with reserved whipped topping. Chill until serving time. Yield: 15 servings.

Approx Per Serving: Cal 364; Prot 5 g; Carbo 37 g; Fiber 1 g;
  T Fat 23 g; 55% Calories from Fat; Chol 69 mg; Sod 129 mg.

Bananas Foster

This is from New Orleans' famous Brennan's Restaurant. —Ginnie Tyson

¹/₄ cup butter
2 tablespoons (heaping) brown sugar
4 bananas, cut into halves lengthwise
1 tablespoon banana liqueur

Cinnamon to taste
1 tablespoon rum
2 tablespoons brandy
6 cups vanilla ice cream

Combine butter and brown sugar in chafing dish or skillet. Cook over medium heat until sugar is melted, stirring frequently. Add bananas. Cook until heated through, stirring gently. Add banana liqueur and cinnamon, stirring gently. Sprinkle with rum and brandy. Ignite. Spoon over vanilla ice cream in serving bowls. Yield: 6 servings.

Approx Per Serving: Cal 451; Prot 6 g; Carbo 57 g; Fiber 2 g;
  T Fat 22 g; 45% Calories from Fat; Chol 80 mg; Sod 184 mg.

It is nice to fix a pretty table for guests—it's nicer to do it for your family.

Frozen Banana Dessert

1 recipe mixture for graham cracker
   pie shell
2 cups sugar
Juice of 3 lemons

3 bananas, mashed
1 8-ounce can crushed pineapple
1 12-ounce can evaporated milk,
   chilled

Prepare graham cracker pie shell crumbs using graham cracker crumb package directions; pat into 9x13-inch baking dish. Combine sugar, lemon juice, bananas and pineapple in bowl; mix well. Whip chilled evaporated milk in bowl. Fold into fruit mixture. Pour into prepared dish. Freeze until firm. Yield: 10 servings.

Approx Per Serving: Cal 390; Prot 4 g; Carbo 74 g; Fiber 1 g;
   T Fat 10 g; 23% Calories from Fat; Chol 10 mg; Sod 201 mg.

Cheesecake

2¹/₂ cups graham cracker crumbs
¹/₂ cup melted butter
4 eggs
1 cup sugar
2 teaspoons vanilla extract

24 ounces cream cheese, softened
2 cups sour cream
2 tablespoons sugar
1 teaspoon vanilla extract

Combine graham cracker crumbs and melted butter in bowl; mix well. Press onto bottom and up sides of 9-inch springform pan. Combine eggs, 1 cup sugar and 2 teaspoons vanilla in mixer bowl; beat well. Add cream cheese; mix well. Pour into graham cracker crumb crust. Bake at 325 degrees for 45 minutes. Cool for 30 minutes. Combine sour cream, 2 tablespoons sugar and 1 teaspoon vanilla in bowl; mix well. Spread over cheesecake. Bake at 325 degrees for 15 minutes. Chill. Remove side of springform pan. Top with favorite pie filling or fresh strawberries. Yield: 8 servings.

Approx Per Serving: Cal 835; Prot 14 g; Carbo 63 g; Fiber 1 g;
   T Fat 60 g; 64% Calories from Fat; Chol 256 mg; Sod 645 mg.

Light Microwave Cheesecake

15 ounces ricotta cheese
1 cup plain low-fat yogurt
3 egg whites
¹/₃ cup sugar

1 teaspoon vanilla extract
¹/₂ teaspoon almond extract
1 9-inch graham cracker pie shell
10 fresh strawberries

Beat first 6 ingredients in glass bowl until smooth. Microwave on High for 4 to 7 minutes or until very hot, stirring every 2 minutes with whisk. Pour into pie shell in glass dish. Microwave on Medium for 7 to 15 minutes or until center is almost set, rotating dish ¹/₄ turn every 3 minutes. Chill for 6 hours or longer or until firm. Garnish with fresh strawberries. Yield: 10 servings.

Approx Per Serving: Cal 288; Prot 8 g; Carbo 31 g; Fiber 1 g;
   T Fat 15 g; 45% Calories from Fat; Chol 23 mg; Sod 258 mg.

Cherry Ping

1/2 cup sugar
1/4 cup all-purpose flour
1/4 cup whole wheat flour
1 teaspoon baking powder
1 teaspoon vanilla extract
1 egg, beaten
2 16-ounce cans water-pack pitted
   tart red cherries

1/3 cup sugar
1 1/2 tablespoons cornstarch
1/8 teaspoon nutmeg
2 teaspoons lemon juice
1/8 teaspoon almond extract
1 teaspoon sifted confectioners' sugar

Combine 1/2 cup sugar, all-purpose flour, whole wheat flour and baking powder in bowl; mix well. Add vanilla and egg, stirring just until dry ingredients are moistened. Drain cherries, reserving 1/2 cup liquid. Place cherries in 8-inch square baking dish. Combine 1/3 cup sugar, cornstarch and nutmeg in bowl; mix well. Add reserved cherry liquid, lemon juice and almond extract gradually, stirring with wire whisk to blend. Pour over cherries. Drop flour mixture by tablespoonfuls onto mixture. Bake at 375 degrees for 40 minutes or until top sounds hollow when tapped. Cool in pan for several minutes. Remove to wire rack to cool for 20 minutes. Sprinkle with confectioners' sugar. Yield: 6 servings.

Approx Per Serving: Cal 222; Prot 3 g; Carbo 51 g; Fiber 1 g;
    T Fat 1 g; 5% Calories from Fat; Chol 36 mg; Sod 78 mg.

Neiman Marcus Dessert Squares

1 2-layer package butter-recipe
   fudge cake mix
3 eggs, beaten
1 cup broken pecans
1/2 cup margarine, softened

1 1-pound package confectioners'
   sugar
1 egg, slightly beaten
8 ounces cream cheese, softened

Combine cake mix, 3 eggs, pecans and margarine in bowl; stir by hand until well mixed. Pour into buttered 9x13-inch baking dish. Combine confectioners' sugar, 1 egg and cream cheese in bowl. Mix until smooth. Spoon into prepared dish. Bake at 350 degrees for 35 minutes or until set. Cool. Cut into squares. Yield: 15 servings.

Approx Per Serving: Cal 468; Prot 5 g; Carbo 66 g; Fiber 1 g;
    T Fat 22 g; 41% Calories from Fat; Chol 73 mg; Sod 327 mg.

Do unto others as though you were the others.

Crème au Café

4 eggs
Salt to taste
¹/₂ cup sugar
3 5-ounce cans evaporated milk

2 cups water
1 teaspoon almond extract
2 teaspoons instant coffee granules

Beat eggs with salt lightly in bowl. Add sugar, evaporated milk, water and almond extract, mixing well. Stir in instant coffee granules. Pour into 6 buttered custard cups. Place in pan of water 1-inch deep. Bake at 300 degrees for 1 hour and 15 minutes or until custard is set. Yield: 6 servings.

Approx Per Serving: Cal 215; Prot 9 g; Carbo 24 g; Fiber <1 g;
T Fat 9 g; 38% Calories from Fat; Chol 163 mg; Sod 122 mg.

Dot Council's Custard

4 eggs or egg substitute
1 cup (scant) sugar
2 cups half and half

1 teaspoon vanilla extract
Nutmeg to taste

Beat eggs, sugar, half and half and vanilla in bowl. Pour into 6 buttered custard cups; sprinkle with nutmeg. Place in pan of water 1 inch deep. Bake at 350 degrees for 30 to 45 minutes or until custard is set. Cool slightly. Chill in refrigerator. Yield: 6 servings.

Approx Per Serving: Cal 288; Prot 6 g; Carbo 37 g; Fiber 0 g;
T Fat 13 g; 40% Calories from Fat; Chol 172 mg; Sod 80 mg.

Kansas Dirt Cake Dessert

1 1¹/₄-pound package chocolate
   cream sandwich cookies
¹/₂ cup melted margarine
1 cup confectioners' sugar
3 ounces cream cheese, softened

2 4-ounce packages vanilla instant
   pudding mix
3¹/₂ cups milk
12 ounces whipped topping

Place cookies several at a time in blender container. Process until crumbled. Combine margarine, confectioners' sugar and cream cheese in mixer bowl; mix well. Add pudding mix and milk; beat well. Fold in whipped topping. Alternate layers of cookie crumbs and pudding mixture in buttered 9x13-inch dish, beginning and ending with cookie crumbs. Chill until serving time. Yield: 12 servings.

Approx Per Serving: Cal 565; Prot 6 g; Carbo 72 g; Fiber 1 g;
T Fat 29 g; 46% Calories from Fat; Chol 17 mg; Sod 497 mg.

Dream Dessert

1 3-ounce package lime gelatin
1 cup boiling water
1/2 cup cold water
1 cup graham cracker crumbs
1/4 cup melted butter
1 3-ounce package pineapple gelatin
1/4 cup sugar
1 cup boiling water
1/2 cup cold water

2 cups whipping cream, whipped
1 8-ounce can pineapple tidbits,
   drained
1 8-ounce can sliced peaches,
   drained
1 cup miniature marshmallows
10 maraschino cherries, cut into
   halves

Dissolve lime gelatin in 1 cup boiling water in bowl. Stir in 1/2 cup cold water. Pour into 8x8-inch pan. Chill in refrigerator until set. Combine graham cracker crumbs and melted butter in bowl; mix well. Press into buttered 9-inch springform pan. Chill in refrigerator. Dissolve pineapple gelatin and sugar in 1 cup boiling water in bowl. Stir in 1/2 cup cold water. Chill until partially set. Cut congealed lime gelatin into cubes. Fold lime gelatin cubes, whipped cream, pineapple, peaches, marshmallows and cherries into partially congealed pineapple gelatin. Pour into prepared pan. Chill overnight. Remove side of springform pan. Yield: 15 servings.

Approx Per Serving: Cal 258; Prot 3 g; Carbo 29 g; Fiber 1 g;
     T Fat 16 g; 53% Calories from Fat; Chol 52 mg; Sod 127 mg.

Dump Cake Dessert

1/2 cup margarine
1 2-layer package white cake mix
2 16-ounce cans crushed pineapple

2 21-ounce cans pie filling
1 cup chopped pecans

Cut margarine into cake mix in bowl until crumbly. Layer undrained pineapple, pie filling, pecans and cake mix mixture into buttered 9x13-inch baking dish. Bake at 350 degrees for 65 minutes or until dessert tests done. Cut into squares; invert onto serving plates. Garnish with whipped topping. Yield: 20 servings.

Approx Per Serving: Cal 282; Prot 2 g; Carbo 46 g; Fiber 2 g;
     T Fat 11 g; 34% Calories from Fat; Chol 0 mg; Sod 217 mg.

A budget is an attempt to live below your yearnings.

Easy Fruit Cobbler

1/2 cup butter
1 cup sugar
1 cup self-rising flour
1 teaspoon baking powder

1/2 teaspoon salt
1 cup milk
1   20-ounce can cherry pie filling

Melt butter in 8x8-inch baking dish in 350-degree oven. Combine sugar, flour, baking powder and salt in bowl; mix well. Add milk; mix well. Pour into prepared baking dish. Top with pie filling. Bake at 350 degrees for 25 minutes or until golden brown. May substitute other fruit pie fillings for cherry. Yield: 8 servings.

Approx Per Serving: Cal 340; Prot 3 g; Carbo 56 g; Fiber 1 g;
    T Fat 13 g; 33% Calories from Fat; Chol 35 mg; Sod 474 mg.

Lemon Torte

1   3-ounce package lemon gelatin
1/2 cup boiling water
1 1/2 to 2 cups graham cracker crumbs
3/4 cup melted butter

1   12-ounce can evaporated milk, chilled
3 tablespoons lemon juice
1 cup sugar

Dissolve gelatin in boiling water in bowl. Let stand at room temperature. Reserve 1/2 cup graham cracker crumbs. Combine remaining graham cracker crumbs and butter in bowl; mix well. Press into buttered springform pan. Beat chilled evaporated milk in mixer bowl until thick. Add lemon juice, sugar and lemon gelatin. Pour into prepared pan. Top with reserved graham cracker crumbs. Chill for 8 hours. Remove side of springform pan. Yield: 6 servings.

Approx Per Serving: Cal 633; Prot 8 g; Carbo 83 g; Fiber 1 g;
    T Fat 32 g; 44% Calories from Fat; Chol 79 mg; Sod 545 mg.

Oreo Cookie Dessert

1   16-ounce package Oreo cookies, crushed
1 cup chopped pecans

8 ounces whipped topping
1/2 gallon vanilla ice cream, softened

Combine cookie crumbs and pecans in bowl; mix well. Fold in whipped topping and ice cream. Pour into 9x13-inch dish. Freeze overnight. Yield: 16 servings.

Approx Per Serving: Cal 368; Prot 5 g; Carbo 41 g; Fiber 1 g;
    T Fat 21 g; 51% Calories from Fat; Chol 30 mg; Sod 196 mg.

Baked Peaches and Cream

1/4 cup sugar
1/4 cup packed brown sugar
1 teaspoon cinnamon
1 tablespoon flour
1/4 cup butter
2 pounds fresh peaches, peeled, sliced

3/4 cup flour
1 teaspoon baking powder
1/8 teaspoon salt
1/4 cup sugar
1 cup whipping cream, whipped

Combine 1/4 cup sugar, brown sugar, cinnamon and 1 tablespoon flour in bowl; mix well. Cut in butter until crumbly. Add peaches, tossing to mix. Pour into buttered 1 1/2-quart baking dish. Combine 3/4 cup flour, baking powder, salt and 1/4 cup sugar in bowl; mix well. Fold into whipped cream. Spread over peach mixture. Bake at 425 degrees for 30 minutes. Cool for 1 hour. Yield: 6 servings.

Approx Per Serving: Cal 439; Prot 4 g; Carbo 59 g; Fiber 3 g;
T Fat 23 g; 45% Calories from Fat; Chol 75 mg; Sod 185 mg.

Flamed Louisiana Peaches

4 fresh peaches, sliced
1/4 cup butter
2 tablespoons Amaretto liqueur

3 tablespoons rum
1 1/2 quarts vanilla ice cream

Sauté peaches in butter in chafing dish. Stir in liqueur. Heat rum in small saucepan. Ignite. Pour over peaches. Serve over ice cream when flame subsides. Yield: 6 servings.

Approx Per Serving: Cal 397; Prot 5 g; Carbo 41 g; Fiber 1 g;
T Fat 22 g; 52% Calories from Fat; Chol 80 mg; Sod 181 mg.

Peachy Delight

1 cup flour
1 tablespoon sugar
1/2 cup margarine
1/4 cup chopped pecans
1 cup sugar
8 ounces cream cheese, softened

9 ounces whipped topping
3 cups sliced fresh peaches
1 cup sugar
1/4 cup cornstarch
1 1/2 cups water
1 3-ounce package peach gelatin

Combine flour and 1 tablespoon sugar in bowl; mix well. Cut in margarine until crumbly. Stir in pecans. Press into buttered 9x13-inch baking dish. Bake at 350 degrees for 20 minutes. Cool. Combine 1 cup sugar and cream cheese in mixer bowl; mix well. Fold in whipped topping. Spread over cooled crust. Top with peaches. Combine 1 cup sugar, cornstarch and water in saucepan; mix well. Cook over medium heat until thickened, stirring constantly. Stir in gelatin until dissolved. Spread over top of peaches. Chill until serving time. Yield: 12 servings.

Approx Per Serving: Cal 443; Prot 4 g; Carbo 61 g; Fiber 1 g;
T Fat 21 g; 42% Calories from Fat; Chol 21 mg; Sod 174 mg.

Pots de Crème

1 cup chocolate chips
2 egg yolks
1/2 cup whipping cream, scalded

1¹/₂ cups half and half, scalded
Brandy or rum to taste

Combine chocolate chips, egg yolks, hot whipping cream and hot half and half in blender container. Process until chocolate chips are melted and mixture is well blended. Add brandy or rum; mix well. Pour into 4 pot de crème cups. Chill, covered with waxed paper, until serving time. Garnish with whipped cream.
Yield: 4 servings.

Approx Per Serving: Cal 467; Prot 6 g; Carbo 29 g; Fiber 1 g;
    T Fat 40 g; 71% Calories from Fat; Chol 181 mg; Sod 58 mg.

Pumpkin Pie Squares

1 cup sifted flour
1/2 cup oats
1/2 cup packed brown sugar
1/2 cup butter, softened
1   16-ounce can pumpkin
1   12-ounce can evaporated milk
2 eggs

³/₄ cup sugar
1/2 teaspoon salt
1 teaspoon cinnamon
2 tablespoons butter
1/2 cup packed brown sugar
1 cup chopped pecans

Combine flour, oats, 1/2 cup brown sugar and 1/2 cup butter in mixer bowl; mix on low speed until crumbly. Press into ungreased 9x13-inch baking dish. Bake at 350 degrees for 15 minutes. Combine pumpkin, evaporated milk and eggs in mixer bowl; mix well. Add sugar, salt and cinnamon; mix well. Pour into baked crust. Bake at 350 degrees for 20 minutes. Cut 2 tablespoons butter into 1/2 cup brown sugar until crumbly. Stir in pecans. Sprinkle over top. Bake for 15 to 20 minutes longer or until brown. Yield: 10 servings.

Approx Per Serving: Cal 476; Prot 7 g; Carbo 62 g; Fiber 2 g;
    T Fat 24 g; 44% Calories from Fat; Chol 84 mg; Sod 268 mg.

*Don't wait for a crisis to discover
what's important in your life.*

Pumpkin Torte

1½ cups graham cracker crumbs
⅓ cup sugar
½ cup margarine
2 eggs
¾ cup sugar
8 ounces cream cheese, softened
2 cups pumpkin
3 egg yolks
½ cup sugar

½ cup milk
½ teaspoon salt
1 teaspoon cinnamon
1 envelope unflavored gelatin
¼ cup water
3 egg whites
¼ cup sugar
16 ounces whipped topping
½ cup chopped pecans

Combine graham cracker crumbs and ⅓ cup sugar in bowl; mix well. Cut in margarine until crumbly. Press into buttered 9x13-inch baking dish. Combine eggs, ¾ cup sugar and cream cheese in mixer bowl; mix well. Pour into prepared pan. Bake at 350 degrees for 25 minutes. Cool to room temperature. Combine pumpkin, egg yolks, ½ cup sugar, milk, salt and cinnamon in saucepan; mix well. Cook over medium heat until thickened, stirring constantly. Soften gelatin in ¼ cup water. Add to hot mixture, stirring until dissolved. Cool. Beat egg whites until soft peaks form. Add ¼ cup sugar gradually, beating until stiff peaks form. Fold into cooled pumpkin mixture. Spread over cooled crust. Top with whipped topping; sprinkle with pecans. Chill until serving time. Yield: 12 servings.

Approx Per Serving: Cal 519; Prot 7 g; Carbo 55 g; Fiber 2 g;
   T Fat 31 g; 53% Calories from Fat; Chol 111 mg; Sod 368 mg.

Margland II's Watermelon Sorbet

3 quarts seeded ½-inch watermelon
   cubes

3 tablespoons sugar
1 tablespoon fresh lemon juice

Place watermelon cubes in bowl. Sprinkle with sugar and lemon juice. Place in plastic freezer bag. Freeze for 4 hours to overnight. Purée frozen watermelon in blender 2 cups at a time until fluffy. Spoon into parfait glasses. Garnish with fresh mint. Yield: 6 servings.

Approx Per Serving: Cal 125; Prot 2 g; Carbo 29 g; Fiber 1 g;
   T Fat 1 g; 9% Calories from Fat; Chol 0 mg; Sod 6 mg.

Faith is the best antidote for fear.

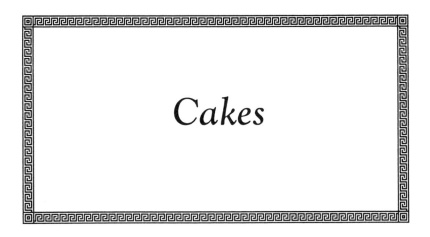

Cakes

German Apple Cake

5 tart apples, peeled, sliced
5 tablespoons sugar
2 teaspoons cinnamon
3 cups flour
2¹/₂ cups sugar
¹/₂ teaspoon salt
1¹/₂ teaspoons baking soda
1¹/₂ teaspoons baking powder

4 eggs
1 cup oil
2 teaspoons vanilla extract
¹/₃ cup orange juice
1¹/₂ cups confectioners' sugar
3 tablespoons butter, softened
1¹/₂ teaspoons vanilla extract
1 or 2 tablespoons water

Place apples in bowl. Combine 5 tablespoons sugar and cinnamon in bowl. Add to apples, tossing to coat. Combine flour, 2¹/₂ cups sugar, salt, baking soda, baking powder, eggs and oil in mixer bowl; mix well. Add 2 teaspoons vanilla and orange juice; mix well. Alternate layers of ¹/₃ of the batter and ¹/₂ of the apples in greased and floured 10-inch tube pan, beginning and ending with batter. Bake at 350 degrees for 1¹/₂ to 1³/₄ hours or until cake tests done. Cool in pan for 10 minutes. Invert onto serving plate to cool completely. Combine confectioners' sugar, butter and 1¹/₂ teaspoons vanilla in mixer bowl; mix well. Add water; mix well. Drizzle over cooled cake. Yield: 12 servings.

Approx Per Serving: Cal 602; Prot 5 g; Carbo 95 g; Fiber 2 g;
    T Fat 23 g; 34% Calories from Fat; Chol 79 mg; Sod 282 mg.

Mama's Fresh Apple Cake

1¹/₂ cups oil
2 eggs
2 cups sugar
1 teaspoon vanilla extract
2¹/₂ cups sifted flour
1 teaspoon baking soda

2 teaspoons baking powder
1 teaspoon salt
3 cups chopped tart apples
1 cup chopped pecans
Easy Caramel Frosting

Combine oil, eggs, sugar and vanilla in mixer bowl; mix well. Sift flour, baking soda, baking powder and salt together. Add to egg mixture gradually, beating well. Fold in apples and pecans. Pour cake batter into waxed paper-lined 9x13-inch cake pan. Bake at 350 degrees for 55 to 60 minutes or until cake tests done. Frost with Easy Caramel Frosting. Yield: 15 servings.

Approx Per Serving: Cal 601; Prot 4 g; Carbo 73 g; Fiber 2 g;
T Fat 35 g; 50% Calories from Fat; Chol 46 mg; Sod 455 mg.

Easy Caramel Frosting

¹/₂ cup butter
¹/₂ teaspoon salt
2 tablespoons evaporated milk

1 cup packed brown sugar
1 cup confectioners' sugar

Combine butter, salt and evaporated milk in saucepan. Heat over medium heat until butter is melted, stirring frequently. Add brown sugar, stirring until brown sugar dissolves. Stir in enough confectioners' sugar to make of spreading consistency. Yield: 15 servings.

Approx Per Serving: Cal 156; Prot <1 g; Carbo 26 g; Fiber 0 g;
T Fat 6 g; 35% Calories from Fat; Chol 17 mg; Sod 133 mg.

Banana Nut Cake

2 small bananas, mashed
1 2-layer package yellow cake mix
1 4-ounce package banana cream
   instant pudding mix

4 eggs
1 cup water
¹/₄ cup oil
¹/₂ cup chopped pecans

Combine bananas, cake mix, pudding mix, eggs and water in mixer bowl; mix well. Add oil; beat for 2 minutes. Stir in pecans. Pour into greased and floured tube pan. Bake at 350 degrees for 60 to 70 minutes or until cake tests done. Cool in pan for several minutes. Remove to serving dish. Yield: 12 servings.

Approx Per Serving: Cal 330; Prot 4 g; Carbo 49 g; Fiber 1 g;
T Fat 13 g; 36% Calories from Fat; Chol 71 mg; Sod 348 mg.

Carrot Cake

2 cups flour
2 teaspoons baking powder
1 teaspoon baking soda
1 teaspoon salt
2 teaspoons cinnamon
2 cups sugar

1½ cups oil
4 eggs
2 cups grated carrots
1   8-ounce can crushed pineapple
1 cup chopped pecans

Sift flour, baking powder, baking soda, salt, cinnamon and sugar together into mixer bowl. Add oil; beat for 2 minutes. Add eggs; beat well. Stir in carrots, pineapple and pecans. Pour into greased and floured tube cake pan. Bake at 350 degrees for 30 to 35 minutes or until cake tests done. Cool in pan for several minutes. Remove to serving plate. Yield: 12 servings.

Approx Per Serving: Cal 562; Prot 5 g; Carbo 57 g; Fiber 2 g;
   T Fat 36 g; 57% Calories from Fat; Chol 71 mg; Sod 332 mg.

Chocolate Chip Cake

1   2-layer package butter-recipe cake
   mix
1   4-ounce package chocolate instant
   pudding mix
½ cup oil

1 teaspoon vanilla extract
4 eggs
1 cup sour cream
2 cups chocolate chips

Combine cake mix, pudding mix, oil, vanilla, eggs and sour cream in bowl; mix well. Stir in chocolate chips. Pour into greased and floured bundt pan. Bake at 325 degrees for 50 to 60 minutes or until cake tests done. Cool in pan for several minutes. Remove to serving plate. Yield: 12 servings.

Approx Per Serving: Cal 520; Prot 6 g; Carbo 63 g; Fiber 1 g;
   T Fat 29 g; 49% Calories from Fat; Chol 80 mg; Sod 262 mg.

Chocolate-Mayonnaise Cakes

1 cup mayonnaise
1 cup cold water
1 teaspoon vanilla extract
2 cups flour

1 cup sugar
1½ to 2 tablespoons baking cocoa
1½ teaspoons baking soda
⅛ teaspoon salt

Combine mayonnaise, cold water and vanilla in mixer bowl; beat well. Sift flour, sugar, baking cocoa, baking soda and salt together. Add to mayonnaise mixture; beat for 2 minutes. Pour into 2 greased and floured 9-inch cake pans. Bake at 350 degrees for 20 to 25 minutes or until cakes test done. Cool in pan for several minutes. Remove to wire rack to cool completely. Yield: 12 servings.

Approx Per Serving: Cal 275; Prot 3 g; Carbo 34 g; Fiber 1 g;
   T Fat 15 g; 48% Calories from Fat; Chol 11 mg; Sod 231 mg.

Chocolate Sheath Cake

2 cups flour
2 cups sugar
1 cup margarine
1 cup water
¼ cup baking cocoa
½ teaspoon cinnamon

½ cup buttermilk
2 eggs, slightly beaten
1 teaspoon baking soda
1 teaspoon vanilla extract
Cocoa-Pecan Frosting

Combine flour and sugar in mixer bowl; mix well. Combine 1 cup margarine, water, baking cocoa and cinnamon in saucepan. Bring to a boil, stirring occasionally. Pour over flour mixture; mix well. Add buttermilk, eggs, baking soda and vanilla; mix well. Pour into greased 11x16-inch cake pan. Bake at 400 degrees for 30 minutes. Spread Cocoa-Pecan Frosting over hot cake. Yield: 15 servings.

Approx Per Serving: Cal 546; Prot 4 g; Carbo 79 g; Fiber 2 g;
    T Fat 25 g; 41% Calories from Fat; Chol 30 mg; Sod 291 mg.

Cocoa-Pecan Frosting

½ cup margarine
6 tablespoons milk
¼ cup baking cocoa
1   1-pound package confectioners'
    sugar

1 cup chopped pecans
1 teaspoon vanilla extract

Combine margarine, milk and baking cocoa in saucepan. Bring to a boil, stirring occasionally. Remove from heat. Add confectioners' sugar, mixing well. Stir in pecans and vanilla. Yield: 15 servings.

Approx Per Serving: Cal 255; Prot 1 g; Carbo 39 g; Fiber 1 g;
    T Fat 12 g; 40% Calories from Fat; Chol 1 mg; Sod 75 mg.

*Any person who is always feeling sorry
for himself, should be.*

Old-Fashioned Chocolate Cake

1 cup margarine, softened
1 cup sugar
1 cup packed brown sugar
2 eggs, beaten
1¼ cups buttermilk
3 cups flour

¼ cup baking cocoa
2 teaspoons baking soda
½ cup hot water
2 teaspoons cinnamon
½ teaspoon ground cloves
Fudge Frosting

Cream margarine, sugar and brown sugar in mixer bowl until light and fluffy. Add eggs; beat well. Add buttermilk and flour alternately, beating well after each addition. Combine baking cocoa and baking soda in bowl. Add hot water, stirring until bubbly. Add to creamed mixture. Add cinnamon and cloves; beat well. Pour into greased and floured 9x13-inch cake pan. Bake at 325 degrees for 1 hour or until cake tests done. Frost with Fudge Frosting. Yield: 15 servings.

Approx Per Serving: Cal 477; Prot 5 g; Carbo 79 g; Fiber 1 g;
    T Fat 17 g; 31% Calories from Fat; Chol 30 mg; Sod 330 mg.

Fudge Frosting

2 cups sugar
2 tablespoons baking cocoa
¼ cup milk

¼ cup margarine
1 teaspoon vanilla extract

Combine sugar, baking cocoa and milk in saucepan. Bring to a boil. Boil for 2 minutes, stirring frequently. Remove from heat. Stir in margarine and vanilla. Beat until of spreading consistency. Yield: 15 servings.

Approx Per Serving: Cal 135; Prot <1 g; Carbo 27 g; Fiber <1 g;
    T Fat 3 g; 21% Calories from Fat; Chol 1 mg; Sod 38 mg.

It takes rain and sunshine to make a rainbow.

Chocolate-Zucchini Cake

¹/₂ cup margarine
¹/₂ cup oil
1³/₄ cups sugar
2 eggs
1 teaspoon vanilla extract
¹/₂ cup sour milk
2¹/₂ cups flour
¹/₄ cup baking cocoa

¹/₂ teaspoon baking powder
1 teaspoon baking soda
¹/₂ teaspoon cinnamon
¹/₂ teaspoon ground cloves
2 cups finely chopped seeded
  zucchini
¹/₂ cup chocolate chips

Cream margarine, oil and sugar in mixer bowl until light and fluffy. Add eggs, vanilla and sour milk; beat well. Mix flour, baking cocoa, baking powder, baking soda, cinnamon and cloves together. Add to creamed mixture; mix well. Stir in zucchini. Pour into greased and floured 9x13-inch cake pan. Sprinkle with chocolate chips. Bake at 325 degrees for 40 to 45 minutes or until cake tests done. Yield: 15 servings.

Approx Per Serving: Cal 336; Prot 4 g; Carbo 44 g; Fiber 1 g;
  T Fat 17 g; 44% Calories from Fat; Chol 30 mg; Sod 152 mg.

Texas Chocolate Cake

2 cups flour
2 cups sugar
1 teaspoon baking soda
1 cup water
¹/₄ cup baking cocoa

1 cup margarine
¹/₂ cup buttermilk
2 eggs
¹/₂ teaspoon salt
1 teaspoon vanilla extract

Combine flour, sugar and baking soda in mixer bowl; mix well. Combine water, baking cocoa and margarine in saucepan. Bring to a boil, stirring until well mixed. Cool for 5 minutes. Add to flour mixture; mix well. Add buttermilk, eggs, salt and vanilla; beat well. Pour into greased 9x13-inch cake pan. Bake at 400 degrees for 20 minutes or until cake tests done. Yield: 15 servings.

Approx Per Serving: Cal 290; Prot 3 g; Carbo 41 g; Fiber 1 g;
  T Fat 13 g; 41% Calories from Fat; Chol 29 mg; Sod 288 mg.

*Whoever has a heart full of love always
has something to give.*

Nelson's Devil's Food Cake

This recipe was given to me by Mrs. M. L. Nelson
of Blevins, Arkansas in the late 1930s. Her husband served on the
Blevins School Board for a number of years. —Dorothy Bradford Ward

1/2 cup butter, softened
2 cups sugar
2 eggs
2 cups flour
3/4 cup baking cocoa
1 teaspoon cinnamon

1 teaspoon nutmeg
1 cup buttermilk
1 teaspoon baking soda
1/2 cup boiling water
1 teaspoon vanilla extract
Devil's Food Frosting

Cream butter and sugar in mixer bowl until light and fluffy. Add eggs; beat well. Sift flour, baking cocoa, cinnamon and nutmeg together. Add to creamed mixture alternately with mixture of buttermilk and baking soda, beating well after each addition. Add boiling water and vanilla; mix well. Pour into greased and floured 9x13-inch cake pan. Bake at 350 degrees for 15 minutes or until cake tests done. Cool to room temperature. Frost with Devil's Food Frosting. Yield: 15 servings.

Approx Per Serving: Cal 424; Prot 5 g; Carbo 72 g; Fiber 2 g;
 T Fat 15 g; 30% Calories from Fat; Chol 64 mg; Sod 193 mg.

Devil's Food Frosting

1/3 cup baking cocoa
2 cups sugar
3/4 cup milk

2 tablespoons corn syrup
1/2 cup butter

Sift baking cocoa and sugar into heavy saucepan. Add milk, corn syrup and butter. Bring to a boil. Boil for 5 to 8 minutes or until thickened, stirring constantly. Remove from heat; beat until creamy. Yield: 15 servings.

Approx Per Serving: Cal 177; Prot 1 g; Carbo 30 g; Fiber 1 g;
 T Fat 7 g; 33% Calories from Fat; Chol 18 mg; Sod 59 mg.

Only when you are silent can you
learn something new.

Easy Devil's Food Cake

1/2 cup shortening
1 cup sugar
1 egg, beaten
1/2 cup baking cocoa
1 1/2 cups flour

1/4 teaspoon salt
1 cup buttermilk
1 teaspoon baking soda
1 teaspoon vanilla extract

Cream shortening and sugar in mixer bowl until light and fluffy. Add egg; beat well. Sift baking cocoa, flour and salt together. Add to creamed mixture alternately with mixture of buttermilk and baking soda, beating well after each addition. Add vanilla; mix well. Pour into 2 greased and floured 8-inch cake pans. Bake at 350 degrees for 15 minutes or until layers test done. Cool in pan for several minutes. Remove to wire rack to cool. Spread with favorite icing before cake cools completely. Yield: 12 servings.

Approx Per Serving: Cal 222; Prot 3 g; Carbo 31 g; Fiber 1 g;
    T Fat 10 g; 39% Calories from Fat; Chol 19 mg; Sod 141 mg.

Hot Fudge Cake

1 2-layer package milk chocolate
   cake mix
1 gallon vanilla ice cream
1 16-ounce can chocolate syrup

1 14-ounce can sweetened
   condensed milk
1/2 cup butter

Bake chocolate cake using package directions for 9x13-inch cake pan. Cool to room temperature. Cut cake to size of ice cream. Layer cake, ice cream and cake in freezer container. Freeze until firm. Combine chocolate syrup, condensed milk and butter in double boiler. Cook over boiling water until thickened, stirring constantly. Slice cake into servings; top with chocolate syrup. Freeze leftover cake. Store leftover chocolate syrup in refrigerator. Yield: 12 servings.

Approx Per Serving: Cal 928; Prot 14 g; Carbo 135 g; Fiber 1 g;
    T Fat 41 g; 38% Calories from Fat; Chol 111 mg; Sod 501 mg.

He who hesitates gets leftovers.

Christmas Cake

This cake has been in the Sisk family for many years and
is always served at Christmas. —Mrs. Irvin Sisk, Jr.

2 cups packed brown sugar
1/2 cup butter, softened
1 cup sour cream
3 eggs
1 teaspoon baking soda
2 cups flour

1/2 cup baking cocoa
1 cup chopped English walnuts
1 cup dark raisins
1 teaspoon vanilla extract
Old-Fashioned Caramel Icing

Beat first 4 ingredients in mixer bowl. Sift baking soda, flour and baking cocoa together. Add walnuts and raisins. Add to brown sugar mixture; mix well. Stir in vanilla. Pour into 2 greased and floured 9-inch cake pans. Bake at 350 degrees for 15 minutes or until layers test done. Cool in pan for several minutes. Remove to wire rack to cool completely. Spread Old-Fashioned Caramel Icing between layers and on top and side of cake. Yield: 15 servings.

Approx Per Serving: Cal 589; Prot 6 g; Carbo 94 g; Fiber 2 g;
    T Fat 23 g; 34% Calories from Fat; Chol 98 mg; Sod 210 mg.

Old-Fashioned Caramel Icing

1/2 cup sugar
3/4 cup milk
2 cups sugar

1/2 cup butter
1 egg, slightly beaten
1 teaspoon vanilla extract

Caramelize 1/2 cup sugar in heavy skillet over low heat until light brown, stirring constantly. Combine milk, 2 cups sugar, butter and egg in saucepan. Cook over low heat until butter melts, stirring constantly. Increase heat. Cook until mixture boils. Add caramelized sugar. Cook at a rapid boil to 234 to 240 degrees on candy thermometer, soft-ball stage, stirring frequently. Remove from heat. Add vanilla. Beat until of spreading consistency. Yield: 15 servings.

Approx Per Serving: Cal 196; Prot 1 g; Carbo 34 g; Fiber 0 g;
    T Fat 7 g; 31% Calories from Fat; Chol 32 mg; Sod 62 mg.

No kindness is ever wasted.

Coconut-Black Walnut Pound Cake

My mother always made a black walnut cake for Christmas.
Now, 60 years later, my family still enjoys her recipe. —Lucille Burkett

1 cup oil
2 cups sugar
4 eggs, beaten
3 cups flour
1/2 teaspoon baking soda
2 1/2 teaspoons baking powder
1 cup buttermilk
2 teaspoons coconut extract

1 teaspoon black walnut extract
1 cup chopped black walnuts
1 cup flaked coconut
1 cup sugar
1/2 cup water
1 teaspoon coconut extract
2 tablespoons margarine

Cream oil and 2 cups sugar in mixer bowl until light and fluffy. Add eggs; beat well. Mix flour, baking soda and baking powder together. Add to creamed mixture alternately with buttermilk, beating well after each addition. Stir in flavorings, walnuts and coconut. Pour into greased and floured 10-inch tube pan. Bake at 325 degrees for 65 minutes or until cake tests done. Cool in pan for several minutes. Remove to serving plate. Combine 1 cup sugar and water in saucepan. Bring to a boil. Simmer for 5 minutes, stirring frequently. Remove from heat. Stir in 1 teaspoon coconut extract and margarine. Drizzle over cake. Yield: 16 servings.

Approx Per Serving: Cal 462; Prot 7 g; Carbo 60 g; Fiber 2 g;
    T Fat 23 g; 44% Calories from Fat; Chol 54 mg; Sod 130 mg.

Coconut Cake

1 2-layer package yellow cake mix
1 16-ounce can cream of coconut
1 14-ounce can sweetened
   condensed milk

16 ounces whipped topping
1 cup flaked coconut

Bake cake using package directions for 9x13-inch cake pan. Pierce holes in hot cake. Pour cream of coconut and condensed milk over cake. Cool to room temperature. Spread whipped topping over top; sprinkle with coconut. Chill until serving time. Yield: 12 servings.

Approx Per Serving: Cal 639; Prot 8 g; Carbo 83 g; Fiber 1 g;
    T Fat 33 g; 45% Calories from Fat; Chol 11 mg; Sod 267 mg.

Life is what happens when you're
making other plans.

Earthquake Cake

1 cup coconut
1 cup chopped pecans
1 2-layer package German chocolate
   cake mix
8 ounces cream cheese, softened

1 1-pound package confectioners'
   sugar
1/2 cup butter, softened
1 teaspoon vanilla extract

Sprinkle coconut and pecans in buttered 9x13-inch cake pan. Prepare chocolate cake using package directions. Pour into prepared pan. Bake at 350 degrees for 1 hour or until cake tests done. Cool to room temperature. Combine cream cheese, confectioners' sugar, butter and vanilla in mixer bowl. Beat until of spreading consistency. Spread over cooled cake. Yield: 15 servings.

Approx Per Serving: Cal 531; Prot 4 g; Carbo 68 g; Fiber 1 g;
    T Fat 28 g; 47% Calories from Fat; Chol 77 mg; Sod 434 mg.

Gingerbread with Hot Buttered Rum Sauce

2 cups flour
1 1-pound package light brown
   sugar
3/4 cup margarine
2 teaspoons ginger
2 teaspoons cinnamon
1 teaspoon nutmeg

1 teaspoon baking soda
2 eggs
1 cup buttermilk
1/2 cup finely chopped pecans
8 ounces whipped topping
Hot Buttered Rum Sauce

Combine flour and brown sugar in bowl; mix well. Cut in margarine until crumbly. Reserve 1 cup mixture. Add ginger, cinnamon, nutmeg and baking soda to remaining mixture; mix well. Add eggs; mix well. Stir in buttermilk. Pour into ungreased 8x12-inch cake pan. Sprinkle with reserved brown sugar mixture. Sprinkle pecans on top. Bake at 350 degrees for 30 to 40 minutes or until cake tests done. Cool slightly. Cut into squares. Top with whipped topping; drizzle with Hot Buttered Rum Sauce. Yield: 15 servings.

Approx Per Serving: Cal 464; Prot 4 g; Carbo 61 g; Fiber 1 g;
    T Fat 23 g; 45% Calories from Fat; Chol 32 mg; Sod 286 mg.

Hot Buttered Rum Sauce

1 cup sugar
1/2 cup evaporated milk

1/2 cup margarine
1/2 teaspoon rum extract

Combine sugar, evaporated milk and margarine in saucepan. Cook over medium heat until sugar and margarine are melted and mixture thickens, stirring frequently. Remove from heat. Stir in rum extract. Yield: 15 servings.

Approx Per Serving: Cal 117; Prot 1 g; Carbo 14 g; Fiber 0 g;
    T Fat 7 g; 50% Calories from Fat; Chol 2 mg; Sod 81 mg.

Grandma Baker's Cake

My mother made this during the Great Depression. —Bonnie B. Harris

⅓ cup shortening
1 cup sugar
2 eggs
1 teaspoon vanilla extract

1¼ cups flour
1 tablespoon baking powder
½ cup milk

Cream shortening and sugar by hand in bowl until light and fluffy. Add eggs and vanilla; mix well. Add mixture of flour and baking powder alternately with milk, stirring just until mixed. Pour into buttered 9x9-inch cake pan. Bake at 350 degrees for 30 minutes or until cake tests done. Serve with fresh or canned fruit. Yield: 9 servings.

Approx Per Serving: Cal 245; Prot 4 g; Carbo 37 g; Fiber <1 g;
    T Fat 9 g; 35% Calories from Fat; Chol 49 mg; Sod 132 mg.

Mexican Fruitcake

2 cups flour
2 cups sugar
2 teaspoons baking soda
1 20-ounce can crushed pineapple
½ cup chopped pecans

2 eggs, beaten
8 ounces cream cheese, softened
¼ cup margarine, softened
2 cups confectioners' sugar
2 teaspoons vanilla extract

Sift flour, sugar and baking soda together into mixer bowl. Add undrained crushed pineapple, pecans and eggs; mix well. Pour into greased and floured 9x13-inch cake pan. Bake at 325 degrees for 45 minutes or until cake tests done. Cool to room temperature. Combine cream cheese, margarine, confectioners' sugar and vanilla in mixer bowl; mix well. Spread over cooled cake. Chill until serving time. Flavor is enhanced after 2 or 3 days. Yield: 15 servings.

Approx Per Serving: Cal 373; Prot 4 g; Carbo 64 g; Fiber 1 g;
    T Fat 12 g; 28% Calories from Fat; Chol 45 mg; Sod 201 mg.

Many can rise to the occasion, but few
know when to sit down.

Mississippi Mud Cake

1/4 cup baking cocoa
1 1/2 cups flour
1 cup butter, softened
2 cups sugar
4 eggs
1 teaspoon vanilla extract
1 7-ounce can coconut
1 1/2 cups chopped pecans

1 7-ounce jar marshmallow creme
1/3 cup margarine
1/2 cup evaporated milk
1 1-pound package confectioners' sugar
1/3 cup baking cocoa
1 teaspoon vanilla extract

Mix 1/4 cup baking cocoa and flour together. Cream butter and sugar in mixer bowl until light and fluffy. Add eggs; beat well. Add flour mixture; mix well. Stir in 1 teaspoon vanilla, coconut and pecans. Pour into greased 9x13-inch cake pan. Bake at 350 degrees for 30 minutes. Spread marshmallow creme over hot cake. Cool to room temperature. Combine margarine, evaporated milk, confectioners' sugar, 1/3 cup baking cocoa and 1 teaspoon vanilla in mixer bowl; beat until of spreading consistency. Spread over cooled cake. Yield: 15 servings.

Approx Per Serving: Cal 655; Prot 6 g; Carbo 93 g; Fiber 4 g;
     T Fat 31 g; 42% Calories from Fat; Chol 92 mg; Sod 190 mg.

Chocolate Cherry Ring

2 cups flour
3/4 cup sugar
1 teaspoon baking soda
1 teaspoon cinnamon
1/8 teaspoon salt
2 eggs, beaten

1/2 cup oil
2 teaspoons vanilla extract
1 21-ounce can cherry pie filling
1 cup semi-sweet chocolate chips
1 cup chopped walnuts

Combine flour, sugar, baking soda, cinnamon and salt in mixer bowl. Mix eggs, oil and vanilla together in bowl. Add to flour mixture; beat well. Fold in pie filling, chocolate chips and walnuts. Pour into greased and floured 10-inch bundt cake pan. Bake at 350 degrees for 1 hour or until surface is brown and cracked. Cool in pan for several minutes. Remove to wire rack to cool completely. Garnish with sifted confectioners' sugar. Serve with whipped cream or ice cream. Yield: 10 servings.

Approx Per Serving: Cal 483; Prot 6 g; Carbo 61 g; Fiber 3 g;
     T Fat 26 g; 46% Calories from Fat; Chol 43 mg; Sod 145 mg.

*The world stands aside to let anyone pass who
knows where he's going.*

Oatmeal-Chocolate Chip Cake

This easy and moist cake was one of the first my daughter
learned to make. —Wanda Williams

1³/₄ cups boiling water
1 cup oats
1 cup packed brown sugar
1 cup sugar
¹/₂ cup margarine
2 eggs, slightly beaten

1³/₄ cups flour
1 teaspoon baking soda
¹/₂ teaspoon salt
1 tablespoon baking cocoa
2 cups chocolate chips
³/₄ cup chopped walnuts

Pour boiling water over oats in bowl. Let stand for 10 minutes. Add brown sugar, sugar and margarine, stirring until margarine is melted. Add eggs; mix well. Sift flour, baking soda, salt and baking cocoa together. Add to sugar mixture; mix well. Stir in 1 cup chocolate chips. Pour into greased and floured 9x13-inch cake pan. Sprinkle remaining 1 cup chocolate chips and walnuts over top. Bake at 350 degrees for 35 to 40 minutes or until cake tests done. Yield: 15 servings.

Approx Per Serving: Cal 412; Prot 5 g; Carbo 60 g; Fiber 2 g;
    T Fat 19 g; 40% Calories from Fat; Chol 28 mg; Sod 219 mg.

Orange Slice Cake

1 pound chopped dates
1 pound orange slice candy, chopped
2 cups chopped pecans
1   7-ounce can flaked coconut
3¹/₂ cups flour
1 cup margarine, softened

2 cups sugar
4 eggs
¹/₂ cup buttermilk
1 teaspoon baking soda
2 cups confectioners' sugar
1 cup orange juice

Combine dates, orange slice candy, pecans and coconut in bowl. Sift flour over mixture; toss to coat. Cream margarine and sugar in mixer bowl until light and fluffy. Beat in eggs 1 at a time. Add mixture of buttermilk and baking soda; mix well. Pour into flour mixture, stirring to mix. Pour into greased and floured tube pan. Bake at 250 degrees for 3 hours. Cool in pan for several minutes. Invert onto serving plate. Combine confectioners' sugar and orange juice in bowl; mix well. Drizzle over hot cake. Yield: 12 servings.

Approx Per Serving: Cal 958; Prot 9 g; Carbo 154 g; Fiber 7 g;
    T Fat 36 g; 33% Calories from Fat; Chol 71 mg; Sod 314 mg.

There is no machine that can take the place
of a good neighbor.

Buttermilk Pound Cake

This was the favorite cake of my daughter Vicki Rush,
cancer victim, June 7, 1992. —Clara Jacobs

³/₄ cup shortening	¹/₂ teaspoon baking soda
2 cups sugar	¹/₈ teaspoon salt
3 eggs	1 cup buttermilk
2 cups flour	1 teaspoon almond extract
1 teaspoon baking powder	1 teaspoon vanilla extract

Cream shortening and sugar in mixer bowl until light and fluffy. Beat in eggs 1 at a time. Sift flour, baking powder, baking soda and salt together. Add alternately with buttermilk to creamed mixture, beating constantly. Add flavorings. Pour into greased and floured tube pan. Bake at 350 degrees for 45 minutes. Cool in pan. Invert onto serving plate. Yield: 12 servings.

Approx Per Serving: Cal 348; Prot 4 g; Carbo 51 g; Fiber 1 g;
    T Fat 15 g; 37% Calories from Fat; Chol 54 mg; Sod 124 mg.

Golden Pound Cake

1 2-layer package yellow cake mix	¹/₂ cup oil
1 4-ounce package vanilla instant pudding mix	4 eggs

Combine all ingredients in mixer bowl. Beat for 2 minutes at medium speed. Pour into greased and floured tube pan. Bake at 350 degrees for 45 to 55 minutes. Cool in pan for several minutes. Invert onto serving plate. Yield: 12 servings.

Approx Per Serving: Cal 324; Prot 4 g; Carbo 45 g; Fiber <1 g;
    T Fat 15 g; 40% Calories from Fat; Chol 71 mg; Sod 348 mg.

Sour Cream Pound Cake

1¹/₂ cups butter, softened	¹/₂ teaspoon salt
3 cups sugar	¹/₄ teaspoon baking soda
6 eggs	1 cup sour cream
3 cups flour	1¹/₂ teaspoons vanilla extract

Cream butter and sugar in mixer bowl until light and fluffy. Beat in eggs 1 at a time. Mix flour, salt and baking soda together. Add to creamed mixture alternately with sour cream, beating well. Stir in vanilla. Pour into greased tube pan. Bake at 300 degrees for 1 hour and 20 minutes or until cake tests done. Do not open oven during baking. Cool in pan for several minutes. Invert onto serving plate. Yield: 12 servings.

Approx Per Serving: Cal 592; Prot 7 g; Carbo 75 g; Fiber 1 g;
    T Fat 30 g; 45% Calories from Fat; Chol 177 mg; Sod 346 mg.

Prune Cake

2 cups self-rising flour
2 cups sugar
1 teaspoon nutmeg
1 teaspoon ground cloves
1 teaspoon cinnamon
4 eggs
1 cup cooked seeded prunes

1 cup oil
1 cup buttermilk
1½ cups sugar
1 cup buttermilk
½ teaspoon baking soda
¼ cup butter
1 teaspoon vanilla extract

Combine flour, 2 cups sugar, nutmeg, cloves and cinnamon in bowl; mix well. Beat in eggs 1 at a time. Add prunes, oil and 1 cup buttermilk; mix well. Pour into greased 9x13-inch cake pan. Bake at 325 degrees for 45 to 60 minutes or until cake tests done. Combine 1½ cups sugar, 1 cup buttermilk, baking soda and butter in saucepan. Bring to a boil. Simmer for 3 minutes, stirring constantly. Stir in vanilla. Pour over hot cake. Yield: 15 servings.

Approx Per Serving: Cal 444; Prot 5 g; Carbo 65 g; Fiber 1 g;
    T Fat 20 g; 39% Calories from Fat; Chol 66 mg; Sod 287 mg.

Rum Cake

1 2-layer package golden butter
   cake mix
1 cup water
1 4-ounce package vanilla instant
   pudding mix
½ cup oil
4 eggs

½ teaspoon rum extract
¾ cup chopped pecans
1 cup sugar
½ cup butter
½ cup water
½ teaspoon rum extract

Combine cake mix, water, pudding mix, oil, eggs, ½ teaspoon rum extract and pecans in bowl; mix well. Pour into greased and floured bundt pan. Bake at 325 degrees for 1 hour or until cake tests done. Combine sugar, butter and water in saucepan. Bring to a boil. Simmer for 3 to 4 minutes or until thickened, stirring constantly. Stir in ½ teaspoon rum extract. Pour over hot cake. Let stand for 30 minutes before removing from pan. Yield: 15 servings.

Approx Per Serving: Cal 413; Prot 4 g; Carbo 51 g; Fiber <1 g;
    T Fat 22 g; 48% Calories from Fat; Chol 73 mg; Sod 251 mg.

*How silent the woods would be if only
the best birds sang.*

Scratch Cake for-a-Bride

This recipe was given by a mother-in-law to a young bride
who could not cook. —Rev. N. Lorene Pritchett

1 cup sugar
2 eggs
1/2 cup evaporated milk
1/2 cup milk
1 teaspoon vanilla extract
6 tablespoons melted margarine
1 1/4 cups self-rising flour

1 teaspoon baking powder
1/4 teaspoon salt
1 cup sugar
1/4 cup baking cocoa
2 tablespoons melted margarine
1/4 cup evaporated milk
1 teaspoon vanilla extract

Combine 1 cup sugar, eggs, 1/2 cup evaporated milk, milk, 1 teaspoon vanilla and 6 tablespoons margarine in mixer bowl; mix well. Mix flour, baking powder and salt together. Add to sugar mixture; mix well. Pour into 2 greased and floured 9-inch cake pans. Bake at 350 degrees for 25 minutes or until cake tests done. Cool in pan for several minutes. Remove to wire rack to cool completely. Combine 1 cup sugar, baking cocoa and 2 tablespoons margarine in saucepan; mix well. Add 1/4 cup evaporated milk. Cook over medium heat until thickened, stirring constantly. Stir in 1 teaspoon vanilla. Spread between layers and over top and side of cooled cake. Yield: 12 servings.

Approx Per Serving: Cal 289; Prot 4 g; Carbo 46 g; Fiber 1 g;
    T Fat 11 g; 34% Calories from Fat; Chol 42 mg; Sod 329 mg.

Mom's Spice Cakes

3 eggs, slightly beaten
2 cups sugar
2 cups self-rising flour
1 cup oil
1   8-ounce jar junior size baby food
    prunes

1 teaspoon cinnamon
1 teaspoon nutmeg
1 teaspoon vanilla extract
1 cup chopped pecans

Combine eggs, sugar, flour, oil, baby food prunes, cinnamon, nutmeg and vanilla in mixer bowl. Beat at medium speed for 2 minutes. Stir in pecans. Pour into 2 greased and floured 5x9-inch loaf pans. Bake at 325 degrees for 1 hour or until loaves test done. Serve with butter or cream cheese. Yield: 24 servings.

Approx Per Serving: Cal 231; Prot 2 g; Carbo 27 g; Fiber 1 g;
    T Fat 13 g; 50% Calories from Fat; Chol 27 mg; Sod 122 mg.

Because things go wrong is no reason
you must go with them.

Sour Cream Spice Cake

2 cups flour
1¹/₂ cups packed brown sugar
1¹/₄ teaspoons baking soda
1 teaspoon baking powder
1 teaspoon salt
2 teaspoons cinnamon
³/₄ teaspoon ground cloves
¹/₂ teaspoon nutmeg
¹/₂ cup butter, softened

¹/₄ cup shortening
2 eggs, beaten
1 cup sour cream
¹/₂ cup water
1 cup chopped raisins
¹/₂ cup chopped walnuts
1 package vanilla whipped frosting
  mix

Combine flour, brown sugar, baking soda, baking powder, salt, cinnamon, cloves, nutmeg, butter, shortening, eggs, sour cream, water, raisins and walnuts in mixer bowl. Beat at low speed for 30 seconds. Beat at high speed for 3 minutes. Pour into greased and floured 9x13-inch cake pan. Bake at 350 degrees for 40 to 45 minutes or until cake tests done. Cool to room temperature. Prepare frosting mix using package directions. Spread over cooled cake. Yield: 15 servings.

Approx Per Serving: Cal 479; Prot 4 g; Carbo 71 g; Fiber 1 g;
    T Fat 21 g; 39% Calories from Fat; Chol 52 mg; Sod 386 mg.

Sugarplum Cake

2 cups flour
1¹/₂ cups sugar
2¹/₂ teaspoons baking powder
1¹/₄ teaspoons baking soda
1 teaspoon salt
1 teaspoon each cinnamon, nutmeg
  and allspice

1 cup buttermilk
³/₄ cup oil
3 eggs
1 cup chopped cooked prunes
1 cup chopped pecans
Butter Sauce

Combine first 12 ingredients in mixer bowl. Beat at low speed for 3 to 5 minutes or until mixed well. Stir in pecans. Pour into greased 9x13-inch cake pan. Bake at 350 degrees for 35 to 40 minutes or until cake tests done. Serve warm with Butter Sauce. Yield: 12 servings.

Approx Per Serving: Cal 549; Prot 6 g; Carbo 67 g; Fiber 2 g;
    T Fat 30 g; 48% Calories from Fat; Chol 54 mg; Sod 472 mg.

Butter Sauce

1 cup sugar
2 tablespoons cornstarch
¹/₂ cup buttermilk

¹/₂ cup margarine
1 teaspoon vanilla extract

Combine sugar, cornstarch, buttermilk and margarine in saucepan. Bring to a boil. Cook for 1 minute, stirring constantly. Stir in vanilla. Serve warm. Yield: 12 servings.

Approx Per Serving: Cal 142; Prot <1 g; Carbo 18 g; Fiber <1 g;
    T Fat 8 g; 48% Calories from Fat; Chol <1 mg; Sod 100 mg.

Cookies

Butterscotch Brownies

1/2 cup shortening
2 cups packed dark brown sugar
2 eggs, beaten
1 teaspoon vanilla extract

2 cups flour, sifted
2 teaspoons baking powder
1/2 teaspoon salt
1 cup chopped pecans

Cream shortening and brown sugar in mixer bowl until light and fluffy. Beat in eggs and vanilla. Reserve 1/4 cup flour. Sift remaining flour, baking powder and salt together. Add to creamed mixture; mix well. Coat pecans with reserved flour. Stir into mixture. Press into greased 9x13-inch baking dish. Bake at 350 degrees for 30 minutes. Do not overbake. Store in airtight container. Yield: 15 servings.

Approx Per Serving: Cal 323; Prot 3 g; Carbo 50 g; Fiber 1 g;
    T Fat 13 g; 36% Calories from Fat; Chol 28 mg; Sod 141 mg.

Muffin Brownies

1 cup margarine
4 ounces semisweet chocolate
4 eggs, beaten
1 3/4 cups sugar

1 cup flour
1 teaspoon vanilla extract
1 1/2 cups chopped pecans

Melt margarine and chocolate in saucepan over low heat, stirring frequently. Cool slightly. Combine chocolate mixture, eggs and sugar in mixer bowl; beat well. Add flour and vanilla; mix well. Stir in pecans. Spoon into greased or paper-lined muffin cups. Bake at 325 degrees for 30 minutes or until muffins test done. Yield: 24 servings.

Approx Per Serving: Cal 229; Prot 2 g; Carbo 23 g; Fiber 1 g;
    T Fat 15 g; 57% Calories from Fat; Chol 36 mg; Sod 101 mg.

Turtle Brownies

1 2-layer package German chocolate
  cake mix
1/3 cup evaporated milk
3/4 cup melted margarine

1 14-ounce package caramels
1/3 cup evaporated milk
2 cups chocolate chips
1 cup chopped pecans

Combine cake mix, 1/3 cup evaporated milk and margarine in bowl; mix until lumpy. Pour half the batter into greased 9x13-inch baking dish. Bake at 325 degrees for 17 minutes. Melt caramels in 1/3 cup evaporated milk in saucepan over low heat, stirring frequently. Pour over baked layer; sprinkle with chocolate chips and pecans. Pour remaining batter over top. Bake at 325 degrees for 25 to 27 minutes or until brownies test done. Yield: 15 servings.

Approx Per Serving: Cal 515; Prot 5 g; Carbo 64 g; Fiber 2 g;
    T Fat 30 g; 49% Calories from Fat; Chol 4 mg; Sod 501 mg.

Festive Caramel Bars

32 caramel candy squares
1 5-ounce can evaporated milk
1 cup flour
1 cup quick-cooking oats
1/2 cup packed brown sugar
1/2 teaspoon baking soda

1/4 teaspoon salt
1/2 cup melted margarine
1 cup chopped pecans
1 1/2 cups "M & M's" Plain or Peanut
  Chocolate Candies

Melt caramels in evaporated milk in heavy saucepan over low heat, stirring frequently. Combine flour, oats, brown sugar, baking soda and salt in bowl; mix well. Add margarine, stirring until crumbly. Stir in pecans. Reserve 1 cup mixture. Press remaining mixture into greased 9x13-inch baking dish. Bake at 375 degrees for 10 minutes. Sprinkle with 1 cup chocolate candies; drizzle with melted caramels. Sprinkle with reserved flour mixture; top with remaining 1/2 cup candies. Bake for 20 to 25 minutes longer or until golden brown. Cool slightly. Chill for 30 minutes. Cut into bars. Yield: 15 servings.

Approx Per Serving: Cal 339; Prot 5 g; Carbo 44 g; Fiber 2 g;
    T Fat 17 g; 44% Calories from Fat; Chol 3 mg; Sod 201 mg.

*Life is not a cup to be drained, but a
measure to be filled.*

Carrot Drop Cookies

1 cup shortening
³/₄ cup sugar
1 teaspoon vanilla extract
1 teaspoon lemon juice
1 cup cooked mashed carrots
¹/₂ teaspoon salt
2¹/₂ cups flour

2 teaspoons baking powder
2 cups confectioners' sugar
Salt to taste
1 tablespoon melted butter
3¹/₂ tablespoons orange juice
1 teaspoon grated orange rind

Cream shortening and sugar in mixer bowl until light and fluffy. Add vanilla, lemon juice and mashed carrots; beat well. Sift ¹/₂ teaspoon salt, flour and baking powder together 3 times. Add to creamed mixture, stirring well. Batter will be very stiff. Drop by teaspoonfuls onto greased cookie sheet. Bake at 400 degrees for 10 minutes. Do not brown. Cool in pan for several minutes. Remove to wire rack to cool completely. Combine confectioners' sugar, salt to taste, butter, orange juice and orange rind in mixer bowl; mix well. Spread on cookies. Yield: 60 servings.

Approx Per Serving: Cal 79; Prot 1 g; Carbo 11 g; Fiber <1 g;
   T Fat 4 g; 41% Calories from Fat; Chol 1 mg; Sod 34 mg.

Angel Nut Bars

1 cup sugar
¹/₂ cup milk
1 cup butter
1 egg, slightly beaten
1 teaspoon vanilla extract
1 cup chopped pecans

1 cup graham cracker crumbs
1   16-ounce package graham crackers
1 cup confectioners' sugar
¹/₄ cup margarine, softened
¹/₂ teaspoon vanilla extract
1 tablespoon (about) milk

Combine sugar, ¹/₂ cup milk, butter, egg, 1 teaspoon vanilla, pecans and 1 cup graham cracker crumbs in saucepan. Bring to a boil, stirring frequently. Layer graham crackers on 10x15-inch cookie sheet. Spread with cooked mixture. Top with graham cracker layer. Combine confectioners' sugar, margarine, ¹/₂ teaspoon vanilla and enough milk to make of spreading consistency in bowl. Beat until smooth. Spread over graham crackers. Let stand until cool. Cut into bars. Yield: 15 servings.

Approx Per Serving: Cal 447; Prot 4 g; Carbo 53 g; Fiber 1 g;
   T Fat 25 g; 50% Calories from Fat; Chol 49 mg; Sod 383 mg.

*Some people think they're generous because they
give away free advice.*

Cheesecake Bars

1/3 cup butter, softened
1/3 cup packed brown sugar
1 cup flour
1 cup finely chopped pecans
8 ounces cream cheese, softened

2 tablespoons milk
1 teaspoon vanilla extract
1/4 cup sugar
1 tablespoon lemon juice
1 egg

Combine butter, brown sugar, flour and pecans in bowl; mix well. Reserve 1 cup mixture. Press remaining mixture into ungreased 8x8-inch baking dish. Bake at 350 degrees for 15 minutes. Combine cream cheese, milk and vanilla in mixer bowl; mix well. Add sugar, lemon juice and egg; beat well. Spread over baked layer; sprinkle with reserved 1 cup mixture. Bake for 25 minutes longer. Cool slightly. Cut into bars. Refrigerate leftovers. Yield: 16 servings.

Approx Per Serving: Cal 202; Prot 3 g; Carbo 17 g; Fiber 1 g;
T Fat 14 g; 62% Calories from Fat; Chol 39 mg; Sod 82 mg.

Chinese Chew Bars

1/2 cup shortening
3 tablespoons brown sugar
1 cup sifted flour
1/2 teaspoon salt
2 eggs, beaten
1 cup packed brown sugar

2 tablespoons flour
1/2 teaspoon baking powder
1/2 cup chopped pecans
1 cup shredded coconut
1 teaspoon vanilla extract

Cream shortening and 3 tablespoons brown sugar in mixer bowl until light and fluffy. Stir in sifted flour and salt. Press into lightly greased 8x8-inch baking dish. Bake at 350 degrees for 15 minutes or until light brown. Remove from oven. Beat eggs and 1 cup brown sugar in bowl. Sift in 2 tablespoons flour and baking powder; mix well. Fold in pecans, coconut and vanilla. Spread over baked layer. Bake for 30 minutes longer. Let stand until cool. Cut into bars. Yield: 32 servings.

Approx Per Serving: Cal 112; Prot 1 g; Carbo 14 g; Fiber 1 g;
T Fat 6 g; 46% Calories from Fat; Chol 13 mg; Sod 55 mg.

*The best angle from which to approach any
problem is the try-angle.*

Chinese Chews

The timing and baking temperatures are very important in this recipe. —Vada Beebe

3 tablespoons sugar
1¹/₂ cups flour
Salt to taste
³/₄ cup butter
1 1-pound package brown sugar

3 eggs, beaten
³/₄ cup coconut
1 cup chopped pecans
¹/₄ teaspoon salt
1 teaspoon vanilla extract

Combine sugar, flour and salt in bowl. Cut in butter until crumbly. Press into greased 9x13-inch baking dish. Bake at 375 degrees for 15 minutes. Combine brown sugar and eggs in mixer bowl; beat well. Stir in coconut, pecans, salt and vanilla. Pour over baked layer. Reduce oven temperature to 350 degrees. Bake for 25 minutes. Yield: 40 servings.

Approx Per Serving: Cal 126; Prot 1 g; Carbo 17 g; Fiber <1 g;
    T Fat 6 g; 45% Calories from Fat; Chol 25 mg; Sod 53 mg.

Chocolate Chip Chews

¹/₂ cup margarine, softened
¹/₂ cup packed brown sugar
1 cup flour
2 eggs, beaten
1 cup packed brown sugar
1¹/₂ teaspoons vanilla extract

2 tablespoons flour
1 teaspoon baking powder
¹/₂ teaspoon salt
1 cup chopped pecans
1 cup chocolate chips

Cream margarine and ¹/₂ cup brown sugar in mixer bowl until light and fluffy. Add 1 cup flour; mix well. Press into greased 9x13-inch baking dish. Bake at 350 degrees for 10 minutes. Combine eggs and 1 cup brown sugar in mixer bowl; mix well. Add vanilla, 2 tablespoons flour, baking powder and salt; mix well. Stir in pecans. Spread over baked layer; sprinkle with chocolate chips. Bake for 25 minutes longer. Cut while warm. Yield: 36 servings.

Approx Per Serving: Cal 131; Prot 1 g; Carbo 18 g; Fiber <1 g;
    T Fat 7 g; 45% Calories from Fat; Chol 12 mg; Sod 78 mg.

*Good nature is the oil that makes the day's
work go without squeaking.*

Chocolate Chip Cookies

$^2/_3$ cup shortening
$^2/_3$ cup butter, softened
1 cup sugar
1 cup packed brown sugar
2 eggs
2 teaspoons vanilla extract

3 cups flour
1 teaspoon baking soda
1 teaspoon salt
1 cup chopped pecans
2 cups semisweet chocolate chips

Cream shortening, butter, sugar and brown sugar in mixer bowl until light and fluffy. Add eggs and vanilla; beat well. Mix flour, baking soda and salt together. Add to creamed mixture; mix well. Stir in pecans and chocolate chips. Drop by tablespoonfuls onto nonstick cookie sheet. Bake at 350 degrees for 10 minutes. Cool in pan for several minutes. Remove to wire rack to cool completely. May bake for 8 minutes for chewy cookies. Yield: 36 servings.

Approx Per Serving: Cal 226; Prot 2 g; Carbo 27 g; Fiber 1 g;
    T Fat 13 g; 51% Calories from Fat; Chol 21 mg; Sod 120 mg.

German Chocolate Thumbprint Cookies

1 cup sugar
1 cup evaporated milk
$^1/_2$ cup butter
1 teaspoon vanilla extract
3 egg yolks, beaten

$1^1/_2$ cups chopped pecans
$1^1/_2$ cups flaked coconut
1   2-layer package German chocolate
    cake mix
$^1/_3$ cup melted butter

Combine sugar, evaporated milk, $^1/_2$ cup butter, vanilla and egg yolks in saucepan; mix well. Cook over medium heat for 10 to 13 minutes or until thickened, stirring constantly. Stir in pecans and coconut. Remove from heat. Cool slightly. Reserve $1^1/_4$ cups coconut mixture. Combine remaining mixture, cake mix and $^1/_3$ cup butter in mixer bowl; mix well. Shape into 1-inch balls; place on nonstick cookie sheet. Press thumbprint into each dough ball; fill indentation with $^1/_2$ teaspoon reserved coconut mixture. Bake at 350 degrees for 10 to 13 minutes or until set. Cool in pan for 5 minutes. Remove to wire rack to cool completely. Yield: 60 servings.

Approx Per Serving: Cal 109; Prot 1 g; Carbo 12 g; Fiber <1 g;
    T Fat 7 g; 53% Calories from Fat; Chol 19 mg; Sod 107 mg.

*Don't wait to do great things, do small
things in a great way.*

Dishpan Cookies

2 cups packed brown sugar
2 cups sugar
2 cups oil
2 teaspoons vanilla extract
4 eggs
4 cups flour

2 teaspoons baking soda
1 teaspoon salt
1½ cups quick-cooking oats
4 cups finely crushed cornflakes
2 cups chocolate chips

Cream brown sugar, sugar and oil in mixer bowl until light and fluffy. Add vanilla and eggs; beat well. Mix flour, baking soda and salt together. Add to creamed mixture; mix well. Stir in oats, cornflakes and chocolate chips. Drop by teaspoonfuls onto nonstick cookie sheet. Bake at 350 degrees for 8 minutes. Cool in pan for several minutes. Remove to wire rack to cool completely. Yield: 90 servings.

Approx Per Serving: Cal 143; Prot 1 g; Carbo 20 g; Fiber <1 g;
    T Fat 7 g; 41% Calories from Fat; Chol 9 mg; Sod 86 mg.

Fruitcake Cookies

½ cup butter, softened
⅔ cup packed brown sugar
1 egg, beaten
1 teaspoon baking soda
1½ tablespoons milk
1½ cups flour
1 teaspoon cinnamon
1 teaspoon nutmeg

1 teaspoon allspice
1 teaspoon cloves
¼ teaspoon salt
¼ cup thawed frozen orange juice
    concentrate
1½ pounds mixed candied fruit
4 cups chopped pecans

Cream butter and brown sugar in mixer bowl until light and fluffy. Add egg; beat well. Mix baking soda and milk together. Sift flour, spices and salt together. Add flour mixture alternately with milk mixture and orange juice concentrate to creamed mixture, beating well after each addition. Stir in candied fruit and pecans. Drop by teaspoonfuls onto greased cookie sheet. Bake at 300 degrees for 20 to 30 minutes or until light brown. Cool in pan for several minutes. Remove to wire rack to cool completely. Yield: 100 servings.

Approx Per Serving: Cal 78; Prot 1 g; Carbo 10 g; Fiber <1 g;
    T Fat 4 g; 47% Calories from Fat; Chol 5 mg; Sod 23 mg.

A smile is a curve that helps to set things straight.

Hazelnut Cookies

1½ cups shelled hazelnuts
½ cup butter, softened
½ cup sugar
2 eggs

½ teaspoon vanilla extract
2 cups flour
2 teaspoons baking powder
½ teaspoon salt

Spread hazelnuts on baking sheet. Toast in 350-degree oven for 10 minutes. Spread on dish towel. Rub together with towel to remove as much brown skin as possible. Grate half the hazelnuts; coarsely chop remaining hazelnuts. Cream butter and sugar in mixer bowl until light and fluffy. Add eggs and vanilla; beat well. Mix flour, baking powder, salt and grated hazelnuts together. Add to creamed mixture; mix well. Add chopped hazelnuts; mix well. Shape dough into two 16-inch long rolls; place on buttered cookie sheet. Bake at 350 degrees for 30 minutes or until light brown. Slice rolls into ½-inch diagonal slices; place on rack on cookie sheet. Bake for 15 minutes longer or until firm. Cool. Store in airtight container.
Yield: 48 servings.

Approx Per Serving: Cal 74; Prot 1 g; Carbo 7 g; Fiber 1 g;
T Fat 5 g; 57% Calories from Fat; Chol 14 mg; Sod 55 mg.

Lemon Bars

2 cups flour
½ cup confectioners' sugar
1 cup margarine
2 cups sugar
1 tablespoon flour
1 teaspoon baking powder

¼ teaspoon salt
4 eggs, well beaten
4 teaspoons grated lemon rind
¼ cup lemon juice
¼ cup confectioners' sugar

Sift 2 cups flour and ½ cup confectioners' sugar into bowl. Cut in margarine until blended. Pat into bottom of 9x13-inch baking dish. Bake at 300 degrees for 25 minutes or until brown. Combine sugar, 1 tablespoon flour, baking powder and salt in bowl. Add eggs, lemon rind and lemon juice; mix well. Pour over baked layer. Bake at 350 degrees for 25 to 30 minutes or until set. Sift remaining ¼ cup confectioners' sugar over top. Cut into bars. Let stand until cool. Yield: 100 servings.

Approx Per Serving: Cal 48; Prot 1 g; Carbo 7 g; Fiber <1 g;
T Fat 2 g; 38% Calories from Fat; Chol 9 mg; Sod 33 mg.

*Life is like an onion; you peel one layer at a time,
and sometimes you weep.*

No-Bake Cookies

*This was the first recipe I ever made as a 9-year-old, while standing
on a chair beside mom in the kitchen. —Sandra Franklin*

2 cups sugar
3 tablespoons baking cocoa
1/2 cup butter or margarine
1/2 cup milk

1/2 cup peanut butter
1 teaspoon vanilla
3 cups quick-cooking oats

Bring first 4 ingredients to a boil in saucepan. Boil for 1 to 2 minutes, stirring constantly. Remove from heat. Add peanut butter, vanilla and oats; mix well. Drop by teaspoonfuls onto waxed paper. Let stand until firm. Yield: 60 servings.

Approx Per Serving: Cal 70; Prot 1 g; Carbo 10 g; Fiber 1 g;
    T Fat 3 g; 37% Calories from Fat; Chol 4 mg; Sod 23 mg.

Oatmeal Lace Cookies

1 cup butter, softened
1 cup packed brown sugar
1 cup sugar
1 cup flour
1 teaspoon salt

2 teaspoons baking powder
2 eggs, beaten
1 teaspoon vanilla extract
1 cup chopped pecans
2 cups oats

Cream butter, brown sugar and sugar in mixer bowl. Add mixture of flour, salt and baking powder. Add eggs and vanilla; mix well. Stir in pecans and oats. Chill in refrigerator. Shape into rolls. Chill, covered, overnight. Cut into slices; place on nonstick cookie sheet. Bake at 375 degrees for 7 to 10 minutes or until light brown. Cool in pan for several minutes. Cool on wire rack. Yield: 60 servings.

Approx Per Serving: Cal 91; Prot 1 g; Carbo 12 g; Fiber <1 g;
    T Fat 5 g; 46% Calories from Fat; Chol 15 mg; Sod 77 mg.

Pecan Squares

2/3 cup confectioners' sugar
2 cups flour
1 cup butter, softened
2/3 cup melted butter

1/2 cup honey
3 tablespoons whipping cream
1/2 cup packed brown sugar
3 1/2 cups coarsely chopped pecans

Combine confectioners' sugar and flour in bowl; mix well. Cut in 1 cup butter until crumbly. Press into greased 9x13-inch baking dish. Bake at 350 degrees for 20 minutes. Combine melted butter, honey and cream in bowl; mix well. Add brown sugar; mix well. Stir in pecans. Spread over baked layer. Bake for 25 minutes longer. Cool completely before cutting into squares. Yield: 36 servings.

Approx Per Serving: Cal 219; Prot 2 g; Carbo 17 g; Fiber 1 g;
    T Fat 17 g; 67% Calories from Fat; Chol 25 mg; Sod 74 mg.

One-Pan Raisin and Spice Bars

1 cup raisins	1 teaspoon baking soda
1 cup water	1 teaspoon cinnamon
1/2 cup shortening	1 teaspoon nutmeg
1 cup sugar	1 teaspoon cloves
1 egg, well beaten	1/2 teaspoon salt
1 3/4 cups flour	1/2 cup confectioners' sugar

Combine raisins, water and shortening in large saucepan. Bring to a boil. Let stand until cool. Add sugar, egg, flour, baking soda, spices and salt; mix well. Pour into greased and floured 9x13-inch baking pan. Bake at 375 degrees for 20 minutes. Let stand until cool. Sprinkle with confectioners' sugar or frost with favorite frosting. Cut into bars. Yield: 20 servings.

Approx Per Serving: Cal 164; Prot 2 g; Carbo 28 g; Fiber 1 g;
    T Fat 6 g; 30% Calories from Fat; Chol 11 mg; Sod 99 mg.

Shortcake Pinwheels

3 cups sifted flour	3/4 cup shortening
4 1/2 teaspoons baking powder	2 eggs, beaten
1 1/2 teaspoons salt	1/2 cup milk
5 tablespoons sugar	1/2 cup melted margarine

Sift flour, baking powder, salt and sugar into mixer bowl. Add shortening; mix well. Combine eggs and milk in bowl. Stir quickly into dry ingredients. Roll into 8x21-inch rectangle on floured surface. Brush with melted margarine. Roll as for jelly roll. Chill, wrapped in waxed paper, for several hours. Cut into 1-inch slices; place cut side down on nonstick cookie sheet. Bake at 450 degrees for 15 minutes. Cool in pan for several minutes. Remove to serving dish. Serve warm with strawberries or cream. Yield: 8 servings.

Approx Per Serving: Cal 491; Prot 7 g; Carbo 42 g; Fiber 1 g;
    T Fat 33 g; 60% Calories from Fat; Chol 55 mg; Sod 743 mg.

The best way to keep happiness is to give it away.

Sugar Cookies

1 cup margarine, softened
1 cup confectioners' sugar
1 cup sugar
1 cup oil
1 tablespoon vanilla extract
1 teaspoon almond extract

1 teaspoon cream of tartar
1/2 teaspoon salt
1 teaspoon baking soda
41/2 cups flour
1/2 cup sugar

Cream margarine, confectioners' sugar and 1 cup sugar in mixer bowl until light and fluffy. Add oil and extracts; mix well. Mix cream of tartar, salt, baking soda and flour together. Add to creamed mixture; mix well. Chill for several hours. Shape into 1-inch balls; place on nonstick cookie sheet. Flatten with bottom of glass; sprinkle with sugar. Bake at 350 degrees for 10 to 15 minutes or until light brown. Cool in pan for several minutes. Remove to wire rack to cool completely. May sprinkle with tinted sugar for Christmas. Yield: 50 servings.

Approx Per Serving: Cal 146; Prot 1 g; Carbo 17 g; Fiber <1 g;
    T Fat 8 g; 50% Calories from Fat; Chol 0 mg; Sod 81 mg.

Tea Cakes

My grandmother, Mrs. Annie Morgan of Bluff City, kept these cookies in a bin in her cabinet. During World War II, my mother and I lived with her and my grandfather. One of my favorite memories is coming home to these cookies every day after school. —Mrs. Charlotte Woody

11/4 cups butter, softened
3 cups sugar
5 eggs
1 cup sour cream
2 tablespoons vanilla extract

1 teaspoon baking soda
1 teaspoon cream of tartar
4 to 5 cups flour
1/2 cup sugar

Cream butter and 3 cups sugar in mixer bowl until light and fluffy. Add eggs, sour cream and vanilla; beat well. Add baking soda and cream of tartar; mix well. Add enough flour to make a stiff batter. Drop by teaspoonfuls onto nonstick cookie sheet; sprinkle with sugar. Bake at 350 degrees for 15 to 20 minutes or until light brown. Cool in pan for several minutes. Remove to wire rack to cool completely.
Yield: 48 servings.

Approx Per Serving: Cal 166; Prot 2 g; Carbo 25 g; Fiber <1 g;
    T Fat 7 g; 35% Calories from Fat; Chol 37 mg; Sod 68 mg.

Pies

Almond Cream Pie

1 cup milk
3 egg yolks, beaten
³/4 cup sugar
3 tablespoons cornstarch
¹/4 teaspoon salt
1 cup milk

¹/2 cup sliced almonds
1 teaspoon almond extract
2 tablespoons butter
1 baked 9-inch pie shell
3 egg whites
6 tablespoons sugar

Heat 1 cup milk in saucepan until warm. Stir in mixture of egg yolks, ³/4 cup sugar, cornstarch, salt and 1 cup milk. Cook until thickened, stirring constantly; remove from heat. Stir in almonds, flavoring and butter. Let stand for 10 minutes; mix well. Pour into pie shell. Beat egg whites in mixer bowl until soft peaks form. Add 6 tablespoons sugar gradually, beating until stiff peaks form. Spread over pie, sealing to edge. Bake at 400 degrees for 5 minutes or until brown. Cool. May substitute whipped topping for meringue. Yield: 8 servings.

Approx Per Serving: Cal 359; Prot 7 g; Carbo 45 g; Fiber 1 g;
    T Fat 18 g; 43% Calories from Fat; Chol 96 mg; Sod 277 mg.

Your life either sheds light or casts a shadow.

Banana-Blueberry Pie

3 ounces cream cheese, softened
1/2 cup sugar
1 envelope whipped topping mix
2 bananas, sliced

1 baked 9-inch pie shell
1/2 21-ounce can blueberry pie
   filling

Beat cream cheese and sugar together in bowl. Prepare whipped topping mix using package directions. Fold into cream cheese mixture. Layer bananas and cream cheese mixture in baked pie shell. Chill in refrigerator for 30 minutes. Top with blueberry pie filling. Chill for 3 to 4 hours before serving. Yield: 8 servings.

Approx Per Serving: Cal 297; Prot 3 g; Carbo 42 g; Fiber 2 g;
   T Fat 14 g; 41% Calories from Fat; Chol 14 mg; Sod 194 mg.

Buttermilk Pie

1/4 cup butter, softened
2 cups sugar
3 tablespoons flour
3 eggs, beaten

1 cup buttermilk
1 teaspoon vanilla extract
1/2 teaspoon nutmeg
1 unbaked 9-inch pie shell

Cream butter and sugar in mixer bowl until light and fluffy. Add flour and eggs; mix well. Stir in buttermilk, vanilla and nutmeg. Pour into pie shell. Bake at 350 degrees for 45 minutes. Let stand until cool. Yield: 8 servings.

Approx Per Serving: Cal 410; Prot 5 g; Carbo 64 g; Fiber 1 g;
   T Fat 16 g; 34% Calories from Fat; Chol 97 mg; Sod 245 mg.

Toasted Coconut Pie

3 eggs, beaten
1 1/2 cups sugar
1/2 cup melted margarine
4 teaspoons lemon juice

1 teaspoon vanilla extract
1 3-ounce can flaked coconut
1 unbaked 9-inch pie shell

Combine eggs, sugar, margarine, lemon juice and vanilla in mixer bowl; beat well. Stir in coconut. Pour into unbaked pie shell. Bake at 350 degrees for 40 to 45 minutes or until knife inserted near center comes out clean. Cool before serving. Garnish with whipped cream and toasted coconut. Yield: 8 servings.

Approx Per Serving: Cal 438; Prot 4 g; Carbo 52 g; Fiber 2 g;
   T Fat 24 g; 49% Calories from Fat; Chol 80 mg; Sod 300 mg.

German's Sweet Chocolate Pie

4 ounces German's sweet chocolate
1/4 cup margarine
1   5-ounce can evaporated milk
1 1/2 cups sugar
3 tablespoons cornstarch
1/8 teaspoon salt

2 eggs
1 teaspoon vanilla extract
1 unbaked 10-inch pie shell
1 1/3 cups flaked coconut
1/2 cup chopped pecans

Melt chocolate and margarine in saucepan over low heat, stirring to mix. Remove from heat. Add evaporated milk gradually. Combine sugar, cornstarch and salt in bowl; mix well. Beat in eggs and vanilla. Add chocolate mixture gradually, beating well after each addition. Pour into unbaked pie shell. Combine coconut and pecans in bowl. Sprinkle over pie. Bake at 375 degrees for 45 minutes or until top is puffed. Cool for 4 hours before serving. Yield: 10 servings.

Approx Per Serving: Cal 444; Prot 5 g; Carbo 55 g; Fiber 2 g;
    T Fat 25 g; 48% Calories from Fat; Chol 47 mg; Sod 234 mg.

Fudge Pie

2 ounces unsweetened chocolate
1/2 cup butter
1 cup sugar
2 eggs, beaten

1/2 cup flour
1 teaspoon vanilla extract
Salt to taste

Melt chocolate and butter together in saucepan over low heat, stirring to mix. Remove from heat. Add sugar, eggs, flour, vanilla and salt; mix well. Pour into greased pie plate. Bake at 350 degrees for 20 minutes. May substitute 6 tablespoons baking cocoa and 2 tablespoons margarine for chocolate. Yield: 6 servings.

Approx Per Serving: Cal 379; Prot 4 g; Carbo 44 g; Fiber 2 g;
    T Fat 22 g; 51% Calories from Fat; Chol 112 mg; Sod 153 mg.

Cranberry and Apple Pie

1 3/4 cups sugar
1/4 cup flour
3 cups sliced peeled tart apples

2 cups cranberries
1 recipe 2-crust pie pastry
2 tablespoons butter

Combine sugar and flour in bowl; mix well. Layer apples, cranberries and sugar mixture in pastry-lined pie plate, beginning and ending with apples. Dot with butter; cover with remaining pie pastry. Seal and flute edge; cut vents in top. Cover edge with foil to prevent excessive browning. Bake at 425 degrees for 25 minutes. Remove foil. Bake for 15 to 25 minutes longer or until golden brown and juice begins to bubble through vents. Yield: 6 servings.

Approx Per Serving: Cal 595; Prot 4 g; Carbo 98 g; Fiber 4 g;
    T Fat 22 g; 33% Calories from Fat; Chol 10 mg; Sod 402 mg.

Heavenly Pie

2 7-ounce chocolate-almond candy
  bars

18 ounces whipped topping
1 baked 9-inch pie shell

Melt chocolate candy bars in saucepan over low heat. Cool slightly. Fold in whipped topping. Spoon into baked pie shell. Chill until serving time. Yield: 6 servings.

Approx Per Serving: Cal 770; Prot 10 g; Carbo 68 g; Fiber 4 g;
    T Fat 56 g; 62% Calories from Fat; Chol 11 mg; Sod 258 mg.

Homemade Lemon Pie

¼ cup (rounded) shortening
1 cup self-rising flour
3 tablespoons ice water
1 14-ounce can sweetened
  condensed milk
4 egg yolks, beaten

Grated rind of 1 lemon
Juice of 4 lemons
4 egg whites
3 tablespoons confectioners' sugar
2 drops of lemon juice

Cut shortening into flour in bowl until crumbly. Add ice water, stirring until mixture forms a ball. Roll into 9-inch circle on floured surface. Place in greased pie plate. Bake at 400 degrees for 6 to 10 minutes or until light brown. Combine condensed milk and egg yolks in bowl; mix well. Add lemon rind and juice of 4 lemons, beating until thickened. Pour into prepared pie plate. Beat egg whites until soft peaks form. Add confectioners' sugar gradually and 2 drops of lemon juice, beating until stiff peaks form. Spread over pie, sealing to edge. Bake at 400 degrees for 5 minutes or until meringue is brown. Yield: 8 servings.

Approx Per Serving: Cal 327; Prot 9 g; Carbo 44 g; Fiber 1 g;
    T Fat 14 g; 37% Calories from Fat; Chol 123 mg; Sod 261 mg.

*Children need love; especially when
they do not deserve it.*

Lemon Chess Pie

1 cup sugar
1 tablespoon cornmeal
1 tablespoon flour
Salt to taste
¼ cup milk

¼ cup melted margarine
Grated rind and juice of 2 lemons
4 eggs, beaten
1 unbaked 9-inch pie shell

Combine sugar, cornmeal, flour and salt in bowl; mix well. Add milk, margarine, lemon rind and lemon juice; beat well. Add eggs; mix well. Pour into pie shell. Bake at 350 degrees for 30 minutes or until knife inserted near center comes out clean. Do not overbake. Yield: 6 servings.

Approx Per Serving: Cal 420; Prot 7 g; Carbo 51 g; Fiber 1 g;
 T Fat 22 g; 46% Calories from Fat; Chol 143 mg; Sod 324 mg.

Macadamia Pie

1 cup milk
¼ cup sugar
¼ cup chopped toasted macadamia
 nuts
⅛ teaspoon salt
1 teaspoon vanilla extract
⅓ cup milk
3 egg yolks, beaten

1 tablespoon cornstarch
3 egg whites
½ cup sugar
1 baked 8-inch pie shell
1 cup whipping cream, whipped
¼ cup chopped toasted macadamia
 nuts

Combine milk, ¼ cup sugar, ¼ cup macadamia nuts, salt and vanilla in double boiler. Cook over boiling water until mixture is hot to touch; do not boil. Combine remaining ⅓ cup milk, egg yolks and cornstarch in bowl; mix well. Stir a small amount of hot mixture into egg mixture. Stir egg mixture into hot mixture. Cook until thickened, stirring constantly; remove from heat. Beat egg whites until soft peaks form. Add remaining ½ cup sugar gradually, beating until stiff peaks form. Fold gently into cooked mixture. Pour into pie shell. Let stand until cool. Top with whipped cream and remaining ¼ cup macadamia nuts. Yield: 8 servings.

Approx Per Serving: Cal 387; Prot 6 g; Carbo 32 g; Fiber 1 g;
 T Fat 27 g; 61% Calories from Fat; Chol 126 mg; Sod 206 mg.

*When you are in trouble, try to keep your
chin up and your mouth shut.*

Peach Pie

1 29-ounce can peach halves,
    drained
1 unbaked 9-inch pie shell
1/2 cup butter, softened

3/4 cup sugar
1 egg
2 tablespoons flour

Place peach halves cut side up in pie shell. Cream butter and sugar in mixer bowl until light and fluffy. Add egg and flour; mix well. Spread over peaches. Place pie plate on baking sheet to prevent overflow into oven. Bake at 425 degrees for 15 minutes. Reduce oven temperature to 400 degrees. Bake for 30 minutes longer. Yield: 8 servings.

Approx Per Serving: Cal 359; Prot 3 g; Carbo 45 g; Fiber 2 g;
    T Fat 20 g; 48% Calories from Fat; Chol 58 mg; Sod 248 mg.

The Best Pecan Pie

1/2 cup butter
1 cup light corn syrup
1 cup sugar
3 eggs, beaten
1/2 teaspoon lemon juice

1 teaspoon vanilla extract
Salt to taste
1 cup chopped pecans
1 unbaked 9-inch pie shell

Brown butter in saucepan over medium heat until golden brown, stirring constantly to prevent burning. Cool. Beat corn syrup, sugar and eggs in mixer bowl. Add lemon juice, vanilla and salt; mix well. Stir in pecans and browned butter. Pour into unbaked pie shell. Bake at 425 degrees for 10 minutes. Reduce oven temperature to 325 degrees. Bake for 40 minutes longer. Yield: 8 servings.

Approx Per Serving: Cal 555; Prot 5 g; Carbo 69 g; Fiber 1 g;
    T Fat 31 g; 49% Calories from Fat; Chol 111 mg; Sod 279 mg.

Pecan Chiffon Pie

1 cup dark corn syrup
2/3 cup packed brown sugar
3 egg yolks, beaten
1 envelope unflavored gelatin
1/2 cup cold water

1/2 to 3/4 cup chopped pecans
3 egg whites, stiffly beaten
1 cup whipping cream, whipped
1 baked 9-inch pie shell

Combine corn syrup, brown sugar and egg yolks in saucepan; mix well. Cook over low heat until thickened, stirring constantly. Soften gelatin in cold water. Add to hot mixture, stirring until dissolved. Cool to room temperature. Add pecans; mix well. Fold in stiffly beaten egg whites and whipped cream. Pour into baked pie shell. Chill until serving time. Yield: 8 servings.

Approx Per Serving: Cal 526; Prot 6 g; Carbo 66 g; Fiber 1 g;
    T Fat 28 g; 47% Calories from Fat; Chol 121 mg; Sod 209 mg.

Peanut Butter and Banana Pie

1 baked deep-dish 9-inch pie shell
1/2 cup peanut butter
1 cup confectioners' sugar
3 egg yolks, beaten
2/3 cup sugar
1/4 cup cornstarch

1/8 teaspoon salt
2 cups milk, scalded
2 tablespoons margarine
1/2 teaspoon vanilla extract
2 bananas, sliced
3 egg whites, stiffly beaten

Cool pie shell to room temperature. Cut peanut butter into confectioners' sugar in bowl until crumbly. Sprinkle into cooled pie shell. Combine egg yolks, sugar, cornstarch and salt in bowl; beat well. Add a small amount of hot milk to egg mixture. Add egg mixture to hot milk in double boiler. Cook over hot water until thickened, stirring constantly. Remove from heat. Stir in margarine and vanilla. Place banana slices over crumbly mixture in pie shell; pour in cooked mixture. Spread stiffly beaten egg whites over top, sealing to edge. Bake at 350 degrees for 5 minutes or until meringue is light brown. Yield: 8 servings.

Approx Per Serving: Cal 475; Prot 11 g; Carbo 58 g; Fiber 2 g;
    T Fat 24 g; 44% Calories from Fat; Chol 88 mg; Sod 331 mg.

Peanut Butter Pie

2 tablespoons peanut butter
2 tablespoons (or more)
    confectioners' sugar
1 baked 9-inch pie shell

1 4-ounce package butterscotch or
    vanilla instant pudding mix
8 ounces whipped topping

Cut peanut butter into confectioners' sugar in bowl until crumbly, adding additional confectioners' sugar if needed to form pea-sized pieces. Sprinkle into baked pie shell. Prepare pudding mix using package directions. Spoon into prepared pie shell. Chill in refrigerator for 2 to 3 hours or until set. Top with whipped topping. Yield: 6 servings.

Approx Per Serving: Cal 382; Prot 4 g; Carbo 43 g; Fiber 1 g;
    T Fat 22 g; 52% Calories from Fat; Chol 0 mg; Sod 341 mg.

Recipe for trouble: believe all you hear and repeat it.

Pumpkin Pie

1 cup sugar	2 eggs, beaten
1/4 teaspoon salt	1 1/2 cups cooked pumpkin
1/4 teaspoon nutmeg	1 tablespoon melted butter
1/4 teaspoon cinnamon	1 unbaked 9-inch pie shell
1 cup evaporated milk	

Sift sugar, salt and spices into bowl. Beat in half the evaporated milk. Add eggs and remaining evaporated milk; mix well. Add pumpkin and butter; mix well. Pour into pie shell. Bake at 425 degrees for 10 minutes. Reduce oven temperature to 350 degrees. Bake for 20 minutes longer or until knife inserted near center comes out clean. Garnish with whipped topping or ice cream. Yield: 6 servings.

Approx Per Serving: Cal 391; Prot 7 g; Carbo 54 g; Fiber 2 g;
    T Fat 17 g; 39% Calories from Fat; Chol 89 mg; Sod 357 mg.

Old-Fashioned Raisin Pie

2 cups raisins	2 tablespoons cornstarch
2 cups water	1/2 teaspoon cinnamon
1/2 cup packed brown sugar	1 tablespoon vinegar
1/4 teaspoon salt	1 recipe 2-crust pie pastry

Combine raisins and water in saucepan. Cook for 5 minutes over medium heat, stirring occasionally. Combine brown sugar, salt, cornstarch and cinnamon in bowl. Add to raisins, stirring to mix. Cook until thickened, stirring constantly. Remove from heat. Stir in vinegar. Cool slightly. Pour into pastry-lined pie plate. Cover with top pastry; seal edge and cut vents. Bake at 400 degrees for 30 minutes or until golden brown. Yield: 6 servings.

Approx Per Serving: Cal 530; Prot 5 g; Carbo 92 g; Fiber 4 g;
    T Fat 18 g; 30% Calories from Fat; Chol 0 mg; Sod 472 mg.

Strawberry-Cheese Pie

8 ounces cream cheese, softened	1 baked 9-inch pie shell
1 14-ounce can sweetened	1 quart fresh strawberries, hulled
condensed milk	1 16-ounce package prepared
1/3 cup lemon juice	strawberry glaze, chilled
1 teaspoon vanilla extract	

Beat cream cheese in mixer bowl until fluffy. Add condensed milk gradually, beating until smooth. Add lemon juice and vanilla; mix well. Pour into baked pie shell. Chill in refrigerator for 3 hours or until set. Top with strawberries and desired amount of strawberry glaze. Chill until serving time. Yield: 6 servings.

Approx Per Serving: Cal 716; Prot 11 g; Carbo 99 g; Fiber 3 g;
    T Fat 32 g; 39% Calories from Fat; Chol 64 mg; Sod 381 mg.

Strawberry Pie

1½ cups mixed water and strawberry
  juice
1 3-ounce package strawberry
  gelatin

2 tablespoons cornstarch
¾ cup sugar
1 pint fresh strawberries
1 baked 9-inch pie shell

Heat water and strawberry juice in saucepan. Add mixture of gelatin, cornstarch and sugar. Boil for 3 minutes, stirring constantly. Cool slightly. Add strawberries; mix well. Pour into baked pie shell. Chill until serving time. Garnish with whipped cream. Yield: 8 servings.

Approx Per Serving: Cal 256; Prot 3 g; Carbo 46 g; Fiber 2 g;
    T Fat 8 g; 26% Calories from Fat; Chol 0 mg; Sod 174 mg.

Burnt Sugar Pie

½ cup sugar
¼ cup flour
1½ cups sugar
2 egg yolks, beaten
2 cups milk

1 teaspoon vanilla extract
1 baked 9-inch pie shell
2 egg whites
3 tablespoons confectioners' sugar

Brown ½ cup sugar in heavy saucepan over medium heat until amber colored, stirring constantly. Combine flour and 1½ cups sugar in bowl; mix well. Combine egg yolks, milk and vanilla in bowl; mix well. Add to flour mixture; mix well. Stir into browned sugar. Cook until mixture is thickened, stirring constantly. Pour into baked pie shell. Beat egg whites until soft peaks form. Add 3 tablespoons confectioners' sugar gradually, beating until stiff peaks form. Spread over top of pie, sealing to edge. Bake at 350 degrees for 5 minutes or until meringue is light brown. Yield: 8 servings.

Approx Per Serving: Cal 396; Prot 5 g; Carbo 70 g; Fiber 1 g;
    T Fat 11 g; 25% Calories from Fat; Chol 62 mg; Sod 179 mg.

Eggless Sweet Potato Pie

¾ cup butter, softened
¾ cup sugar
⅓ cup milk
1½ cups grated sweet potatoes

2 tablespoons grated orange rind
¾ teaspoon ginger
1 unbaked 9-inch pie shell

Cream butter and sugar in mixer bowl until light and fluffy. Add milk and grated sweet potatoes alternately, beating well after each addition. Beat in orange rind and ginger. Pour into pie shell. Bake at 300 degrees for 45 minutes or until filling is set and pie is golden brown. Serve warm with whipped cream. Yield: 8 servings.

Approx Per Serving: Cal 405; Prot 3 g; Carbo 43 g; Fiber 2 g;
    T Fat 25 g; 55% Calories from Fat; Chol 48 mg; Sod 295 mg.

Et Cetera

The Old Randolph County Courthouse

The Old Randolph County Courthouse

The Old Randolph County Courthouse standing since 1873, is the center of the square in Pocahontas and has long been an object of endearment to present and former residents of Randolph County. The Courthouse was placed on the National Register of Historic Places in the Spring of 1973.

Spiced Apple Butter

¹/₂ bushel apples
2 cups (about) water
1 cup vinegar

8 cups sugar
4 teaspoons cinnamon
1 cup red hot candies

Core apples; cut into quarters. Place in very large saucepan with water. Cook until soft. Press apples through sieve, measuring 16 cups pulp. Combine apple pulp, vinegar, sugar, cinnamon and candies in very large saucepan; mix well. Cook over low heat for 2 hours or until mixture remains in a smooth ball when tested in cool water, stirring frequently. Spoon into hot sterilized jars, leaving ¹/₂ inch headspace; seal with 2-piece lids. Process in boiling water bath for 10 minutes. Yield: 280 servings.

Approx Per Serving: Cal 42; Prot <1 g; Carbo 11 g; Fiber 1 g;
    T Fat <1 g; 2% Calories from Fat; Chol 0 mg; Sod <1 mg.

Processor Apple Chutney

12 tart apples, peeled, cut into quarters
2 large green bell peppers, cut into
    quarters
1 3-ounce can green chilies
2 large onions, cut into quarters
3 cloves of garlic

¹/₂ cup chopped fresh ginger
2 teaspoons salt
¹/₂ teaspoon cayenne pepper
3¹/₂ cups packed dark brown sugar
2¹/₂ cups cider vinegar
1¹/₂ cups raisins

Keep apples in salted water to prevent discoloration. Process drained apples in food processor fitted with steel blade until smooth. Spoon into large kettle. Combine next 7 ingredients in food processor container. Process for 10 to 15 seconds. Add to apples with brown sugar, vinegar and raisins; mix well. Cook over low heat for 3 hours, stirring frequently. Spoon into hot sterilized jars, leaving ¹/₂ inch headspace; seal with 2-piece lids. Yield: 24 servings.

Approx Per Serving: Cal 230; Prot 1 g; Carbo 60 g; Fiber 2 g;
    T Fat <1 g; 1% Calories from Fat; Chol 0 mg; Sod 223 mg.

Bailey's Irish Creme

1³/₄ cups whiskey
1 14-ounce can sweetened
    condensed milk
1 cup whipping cream
4 eggs

2 tablespoons chocolate syrup
2 teaspoons instant coffee granules
1 teaspoon vanilla extract
¹/₂ teaspoon almond extract

Combine whiskey, condensed milk, whipping cream, eggs, chocolate syrup, coffee granules and flavorings in blender container. Process until smooth. Pour into air-tight container. Chill in refrigerator. Yield: 10 servings.

Approx Per Serving: Cal 341; Prot 6 g; Carbo 25 g; Fiber <1 g;
    T Fat 15 g; 38% Calories from Fat; Chol 131 mg; Sod 90 mg.

Cheese Crackers

2 cups flour
2 cups shredded sharp Cheddar
  cheese

2 cups crisp rice cereal
1 cup butter, softened
Cayenne pepper to taste

Combine flour, cheese, cereal, butter and cayenne pepper in bowl; mix well. Shape into small balls. Place on baking sheet. Flatten with fork. Bake at 350 degrees for 5 minutes. Yield: 48 servings.

Approx Per Serving: Cal 77; Prot 2 g; Carbo 5 g; Fiber <1 g;
    T Fat 5 g; 64% Calories from Fat; Chol 15 mg; Sod 76 mg.

Cheese Straws Perfected

10 ounces sharp Cheddar cheese,
  shredded
1¹/₄ cups butter, softened

3 tablespoons plus 1 teaspoon hot
  sauce
2¹/₄ cups flour

Combine cheese, butter and hot sauce in bowl; mix well. Add flour gradually, mixing well after each addition. Press dough through cookie press fitted with straw-type disk onto baking sheet. Bake at 375 degrees for 17 minutes, rotating baking sheets every 5 minutes. Yield: 40 servings.

Approx Per Serving: Cal 106; Prot 2 g; Carbo 6 g; Fiber <1 g;
    T Fat 8 g; 68% Calories from Fat; Chol 24 mg; Sod 98 mg.

Oyster Crackers

1 1-pound package oyster crackers
1 envelope ranch salad dressing mix

1 cup oil

Place crackers in large doubled grocery bag. Combine salad dressing mix and oil in bowl; mix well. Pour over crackers; shake well. Place bag on large tray. Let stand overnight. Pour crackers into large airtight container. Yield: 8 servings.

Approx Per Serving: Cal 489; Prot 5 g; Carbo 42 g; Fiber 1 g;
    T Fat 34 g; 62% Calories from Fat; Chol 0 mg; Sod 954 mg.

*Always speak the truth and you'll never be
concerned with your memory.*

Beginner's Doughnuts

1¹/₂ cups flour
2 teaspoons baking powder
¹/₄ teaspoon salt
¹/₃ teaspoon nutmeg
¹/₂ cup sugar

1 egg, beaten
¹/₂ cup milk
¹/₂ teaspoon vanilla extract
Oil for frying

Sift flour, baking powder, salt, nutmeg and sugar together. Combine egg, milk and vanilla in bowl; mix well. Stir in sifted ingredients just until moistened; do not overmix. Drop by teaspoonfuls into 365-degree oil in skillet. Fry until brown on both sides, turning once. Drain on paper towel. May dust with confectioners' sugar or roll in granulated sugar. Yield: 20 servings.

Approx Per Serving: Cal 62; Prot 1 g; Carbo 13 g; Fiber <1 g;
  T Fat 1 g; 8% Calories from Fat; Chol 12 mg; Sod 66 mg.
  Nutritional information does not include oil for frying.

Kisses

4 egg whites
¹/₂ teaspoon cream of tartar

1 teaspoon vanilla extract
1¹/₄ cups sugar

Beat egg whites in mixer bowl until soft peaks form. Add cream of tartar, vanilla and 1 cup sugar. Beat until stiff peaks form. Fold in remaining ¹/₄ cup sugar gently. Drop by tablespoonfuls onto greased baking sheet. Bake at 300 degrees for 50 to 60 minutes. Do not open oven door. Turn off oven. Let stand until cool. May serve with crushed pineapple, cherries or any desired fruit. Yield: 12 servings.

Approx Per Serving: Cal 87; Prot 1 g; Carbo 21 g; Fiber 0 g;
  T Fat 0 g; 0% Calories from Fat; Chol 0 mg; Sod 17 mg.

Chocolate-Pecan Meringues

2 egg whites
¹/₈ teaspoon salt
¹/₈ teaspoon cream of tartar
³/₄ cup sugar

1 cup semisweet chocolate chips
²/₃ cup chopped pecans
1 teaspoon vanilla extract

Beat egg whites with salt and cream of tartar in mixer bowl until frothy. Add sugar gradually, mixing until stiff peaks form. Fold in chocolate chips, pecans and vanilla. Drop by teaspoonfuls 2 inches apart onto parchment paper-lined baking sheet. Bake at 300 degrees for 25 minutes. Remove with sharp spatula to wire rack to cool. Store in airtight container. Yield: 36 servings.

Approx Per Serving: Cal 56; Prot 1 g; Carbo 7 g; Fiber <1 g;
  T Fat 3 g; 48% Calories from Fat; Chol 0 mg; Sod 11 mg.

Hot Peanuts

2 tablespoons crushed red pepper
3 tablespoons olive oil
4 cloves of garlic, crushed
1   12-ounce can cocktail peanuts

1   12-ounce can Spanish peanuts
1 teaspoon salt
1 teaspoon chili powder

Heat red pepper in olive oil in skillet over medium heat for 1 minute. Stir in garlic. Add peanuts. Cook for 5 minutes. Remove from heat. Stir in salt and chili powder. Drain on paper towels. Yield: 24 servings.

Approx Per Serving: Cal 180; Prot 8 g; Carbo 5 g; Fiber 3 g;
     T Fat 16 g; 73% Calories from Fat; Chol 0 mg; Sod 93 mg.

Peanut Butter Sticks

6 slices thinly sliced white bread
1/2 cup smooth peanut butter

1/4 cup oil
2/3 cup graham cracker crumbs

Cut each bread slice into 5 sticks. Place on baking sheet. Bake at 250 degrees for 30 minutes or until brown. Mix peanut butter and oil in double boiler over boiling water. Dip toasted breadsticks into peanut butter mixture. Coat with graham cracker crumbs. Place on waxed paper. Let stand until cool. Store in airtight container. Yield: 30 servings.

Approx Per Serving: Cal 68; Prot 2 g; Carbo 5 g; Fiber <1 g;
     T Fat 5 g; 58% Calories from Fat; Chol 0 mg; Sod 63 mg.

Spicy Pecans

3 tablespoons butter
2 teaspoons salt
1 pound pecan halves
3 tablespoons Worcestershire sauce

1/4 teaspoon ground red pepper
1/2 teaspoon cinnamon
Tabasco sauce to taste

Melt butter in 9x13-inch baking dish in oven heated to 300 degrees. Stir in salt. Add pecan halves; toss. Mix Worcestershire sauce, red pepper, cinnamon and Tabasco sauce in small bowl. Add to pecans; mix well. Bake for 30 minutes, stirring occasionally. Let stand until cool. Store in airtight container. Yield: 16 servings.

Approx Per Serving: Cal 210; Prot 2 g; Carbo 6 g; Fiber 2 g;
     T Fat 21 g; 86% Calories from Fat; Chol 6 mg; Sod 312 mg.

Cinnamon-Cucumber Pickles

2 gallons large cucumbers
2 cups lime juice
2 gallons water
1 cup vinegar
1 teaspoon alum
1/2 ounce red food coloring
8 cups sugar

3 cups vinegar
2 cups water
16 whole cloves
8 cinnamon sticks
1   3-ounce package red hot
   cinnamon candies

Peel and core cucumbers. Cut into rings. Soak cucumbers in mixture of lime juice and 2 gallons water in very large bowl for 24 hours. Drain; rinse well. Cover cucumbers with cold water. Let stand for 3 hours; drain. Combine with mixture of 1 cup vinegar, alum, food coloring and enough water to cover in very large saucepan. Simmer for 2 hours; drain. Place cucumbers in very large bowl. Combine sugar, 3 cups vinegar, 2 cups water, cloves, cinnamon sticks and candies in large saucepan. Bring to a boil. Pour over cucumbers. Let stand for 24 hours. Drain; reserving syrup. Bring reserved syrup to a boil. Pour over cucumbers. Let stand for 24 hours. Drain; reserving syrup. Bring reserved syrup to a boil. Pack cucumbers into hot sterilized jars. Add boiling syrup, leaving 1/2 inch headspace; seal with 2-piece lids. Process in boiling water bath for 10 minutes. May add additional cinnamon candies to suit personal taste. Yield: 8 pints.

Approx Per Pint: Cal 984; Prot 6 g; Carbo 254 g; Fiber 12 g;
    T Fat 1 g; 1% Calories from Fat; Chol 0 mg; Sod 30 mg.
    Nutritional information does not include alum.

Pickled Saloon Eggs

12 hard-boiled eggs, peeled
3 cups red wine vinegar
1 cup water
1 clove of garlic
1 dried whole red pepper

4 peppercorns
2 whole cloves
1   1-inch piece of gingerroot, cut
   into quarters

Place eggs in large sterilized jar. Combine vinegar, water, garlic, red pepper, peppercorns and cloves in saucepan. Bring to a boil. Simmer for 5 minutes. Let stand until cool. Pour over eggs, covering by 2 inches. Chill, covered, for 1 week, uncovering once daily to allow fumes to escape. Store, covered, in refrigerator. May determine exact amount of pickling solution needed to cover eggs by filling egg-filled jar with water. Drain, measuring discarded water. Use the recipe as a formula for making more or less solution. Note: Boil eggs in heavily salted water for easier peeling. Yield: 12 servings.

Nutritional information for this recipe is not available.

Lemon Curd

3 cups sugar
½ cup margarine

Juice and grated rind of 3 lemons
3 eggs, beaten, strained

Combine first 3 ingredients in double boiler. Cook over hot water until sugar dissolves. Add a small amount of hot mixture to eggs; stir eggs into hot mixture. Cook until mixture coats spoon, stirring frequently. Store in refrigerator. Serve on cake or ice cream. Yield: 20 servings.

Approx Per Serving: Cal 170; Prot 1 g; Carbo 31 g; Fiber <1 g;
      T Fat 5 g; 28% Calories from Fat; Chol 32 mg; Sod 65 mg.

Creamy Pralines

2 cups sugar
½ cup light corn syrup
2 cups pecans
1 cup whipping cream

⅛ teaspoon salt
½ teaspoon vanilla extract
1½ tablespoons margarine

Combine sugar, corn syrup, pecans and whipping cream in saucepan. Cook over high heat to 234 to 240 degrees on candy thermometer, soft-ball stage, stirring constantly with wooden spoon. Remove from heat. Add salt, vanilla and margarine. Beat until thick and glossy. Drop by spoonfuls onto waxed paper. Yield: 50 servings.

Approx Per Serving: Cal 91; Prot <1 g; Carbo 11 g; Fiber <1 g;
      T Fat 5 g; 50% Calories from Fat; Chol 7 mg; Sod 13 mg.

Christmas Pizza

2 cups milk chocolate chips
14 ounces white almond bark,
   chopped
2 cups miniature marshmallows
1 cup crisp rice cereal
1 cup chopped walnuts
1   4-ounce jar maraschino cherries,
   cut into halves

3 tablespoons quartered green
   maraschino cherries
⅓ cup angel flake coconut
2 ounces white almond bark
1 teaspoon oil

Combine chocolate chips and 14 ounces almond bark in glass dish. Microwave on High for 2 minutes. Stir. Microwave for 2 minutes longer or until smooth, stirring 3 times. Stir in marshmallows, cereal and walnuts. Pour into greased 12-inch pizza pan. Top with cherries and coconut. Combine 2 ounces almond bark and oil in small glass bowl. Microwave on High for 30 to 60 seconds or until melted; stir. Drizzle over pizza. Chill until set. Yield: 12 servings.

Approx Per Serving: Cal 430; Prot 7 g; Carbo 48 g; Fiber 3 g;
      T Fat 26 g; 52% Calories from Fat; Chol 6 mg; Sod 92 mg.

Fruit Pizza

2 16-ounce rolls sugar cookie dough
16 ounces cream cheese, softened
1/2 cup confectioners' sugar
1 tablespoon lemon extract
1/2 cup sliced strawberries
1/2 cup sliced bananas
1/2 cup sliced kiwifruit

1/2 cup blueberries
Sections of 1/2 orange
1/2 cup pineapple tidbits
1/2 cup sliced peaches
1/2 cup peach preserves
1/4 cup water

Slice cookie dough. Arrange slightly overlapping on large pizza pan. Bake at 350 degrees for 20 minutes or until light brown. Let stand until cool. Spread with mixture of cream cheese, confectioners' sugar and lemon extract. Arrange fruit on prepared crust. Combine preserves and water in bowl; mix well. Add additional water if needed. Brush over fruit. Chill until serving time. Yield: 14 servings.

Approx Per Serving: Cal 552; Prot 8 g; Carbo 540 g; Fiber 1 g;
T Fat 27 g; 10% Calories from Fat; Chol 35 mg; Sod 463 mg.

Midland Salsa

This delicious recipe has been handed down from generation to generation in a Mexican cook's family. Best salsa I have ever tasted! —Ginger Motes

12 fresh jalapeño peppers
1 bunch cilantro
4 medium green onions
2 16-ounce cans whole tomatoes

1 teaspoon ground cumin
1/2 teaspoon minced garlic
1 teaspoon salt

Process peppers, cilantro and green onions in food processor until finely chopped. Add tomatoes and spices. Process until finely chopped. Store in airtight container in refrigerator. Serve with favorite chips or crackers. May also be used in Mexican dishes. May store in refrigerator for several weeks. Yield: 50 servings.

Approx Per Serving: Cal 6; Prot <1 g; Carbo 1 g; Fiber <1 g;
T Fat <1 g; 8% Calories from Fat; Chol 0 mg; Sod 72 mg.

Tomato Salsa

2 cups chopped fresh tomatoes
1/2 cup minced red onion
1/2 cup chopped fresh cilantro

2 teaspoons chopped jalapeño pepper
2 tablespoons fresh lime juice
Salt and pepper to taste

Combine tomatoes, onion, cilantro, jalapeño pepper and lime juice in bowl; mix well. Stir in salt and pepper. Chill until serving time. Yield: 6 servings.

Approx Per Serving: Cal 19; Prot 1 g; Carbo 4 g; Fiber 1 g;
T Fat <1 g; 8% Calories from Fat; Chol 0 mg; Sod 21 mg.

Charts, Index
&
Order Information

The McCollum-Chidester Home

The McCollum-Chidester Home

The McCollum-Chidester Home was built in 1847 by Peter McCollum, a local Camden businessman. In 1857 Col. John T. Chidester, stagecoach line owner, purchased the home. Thus the name McCollum-Chidester.

The home may be best known for its use as headquarters at various times by Confederate General Sterling Price and Union General Frederick Steele during the Battle at Poison Springs (April, 1864).

It now houses books and other memorabilia of the Old South. It was placed on the National Register of Historic Places in June, 1975.

Substitution Chart

	Instead of	Use
Baking	1 teaspoon baking powder	1/4 teaspoon baking soda plus 1/2 teaspoon cream of tartar
	1 tablespoon cornstarch (for thickening)	2 tablespoons flour or 1 tablespoon tapioca
	1 cup sifted all-purpose flour	1 cup plus 2 tablespoons sifted cake flour
	1 cup sifted cake flour	1 cup minus 2 tablespoons sifted all-purpose flour
	1 cup dry bread crumbs	3/4 cup cracker crumbs
Dairy	1 cup buttermilk	1 cup sour milk or 1 cup yogurt
	1 cup heavy cream	3/4 cup skim milk plus 1/3 cup butter
	1 cup light cream	7/8 cup skim milk plus 3 tablespoons butter
	1 cup sour cream	7/8 cup sour milk plus 3 tablespoons butter
	1 cup sour milk	1 cup milk plus 1 tablespoon vinegar or lemon juice or 1 cup buttermilk
Seasoning	1 teaspoon allspice	1/2 teaspoon cinnamon plus 1/8 teaspoon cloves
	1 cup catsup	1 cup tomato sauce plus 1/2 cup sugar plus 2 tablespoons vinegar
	1 clove of garlic	1/8 teaspoon garlic powder or 1/8 teaspoon instant minced garlic or 3/4 teaspoon garlic salt or 5 drops of liquid garlic
	1 teaspoon Italian spice	1/4 teaspoon each oregano, basil, thyme, rosemary plus dash of cayenne pepper
	1 teaspoon lemon juice	1/2 teaspoon vinegar
	1 tablespoon mustard	1 teaspoon dry mustard
	1 medium onion	1 tablespoon dried minced onion or 1 teaspoon onion powder
Sweet	1 1-ounce square chocolate	1/4 cup cocoa plus 1 teaspoon shortening
	1 2/3 ounces semisweet chocolate	1 ounce unsweetened chocolate plus 4 teaspoons granulated sugar
	1 cup honey	1 to 1 1/4 cups sugar plus 1/4 cup liquid or 1 cup corn syrup or molasses
	1 cup granulated sugar	1 cup packed brown sugar or 1 cup corn syrup, molasses or honey minus 1/4 cup liquid

Equivalent Chart

	When the recipe calls for	Use
Baking	½ cup butter 2 cups butter 4 cups all-purpose flour 4½ to 5 cups sifted cake flour 1 square chocolate 1 cup semisweet chocolate chips 4 cups marshmallows 2¼ cups packed brown sugar 4 cups confectioners' sugar 2 cups granulated sugar	4 ounces 1 pound 1 pound 1 pound 1 ounce 6 ounces 1 pound 1 pound 1 pound 1 pound
Cereal – Bread	1 cup fine dry bread crumbs 1 cup soft bread crumbs 1 cup small bread cubes 1 cup fine cracker crumbs 1 cup fine graham cracker crumbs 1 cup vanilla wafer crumbs 1 cup crushed cornflakes 4 cups cooked macaroni 3½ cups cooked rice	4 to 5 slices 2 slices 2 slices 28 saltines 15 crackers 22 wafers 3 cups uncrushed 8 ounces uncooked 1 cup uncooked
Dairy	1 cup shredded cheese 1 cup cottage cheese 1 cup sour cream 1 cup whipped cream ⅔ cup evaporated milk 1⅔ cups evaporated milk	4 ounces 8 ounces 8 ounces ½ cup heavy cream 1 small can 1 13-ounce can

Fruit	4 cups sliced or chopped apples
	1 cup mashed bananas
	2 cups pitted cherries
	2½ cups shredded coconut
	4 cups cranberries
	1 cup pitted dates
	1 cup candied fruit
	3 to 4 tablespoons lemon juice plus
	  1 tablespoon grated lemon rind
	⅓ cup orange juice plus 2 teaspoons
	  grated orange rind
	4 cups sliced peaches
	2 cups pitted prunes
	3 cups raisins
		4 medium
		3 medium
		4 cups unpitted
		8 ounces
		1 pound
		1 8-ounce package
		1 8-ounce package
		1 lemon
		
		1 orange
		
		8 medium
		1 12-ounce package
		1 15-ounce package

	When the recipe calls for	Use
Meats	4 cups chopped cooked chicken 3 cups chopped cooked meat 2 cups cooked ground meat	1 5-pound chicken 1 pound, cooked 1 pound, cooked
Nuts	1 cup chopped nuts	4 ounces shelled 1 pound unshelled
Vegetables	2 cups cooked green beans 2½ cups lima beans or red beans 4 cups shredded cabbage 1 cup grated carrot 8 ounces fresh mushrooms 1 cup chopped onion 4 cups sliced or chopped potatoes 2 cups canned tomatoes	½ pound fresh or 1 16-ounce can 1 cup dried, cooked 1 pound 1 large 1 4-ounce can 1 large 4 medium 1 16-ounce can

Measurement Equivalents

1 tablespoon = 3 teaspoons
2 tablespoons = 1 ounce
4 tablespoons = ¼ cup
5⅓ tablespoons = ⅓ cup
8 tablespoons = ½ cup
12 tablespoons = ¾ cup
16 tablespoons = 1 cup
1 cup = 8 ounces or ½ pint
4 cups = 1 quart
4 quarts = 1 gallon

1 6½ to 8-ounce can = 1 cup
1 10½ to 12-ounce can = 1¼ cups
1 14 to 16-ounce can = 1¾ cups
1 16 to 17-ounce can = 2 cups
1 18 to 20-ounce can = 2½ cups
1 29-ounce can = 3½ cups
1 46 to 51-ounce can = 5¾ cups
1 6½ to 7½-pound can or Number
  10 = 12 to 13 cups

Metric Equivalents

Liquid	Dry
1 teaspoon = 5 milliliters 1 tablespoon = 15 milliliters 1 fluid ounce = 30 milliliters 1 cup = 250 milliliters 1 pint = 500 milliliters	1 quart = 1 liter 1 ounce = 30 grams 1 pound = 450 grams 2.2 pounds = 1 kilogram

NOTE: *The metric measures are approximate benchmarks for purposes of home food preparation.*

Index

AMERICAN CANCER SOCIETY
ARKANSAS HERITAGE COOKBOOK
901 N. UNIVERSITY
LITTLE ROCK, ARKANSAS 72207
OR CALL TOLL FREE
1-800-ACS-2345

Please send me _____ copies of
Arkansas Heritage: Recipes Past and Present
at $15.00 per copy plus $2.00 each to cover
postage and handling. Enclosed is an
additional donation of $ _____.

Name: _____

Address: _____

City: _____

State: _____

Zip: _____

_____ Check   (Make payable to American Cancer Society.)

_____ VISA

_____ MasterCard

_____ American Express

Account # _____ Expiration Date _____